GROWING UP WAUKEGAN

A true life story about the life experiences
of growing up in a small town

FRED SCHESKE

iUniverse, Inc.
Bloomington

Growing Up Waukegan
A true life story about the life experiences of growing up in a small town
\

iUniverse books may be ordered through booksellers or by contacting:

iUniverse
1663 Liberty Drive
Bloomington, IN 47403
www.iuniverse.com
1-800-Authors (1-800-288-4677)

ISBN: 978-1-4620-1861-1 (sc)
ISBN: 978-1-4620-1862-8 (e)

Printed in the United States of America

iUniverse rev. date: 6/2/2011

Acknowledgements

A special thank you to my wife, Michelle Madoff-Scheske, and to Diann Wilson for encouragement and editing work.

Thanks to Jean Derreberry Starkey and to Carol Amstutz Kozma for recalling names of some individuals mentioned within the book.

Also, thanks to Carol Helvie Cole for providing Scheske family photos and materials.

Pat Jones Fortine sent Army photos long after my discharge. Thanks.

Thanks to Julianne Peterson for providing information.

And to Howard Heyer who answered many questions for information and provided photos, thank you.

Full names of individuals stated in the book have given permission for use. Some full names are used for individuals who are deceased. In other cases only first names are used to protect identity.

Dedication

This book is a chronicle of my life and a legacy to my family. It is dedicated to my wife Michelle, my children Catherine, Daniel and Karenlin, and to my grandchildren, Fred and Deanna. May it serve as an inspiration to them, and to others, in their journey through life.

It is dedicated in loving memory of Margaret.

Foreword

By Bill Wilson

I am honored to write the "Foreword" of *"Growing Up Waukegan"* by my dear friend, Fred Scheske.

Unlike many people I know, I am not a writer. I have a strong Engineering background, much like Fred. A story teller I am, a limerist I pride myself to be. So, I will do my very best to give the author the due respect he deserves for his work.

As Billy Graham wrote in his book *"The Journey"*, "You can't change the past. Whatever has happened in your life so far, good and bad, cannot be altered, and all the decisions and events that have made you what you are today are indelibly inscribed in the story of your life."

This is what Fred did. He told the story of his life. Most people do not have the insight to think that their life is worth telling. Fred did more than that, he walked us through his life in this beautiful accounting of his childhood upbringing. He led us through his stint with the Army after WWII, indulged us with the spirit of his love of his family. He adopted two children and successfully could acclaim that he was married for 48 years. He suffered and went through steps of grief and overcame the death of a spouse, bouncing back to remarry and retire, now at the young age of 81.

Fred and I have been close friends for many years. We share the same childhood upbringing. I am from Johnstown, PA, much like Waukegan, as he has described in his book. We both have large families, and had parents who were hard working during difficult economic times. For sure, we were not born with Silver Spoons in our mouths.

We both have a lot in common, both having chosen Engineering careers, Fred with Motorola and Intel, me with Jones and Laughlin Steel. My career led me to retire after varied assignments in the Steel Industry. Mainly, being the spokesperson for the environmental causes the Steel Industry suffered. Fred and I both survived difficult industries.

For one thing, I know Fred Scheske to be an honorable and trustworthy friend. He is a faithful person, and having him for a friend is one of the greatest blessings in my life.

I wish him much success in the publishing of *"Growing Up Waukegan"*. I hope it encourages many others to write their story. A very special lady told me "You don't have to be a President to write your memoirs." And this is as good as it gets!

Contents

1. A Little History About My Home Town   1
2. Scheske Family Background   5
3. Family Stories   10
4. Greenwood and Glen Flora Grade Schools   21
5. Grade School Stories   24
6. Waukegan Township High School   29
7. WWII Stories   37
8. From High School to US Army Basic Training   41
9. On to Administration School   50
10. Shipment Overseas to Guam   53
11. Finally! A Job Assignment   57
12. Fun Stories While on Guam   66
13. A Memorable Trip to Japan   69
14. Back to Work   72
15. Reflections On Army Service   76
16. On to Civilian Life in Waukegan   78
17. Lake Forest College to University of Nebraska   84
18. My Life Was About to Change   89
19. On My Own at U of N - No GI Bill   93
20. Back to Waukegan!   95
21. Life in Waukegan and Abbott Laboratories   98
22. I Meet My Future Wife   101
23. Wedding in Waukegan   105
24. Our First Home   109
25. Time to Expand Our Family   130
26. First Experience With Death in the Family   133
27. Arizona, Here We Come!   141

28. Our New Arizona Home   143
29. My New Job as a Process Technician   145
30. Our New Tempe Home   148
31. A New Job Role   150
32. Two Trips to Waukegan   152
33. My Pink Slip – Laid Off!   154
34. Our Family Expands   157
35. Yet Another Motorola Job   159
36. A New Career Path   161
37. Orientation Trip to Austin, Texas   163
38. On Shaky Ground   165
39. A Primer: Semiconductor Manufacturing   167
40. Our New Life In Austin, Texas   170
41. A Family Outing   175
42. Back at the Ranch   177
43. The New Phoenix NMOS Operation   179
44. Introduction to the World of Industrial Engineering   186
45. The Big Texas Vacation   188
46. A Bona Fide Training Job Offer – And Decision Time   190
47. It's Back to Texas!   193
48. New Hire Orientation Was Paying Off!   197
49. Joining Intel Corporation   201
50. Family and Work Issues   205
51. Intel's Fab 6 Group Forms   207
52. Intel Encounters a Big Problem   212
53. My Stint in Corporate Education   216
54. A Family Gathering   221
55. Family Matters   222
56. Time For A Change?   225
57. Buying Another House   227

58. Starting A New Training Job   231
59. A Family Calamity   233
60. Another Fab Retrenchment   235
61. A Fab 9 Real-Life Story   238
62. It's Back to Arizona!   240
63. Corporate Education and Development   242
64. Becoming Grandparents!   244
65. Coping With A Job Transfer   246
66. Scheske Family Events   250
67. Nearing the End of My Career   252
68. My Performance Review   255
69. My Corrective Action Plan   258
70. Ah, Retirement!   260
71. Reflections   263
72. On the Home Front   265
73. The Beginning of a Long Hospital Stay   270
74. Funeral and Aftermath   276
75. Hospice of the Valley   278
76. The Feds, Taxes and Lawyers   280
77. Grief Counseling and Therapy   282
78. That First Christmas   284
79. A Trip to Ireland   286
80. Life's Decisions   288
81. My Last Brother Dies   290
82. One Last Try On match.com   292
83. Our Surprise Home   299
84. Back to the Past   302
85. Second Marriage   305
86. Personal Reflections   309
87. When Visiting Waukegan   312

1

A Little History About My Home Town

Waukegan / Wah kee gen / - A town located 35 miles north of Chicago, Illinois and 60 miles south of Milwaukee, Wisconsin. It is an Indian name for the original settlement of *Little Fort* on a bluff overlooking Lake Michigan on its western shore. A pleasant town with good secondary schools, it had an efficient mayor/aldermanic form of government. Factory and retail jobs were readily available. Two good hospitals: Victory Memorial and Saint Therese. Plenty of doctors and dentists kept folks healthy. People felt safe living there. It was a clean town with good streets and infrastructure. Police and Fire Departments kept the city safe and secure with very little crime or disturbance. Waukegan had the best, and coldest, tap water I've ever tasted!

The city boasted two golf courses: Bonnie Brook Municipal and Glen Flora Country Club. It had two wonderful beaches on Lake Michigan and two concrete piers for great Perch fishing. Several city parks were available for picnics and outings. Ball diamonds and tennis courts were available for players. In the winter, the city made several rinks available for ice skating. In short, there were good recreation facilities for families and kids.

The city was proud of its excellent grade schools and its

accredited high school. Education was an important facet of life in Waukegan.

Waukegan produced many notable people. Perhaps the most widely known Waukeganite was Jack Benny. However, Benjamin Kubelsky, aka Jack Benny, was born February 14, 1894 in Chicago and came to Waukegan as a small child. Benny's father was a haberdasher/tailor with a shop at the corner of Water and Genesee Street. There was a theater just up from the corner on Water Street and that is where Jack got his beginning playing the violin and being a comedian. The theater closed long before I was able to attend a show. Another celebrity, Ray Bradbury, is widely acclaimed as an author of science-fiction stories some of which were made into movies. Ray lived on Grand Avenue, east of Jackson Street. With his acceptance as a noted writer, Ray moved from Waukegan. And, there are many other notable Waukeganites, people who made their way through its school system to become successful and productive citizens.

Waukegan had a population of about 33,000 that varied very little over the thirty-two years I lived there. It was a highly industrialized town with several large corporations. Johns-Manville produced building products and automotive brake parts, all containing asbestos. Johnson Motors produced outboard motors for boats. Outboard Marine produced boats with inboard and outboard motors. Public Service produced electricity for Waukegan and northern Illinois communities. Fansteel Metallurgical produced metal and wire products. Abbott Laboratories, located in the adjoining city of North Chicago, produced pharmaceutical products. Next door to Abbott's was American Can Company. All of these companies provided good paying jobs that allowed families to thrive. There was also a leather tanning factory located south of Public Service. It was a stinking factory – I often wondered how anyone could work there.

There were several automobile sales and service companies: Buick, Chevrolet, Pontiac, Oldsmobile, Cadillac, La Salle, Ford, Chrysler/Plymouth, Dodge and Studebaker. Downtown Waukegan boasted many clothing, department and shoe stores plus four movie theaters. Hein's Department store was the elite fashion shop. The Globe Department store was across the street. There were three five & dime stores: Kresge's Woolworth's, and Neisner's. The city boasted two large banks on the corners of Genesee and Washington Street. It also had more than a fair share of taverns, bars and grills in the downtown area. Waukegan had a thriving fishing industry and its harbor provided marina facilities for small boats. There was a facility for off-loading coal from large cargo boats and turning it into coke for the steel industry located south around the bend in Lake Michigan in Gary, Indiana. Additionally, there were many small manufacturing and service concerns located within the city.

September and October were always looked forward to because that was the time Waukegan automobile dealers unveiled their new models. It was almost an evening of entertainment for folks to visit a dealer and gawk at the new cars. Of course, I was among the horde that was "just looking". Wetzel and Turner showed off the new Buicks and Chevys. Reed-Randle unveiled the new Ford cars. Dealers up and down south Genesee Street opened their doors to let people check out all the new features. After not seeing a new car for six years, people were starved for the latest models to look and see, and maybe buy.

Brother Bill, after returning from Army service, inspected the 1948 Ford, put a down payment of $200 on a new four door sedan and was placed on a long waiting list. Brother Erve meanwhile was checking out a new Chevy. After waiting five months and still no new car, Bill went to Reed-Randle and demanded his money back. After a lengthy discussion, the dealer finally refunded his $200. Erve, noting Bill's long and unsuccessful wait, opted to buy a used car. George did not buy a car until years later.

It was relatively easy to find a job in or around Waukegan. Electric street cars and some buses serviced Waukegan and North Chicago, making it convenient to get to work and to shop. During the 1940's a street car ride cost 10 cents and, with a transfer ticket, one could ride from one side of town to the other in about 20 to 25 minutes. Halloween always brought problems for the electric street cars. Kids would tie two shoes together and fling them over the power line. When the street car came by the shoes would dislodge the electrical connection, stopping the car. The conductor would have to get up on top of the car and get the shoes off of the line and reconnect the power cable. Ah, kids! Did I ever do that? I claim memory failure! Several years after WWII, General Motors convinced city powers-to-be that busses were far superior to electric street cars, were quieter and could extend coverage of the city because they were not tied to electric cables. Of course, they did not mention pollution created by diesel buses. Soon after acceptance of buses into the city, the price of a bus ride increased. That's progress for you!

2

Scheske Family Background

As a native Waukeganite, I came into the world April 14, 1929 on a Sunday afternoon in Victory Memorial Hospital. Dr. Samuel Keller, our family physician, was the doctor in attendance. My mother told me years later that I was colicky, a difficult baby to deal with. Older brothers Erve, George and William (Bill), were not happy with my arrival because of my constant wailing. I was the "Oops" baby, coming twelve years after my predecessor Bill, leaving a considerable age gap. My brother, Robert (Bob), followed me a year and a half later in November, 1930.

My parents were of German lineage. My father, Frederick August Scheske, was born in 1892 in Posen, then a city in Germany. He immigrated to the United States with his parents in 1894, finally settling in Milwaukee, Wisconsin. His last name appears to have been changed in the New York port of entry, along with many other immigrants. Record searches indicated the family name may have been Olsheski or Olshewski. My mother, Louise Johanna Wilke, was conceived in Hamburg, Germany, and was born in Wauwatosa, Wisconsin in 1894. My parents were married in Wauwatosa in1912. Oldest brother, Ervin, was born in Milwaukee in 1914, followed by George in 1915 and William in 1917. Twelve years later I was born in Waukegan, followed by Robert, born in 1930. I was the first to be born in a hospital. My older brothers were all born at home, which was common in the early 1900s. To my knowledge, I was the first, and only, baby in the family to be baptized Lutheran.

I cannot remember much interface with my older brothers, due mostly to the age difference. They pulled a lot of pranks and told me they would take me in a wicker baby carriage to Yeoman Park in back of our house on Judge Avenue and push me down the small hills, without anyone guiding the carriage. Great fun (for them)! An old Kodak photo showed me as a small boy taking a drink from a garden hose. Brother George turned on the faucet full bore, overwhelming me with a stream of water. I can't specifically remember the pranks but I'm told they did happen.

Our family moved later from Judge Avenue to Martin Avenue on the west side and then to the north side of Waukegan into a larger house on the northeast corner of Jackson Street and Keith Avenue. All of the "five boys" slept in a huge bedroom on the second floor. Two full sized beds and one twin bed with one chest of drawers and one walk-in closet provided all of our needs. My wardrobe consisted of a couple of shirts, two pairs of pants, coveralls, a few socks and underwear and one pair of shoes. For some family event, perhaps Easter, my parents had bought me a tweed suit but I can't remember why. Worst, I fell one day while running in the suit and tore a slit in my right pant leg. I don't know when my parents found the tear in the pants, but I heard about it from my father.

It was while in the house at 1703 North Jackson that my parents bought our first electric refrigerator. It was a General Electric, maybe 10 or 12 cubic feet interior with the round condenser coil on the top. Prior to the GE fridge we would buy chunks of ice from a vendor. We'd leave a cardboard sign in the front window indicating how big a piece of ice we wanted:

20 or 30 pound block. Food could not remain long in the ice box, maybe two or three days at best. The electric fridge was a blessing for our family.

Every other day in the morning we'd get a quart bottle of milk delivered to the door by Meadow Gold Dairy. The milkman had a horse driven wagon he'd use to deliver his route. If the bottle of milk was not picked up quickly on winter mornings the cream would expand, pushing the cardboard lid up out of the bottle.

My father (Pa) was a shift supervisor in the (asbestos) paper mill at Johns-Manville Corporation. He had transferred to the Waukegan plant when Milwaukee authorities closed the J-M facility for polluting the Milwaukee River with asbestos effluent. He spent 42 years working for Johns-Manville and retired with very little in benefits!

My mother (Ma), Louise Johanna Wilke Scheske, was a housewife who took care of five children: Erve, George, William, Fred and Robert. She often wished for a girl, if for no other reason than to help with the household duties. She was a loving mother, always ready to take care of her kids.

Being of old German descent, there was little outward display of affection by my parents. I cannot recall having seen my parents hugging or kissing each other. And as kids we received little of that as well. Both parents loved to dance and that was as close to hugging as they displayed. The word "love" was never spoken aloud; at least I never heard it from anyone in the family. We were cared for, we were provided food, shelter and clothing, our health care needs were taken care of, but love was never shown outright. And yet, there was caring closeness in the family that was real and evident.

Our father was the disciplinarian who had, as I recall, the fastest right hand in the world. Any ill timed remark or deed on our part and we had a "zinger" from him. Our Mother was kind and caring in that she would listen and then tell us what we had done wrong but no zingers! She was a wonderful cook and baker and prepared good nutritious meals for all of the family. I often wonder how she managed to take care of all of us males in the house. She handled everything!

The Scheske family was a close, helpful group to a point. On one hand, if anyone was in need, the family was there for support. When I was close to down and out after returning from college in Nebraska, my parents and siblings got me on my feet again. Yes, I paid room and board when working but there were times when I was unemployed (and broke). I not only got financial help but also moral support. On the other hand, we were a private family and did not interfere with each other's affairs. Brother George had marital problems with his wife Gladys. We, as a family, did not stick our nose into their business. We had opinions, of course, but pretty much kept them to ourselves. But, the stigma of Gladys' loose behavior inflicted on her husband and their two children can be seen even today. I would have liked to punch her out at one time but decided it was best to stay out of it. They eventually divorced, which affected George greatly.

To celebrate our parent's fortieth wedding anniversary we held a big party on September 27, 1952 in the basement of Bill's house. Aunts and uncles from Milwaukee were invited and drove to Waukegan. Even two cousins attended. Uncle Frank graced us with songs played on his concertina and we sang along. Aunt Marie, feeling no pain, sang some German songs in her operatic voice. Lots of stories and jokes were told that day and it was a terrific celebration!

The Scheske's were, basically, a happy family. We often got together to eat and imbibe. I am not and never was a drinker. My brothers were much like my father, liking their beer. They were masculine and well proportioned. I was skinny and small boned and had many characteristics of my mother. At the start of high school I weighed a whopping 105 pounds and was about 5 feet, 2 inches tall. Dr. Keller began giving me vitamin B12 shots in my freshman year and I suddenly grew to nearly six feet, weighing about 122 pounds. Taking the physical entry exam for the Army in 1947, I barely qualified for acceptance at 125 pounds, the lowest allowable level. I have since blossomed out to a present day 155 pounds – still on the slim side. One of my buddies, Dean Keller, used to joke saying that when he talked to me I must face him – he wanted to see who he was talking to! In spite of my physique anomalies, I have been blessed with good health. And for that I am grateful.

3
Family Stories

Mother's brother, Albert Wilke, came to live with us after losing his job in Milwaukee. He found a job at Johns-Manville, and came to be known as "Unc" (for uncle) by all of us. Unc would work diligently all week and then turn to partying on the weekend. He usually came home polluted, as my mother used to say, in the wee hours on Sunday only to sober up and head for work on Monday. He was an accredited stone and brick mason and was often called upon by contractors to build a fireplace in a home on Saturdays. Since he was non-union, contractors slipped him in on non-construction workdays, usually weekends.

Pa was a confirmed Buick man. He was adamant about only owning a GM Buick. One time in 1936 a salesman somehow convinced him the aerodynamically designed Chrysler sedan was better than a Buick. He drove it for two days and returned it, reclaiming his Buick, never to own any other make of car again. His opinion carried over to all of my brothers who swore by their GM cars. I, on the other hand, bought and drove a variety of makes and models. I'd bought a used 1961 Volkswagen Beetle at one point. Bill had a great dislike for foreign products, having been with Johnson Outboard Motors most of his working life and told me in no uncertain terms what he thought of my car.

Sundays were the only days we went out for a ride as a family. Older brothers Erve, George and Bill had their own friends and rarely accompanied us. My father had a passion for having a few beers and we would usually wind up at the Bally Muck Tavern on Grand Avenue. I have no idea how the name Bally Muck was chosen (sounds gross!). My father knew the owner and he liked to frequent the place. Once in a great while we would drive to Milwaukee to visit my mother's parents. Mother's father, my grandfather Albert Wilke, died in his 50s and so we only visited my grandmother. My father had had a falling out with his father many years prior to his getting married and we seldom even saw his side of the family. Bob and I never spoke with my grandmother (Mother's side) because she only spoke German and we hadn't a clue what she was saying.

Grandma Wilke made it clear, however, that children were to be seen and not heard. So, we played outside by climbing her apple trees. On one visit, Bob and I saw a large rabbit cross Blue Mound Road, a busy highway, in front of Grandma's house and we decided to follow it. We soon lost sight of the rabbit and headed back to the house. Traffic was heavy at that time and we waited to cross. Bob started to run across and I grabbed him before he would have been hit by a passing car. He jumped again and I couldn't stop him this time and boom! He was hit by a car. The driver, a dentist, immediately stopped and ministered to him. My parents ran from the house and found Bob had broken his right leg. My father immediately got him into the car and headed for the nearest hospital in Milwaukee (no emergency personnel or vehicles in those days!). Bob spent nearly a month in the hospital recovering from the fracture. We would drive up to see him each week. My mother stayed with him for the first week and the rest of the family had to batch it for a while. Bob refused to talk to anyone for three weeks. While visiting one time I told him that unless he started talking to us we weren't going to come to the hospital anymore, and he finally began talking.

My father would usually disappear shortly after arriving at Grandma's house, supposedly to visit some of his old Milwaukee friends for a few hours. I often wondered about his "visits" however. I know he had a liking for women and in later years I figured out he would occasionally stray, which greatly angered me. How do I know this? One Saturday morning, my father accompanied Unc, Bob and me on a fishing trip to Lake Michigan. Pa rarely went fishing. On the way we stopped on the far south side of town at Ms. Calhoun's House of Pleasure, located in a row of red brick townhouses. Pa told Bob and me not to leave the car while he and Unc went into the house, not to appear again for a long half hour. Then we went merrily on our way to fish for Perch. As a boy of seven, I did not fully understand what had happened, but remember the event clearly. It wasn't until many years later that I put two and two together. I could not, and still cannot, understand how he could treat my mother that way.

Unc would often take Bob and me fishing on the Stub Pier at Waukegan's North Beach on Lake Michigan. We loved to go anywhere with my uncle because he had a 1935 De Soto convertible with a rumble seat and Bob and I would get to ride in the back. Now that was real fun! Unc called his car the "Puddle Jumper". To go fishing we'd drive first to South Beach where a dealer sold minnows, charging 25 cents for a dozen in a bucket of water. Then we'd drive to the stub pier in front of Johnson Outboard Motors and walk to our spot in the middle where we'd fish for Perch. We developed a system for measuring the fish we caught, grading them as babies (small), pan size (medium) and jumbo (big 'uns). Any fish we'd catch were brought home where Ma would gut and clean them and then fry them for our meal the next day. I hated eating fish because I once got a fish bone caught in my throat; from then on I refused to eat them.

Spring was my favorite time of the year. The sun warming the earth, green grass poking through, and the scent of lilacs was special for me. Apple tree blossoms have a heavenly scent of their own. There were many empty lots along Greenwood Avenue that provided "playgrounds" for kids living nearby. I often took walks in the lots that, while not large, proved exciting to explore. Violets thrived in many places and I picked many bunches to give to my mother. She would always place them in a small vase and place it on the kitchen window sill above the sink. One lot had a small marshy area that grew pussy willows and I would break off a few and take them home. There was a large choke cherry tree on a corner lot that we liked to climb. I'd climbed up in it one day, lost my hold on a branch and fell out of the tree onto the sidewalk below. Luckily I did not break anything but I was sore for days afterwards. I will, however, always remember the sweet smells, the scents of spring in Waukegan.

My greatest fear while exploring was spotting or coming upon a snake. One excursion into a lot on the corner of Jackson and Greenwood walking toward a grove of neglected apple trees, I came face-to-face with a Cotton Mouth snake, coiled, ready to strike. I slowly backed away and high tailed it out of there. I cannot recall ever going into that area again. My inordinate fear of snakes is still with me.

Holidays were always festive for our family. We would always have a live Christmas tree, usually a Balsam Pine, and we'd all help to decorate it with ornaments, many of them old and from Germany. There would often be a quart bottle of Mogen David wine on the table for non-beer drinkers. Bob and I were allowed to have one shot glass full of the sweet wine for dinner. Ma would always prepare a big meal, usually with little or no help. We'd often have roast turkey, sometimes roast goose, for Thanksgiving and Christmas. The table was always loaded with food, all of it prepared from scratch. As a family we'd talk and tell stories and stuff ourselves with food. Then, all of us would leave the table to read the paper, listen to the radio or take a snooze. All of us except Ma, that is. After cooking all morning, she would put food away and clean up the mess we left at the table. Looking back, I wonder how we could let her do that without helping. She never complained, but I can only guess at what she was thinking: *lazy men*!

Men would often appear at our back door at Jackson Street in daytime during the Depression of the 1930s asking for food. We used to call them bums or hobos – now we call them homeless. Ma would always make a fried egg sandwich, wrap it in wax paper and give it to them. She would not, however, allow them into the house. She was always good hearted for people who needed help.

Ma's brother, Albert Wilke, was an alcoholic and would often lose his job because of his drinking problem. He would come to live with us in Waukegan after running into hard times in Milwaukee. Unc was a good guy and always found time to talk to Bob and me. He loved to go unshaven for a few days and would rub Bob's face in the stubble, laughing at Bob's yelling. Unc seemed to get a kick out of helping Bob and I with our homework, especially arithmetic. He was good at figuring out math problems. He loved to fish and hunt and would spend much of his spare time doing that. And his drinking continued even while living with us. He had an opportunity to marry at one time but opted out of the relationship at the last minute. I think the only reason my father allowed him to live with us is that Unc paid room and board, helping with our living expenses during the Depression.

The Great Depression was not easy for our family, but we

always had food, clothing and a roof over our heads. Often on Saturday nights our dinner consisted of a large can or two of Ann-Page (A&P) baked beans mixed with two large cans of Ann-Page Spaghetti. It may not have been gourmet food, but it was good and we had enough to eat. And yes, we had SPAM served once a week. We often had fried eggs, bacon and toast for breakfast – that kept us going.

My father was fortunate in that he had a job with Johns-Manville Corp. throughout the Great Depression and was able to provide for us. I don't recall specific examples of really tough times but I do remember none of the five boys had many clothes or shoes. We got by and we were relatively happy. Many other families got by as well. There weren't many cars sold, clothing stores didn't sell a lot of clothing and real estate was not humming with sales. My parents would buy clothing for us from Gordon's Clothing Store on Genesee Street in downtown Waukegan because they offered credit. When we needed hardware items, we'd head to Tenth Street Hardware in adjoining North Chicago for the same reason. Not many retail stores did that during the Depression.

But people got along, often going out on Saturday night for a few drinks and maybe some dancing. My parents would often go to the J-M Club on Greenwood Avenue to have a two-piece fried chicken dinner with coleslaw and a piece of bread, all for 75 cents. Of course, a 15 cent glass of Schlitz beer would go well with that dinner. I remember riding my bike around side streets near our home looking for soda pop bottles. We could get a nickel back on each bottle we'd turn in to the store. Life was very different then.

Talking about a bicycle, Pa told me one day that he would take me to Kelly Hardware and I could pick a bike from their stock. I think I was about age seven. We drove to Kelly's on Glen Flora and looked at the several bikes parked in front. My eyes immediately went to a red Roll Fast bike sitting in the row of bicycles. I think it cost about $26. It had 24 inch wheels and I was in heaven! Kelly had a great selection of Schwinn bikes, but the Roll Fast just caught my fancy. No headlight, no horn or bell, just a plain-Jane bike, but I loved it. The bike got washed regularly to keep its shine. Later I attached a wire basket to the handle bars so that I could carry groceries home from the store. We had a white, Heinz-57 dog, Tippy, who loved to ride in the basket and I would take him out for a spin occasionally.

Looking back, life was quite simple, and safe, in Waukegan. Weather permitting, we played outside with our friends. No TV, no I-Pod, no electronic games, just physical activities that required walking, running, biking, throwing and catching a ball, etc. The only portable phones then were two tin cans with string stretched taut between them. We didn't wear helmets when riding our bikes (without training wheels). We sat in Unc's De Soto rumble seat no less, without wearing a seat belt. We played bare hands with a few drops of mercury, coated a penny, and felt no ill effects. I ice skated at Victory Park in the winter using too small, hand-me-down hockey skates without any protective gear. And we drank lots of Kool Aid made with white sugar and lived to tell about it!

All five boys in our family were a kind of hobby/craft bunch. Erve loved to draw with pen and ink and was excellent in his skill. He entered a contest sponsored by the *Chicago Tribune* before WWII which entailed selecting a motion picture star each week and drawing a bust profile for each entry. I thought his drawings were superb. He didn't win a prize but his creative efforts were noted. While in service during WWII, Erve submitted GI cartoons to the Army's *YANK Magazine* and won third place in a contest sponsored by the magazine. He continued his artistic ways after returning from war by designing and painting posters.

George was the oil painting artist in the family. I marveled at how he could sketch a drawing on canvas and then paint with oils. His work was excellent, so much so that Ma's sister, Aunt Martha, raved about several of his works and bought them. The war put a damper on his artistry and he never resumed painting after returning home. George was also an airplane aficionado. Before entering the air force, he designed and built a model plane with a six foot wingspan using balsa wood frame covered with silk cloth, painted yellow. This plane, powered by a tiny gasoline engine, actually flew in free flight before a wind gust drove it into a power line, ending in a disastrous crash.

Bill was the athlete and played baseball whenever and wherever he could. In the mid- 1930s he played with a semi-professional Johnson Motors team. The team was coached by Ray Helvie. Ray and Sadie, his wife, were good family friends and we followed the team to watch many Sunday afternoon games. It was a very good team and had an excellent win record against northern Illinois semi-pro teams. Bill signed a contract with the Chicago White Sox and played in their farm system for three years before being drafted into the Army in 1941. Returning from the war, Bill was too old for professional baseball and turned to managing a semi-pro team sponsored by Bally Muck Tavern.

Bob loved to work with wood and became very good at making furniture pieces. One of his high school woodshop projects was to build a large chest of drawers using maple wood. He finished the chest and brought it home, giving it to our parents. It was a beautiful, professional piece of work.

Following George's lead, I became interested in building small model planes and built several. Kelly Hardware on Glen Flora Avenue had a complete selection of models and accessories. I never actually tried to see if any of my rubber band powered model planes would fly outdoors.

Soon after WWII began, we moved from the large North Jackson home to a smaller home just a few blocks away at 613 Atlantic Avenue. It afforded plenty of room for our now much smaller family. And, it was much easier to heat in the winter, having a coal fired hot air furnace that kept us warm.

I worked the summer of 1944 at Johnson Motors reporting to Ray Helvie. His department prepared outboard motor parts for shipment overseas to the armed forces. We cleaned motor parts in solvent, dipped them in cosmolene (rust preventive), wrapped them in heavy oiled paper, and then dipped the wrapped piece in melted wax to seal it from moisture. I was a stock boy, keeping the various stations supplied with materials. We worked ten hour shifts for five days and four hours on Saturdays, a 54 hour work week. Ray was a great supervisor and his entire crew liked him very much.

I earned enough money that summer to not only pay room and board but also saved enough to buy a new motor scooter. It wasn't much of a vehicle, but I licensed it and drove it to high school for my senior year. Gasoline cost 15 cents a gallon and I could drive the scooter to school for several weeks on one gallon of fuel! How about that, Toyota Prius?

Uncle Albert (Ollie or Unc) was a hunter and loved to go out looking for pheasants. After tasting the cooked bird I never acquired a desire to hunt or roast them. Unc passed on his hunting passion to George and Bill and would take them hunting at farms away from town. They would always get permission to hunt on a farm. I never took a liking to hunting. Unc also loved to fish and I often went to Lake Michigan with him. He was a good worker when he was sober, but he loved to party on Saturday night. On one of his Saturday night excursions, Unc made a sharp left turn at the corner of North Avenue and Keith, overturning his car, causing quite a bit of damage. The car was hauled home to our garage on Jackson

Street where it was repaired and sanded, ready for a new paint job and canvas top. When it returned from the paint shop it looked like a new car! It was a beautiful light green with a cream stripe along the side and a tan canvas top. I loved that car!

There was only one summer vacation our family took together. Bill was playing Class AA baseball for a Chicago White Sox Farm team in Wisconsin Rapids, Wisconsin. It never became clear why but he and another player were suddenly released from the club. It appears they may have broken a team curfew rule and the manager "fired them". Bill's contract was immediately picked up by another team in Fond du Lac, Wisconsin. My father was so incensed by this that he proposed we go to where the team was playing and arranged for the trip by car. My father, mother, and the four boys all jammed into the 1939 Buick and headed out. My parents found a large cabin on Lake Winnebago outside Fond du Lac and rented it for several days. Bob and I were about eight and ten years old and we had been warned to stay away from the lake. But not a boat! He and I climbed in and out of the row boat, and on one attempt the boat began moving away from the pier. It was tethered to the pier but could still move away. I had one foot inside the boat and one foot on the pier and suddenly did the splits – into the water. Fortunately, the water was only about two feet deep at that point. Had it been deeper I would have been in deep sauce. I couldn't swim!

The next day we drove to the ballpark to watch Brother Bill play second base for his new team. The team they were playing was: Wisconsin Rapids White Sox! Every time Bill got up to bat my Dad would start shouting and when he would get a hit and be on base my Dad would razz the Rapids' manager. He made quite an impression that day. To make things really great, Fond du Lac won the game.

The summer of 1941 would remain in our memories. It was the last year Bill played professional baseball. WWII was fast approaching and the draft was being set up to bring thousands of young men into the Services. The US Army, Navy and Air Force were taking men into units for training at various bases throughout the United States. Erve and Bill were notified to report for duty the same time in September, 1941. They were to be taken to a reception center in Rockford, Illinois for processing and sent to bases in California for basic training. George did not receive notification and waited until after the New Year to enlist in the Army Air Force. He was immediately sent to San Antonio, Texas for basic training in early 1942.

My parents were distraught – the house had emptied very quickly. None of the boys wrote much. It was only a guess how they were doing in the service. After basic training, Erve joined the 41st Infantry Division and was sent to Northern California for guard duty – making sure no Japanese forces landed on our coast. Bill joined the 40th Infantry Division and was sent to Oregon for similar duty. George was sent from basic training to Air Force gunnery school in Texas and then to radio communications school in Arizona to learn Morse Code. He was eventually assigned to the 8th Air force as a radioman-gunner on a B-24 bomber aircraft. After further training Erve and Bill were sent to the Pacific theater, awaiting orders for combat. George was sent to England for more training awaiting assignment to a specific crew for combat.

4

Greenwood and Glen Flora Grade Schools

Bob and I attended Greenwood Elementary School on North Avenue. It was a square, red brick building set far back from the street. The school's two rooms were on the second floor with an exercise room and an auditorium on the basement floor. Kindergarten and first grade classes were in one room while second through fourth grade classes were in the second room. The "exercise room" had a huge rack full of shiny, varnished wooden dumbbells. I don't ever remember anyone using them. Any student exercise was gotten on the playground, never inside the building.

Each spring the school would hold a "Field Day". Events such as foot races, softball and other contests were held with winners being awarded a blue ribbon. I never won a race even though I thought I was pretty good at running. It was nice to get out of the classroom for a few hours. Miss Hoverson and Miss Thorsen had their hands full overseeing the events.

Bob's little misadventure crossing Blue Mound Road in Milwaukee cost him a semester in grade school. Our brothers Erve, George and Bill had either finished high school or were about to when we started Kindergarten. Greenwood had two teachers: Miss Thorsen and Miss Hoverson. Miss Thorson was a jewel and all of the kids in K-1 loved her. She taught us how to read Dick and Jane books and to tell time! We had a large sand box right in our classroom and were able to play in it at special times. Miss Hoverson on the other hand, had a dual personality, I think. She could be very nice at times and then quickly change into a frightening ogre. When Grade 2 to 4 classes (all in one room) got a bit noisy or unruly, she would remove a three foot rubber hose from a desk drawer, split on one end, and smack it on top of her desk. It was enough to scare the bejabbers out of anyone! She got the class quiet and disciplined very quickly.

Miss Hoverson announced in class one day that the foolishness of throwing Canadian Thistle burrs into girl's hair must stop at once. Apparently there had been some incidents. One day on the way home to lunch I was goaded by some of the "boys" into doing just that. When I returned that afternoon I was brought before the class and disciplined by being sent to the cloakroom for the entire afternoon. I learned a valuable lesson that day. Don't listen to your (so called) buddies! Use common sense.

Miss Hoverson pandered to mothers from the well-to-do families at Parent-Teacher meetings (did fathers ever attend those meetings?). Mothers outside the financial realm, as my mother was, were excluded and rarely even recognized.

Around the age of eight, I believe, I was asked to attend a Boy Scout meeting. One meeting and I was ready to join the group. My parents were not so agreeable. To join I would have to wear a Boy Scout shirt and hat – which cost money. My father put an end to my wanting to join by telling me no. The cost of the items apparently was too much for the family budget.

Shooting marbles (mibs) was a big deal at Greenwood. An open area on the south side of the building provided a place for the big circle in dirt for shooting. I had a small leather pouch to carry my marbles. While not a great shooter, I held my own and kept my stock of about 25 marbles in the pouch at all times.

One day walking home to lunch I was surrounded by three bikers who had laid in wait for me. Billy H, Billy K and Duane H threatened me. They wanted me to know that they were the big boys at school and pushed me around, scaring the hell out of me. I told Ma what happened when I got home and she was on the phone immediately. I don't know who she talked to but when I got back to school from lunch I was nicely asked to play softball with the boys. I never had another problem with them.

It was a great sense of achievement to transfer to Glen Flora Elementary School for Grades 5, 6, 7, and 8. Glen Flora School was located on an enormous lot at the intersection of Jackson Street and Glen Flora Avenue. It was a large rectangular red brick, two story building. Unlike Greenwood School, it housed all eight grades. This raises the question: Why did Greenwood school only teach Grades K through Four? It reduced the size of K through Grade Four classes at Glen Flora but eventually all of the transfers from Greenwood would escalate Grades Five through Eight class sizes.

Glen Flora Principal, Miss Curtis, was very friendly and treated everyone well. Fifth Grade teacher, Miss Schmidt, taught penmanship using the Palmer Method. I remember very well the OOO's and /\/\/\/\/\'s writing exercises with her closely monitoring our progress. Miss Pyle taught our Sixth Grade class. Then we went on to departmental classes in Seventh and Eighth Grades, preparing us for high school. Miss Smith, Miss Palm, Miss Scott, Miss Connelly, Miss Quimby, Miss Sandvik, and Mr. Calkins taught our classes. At the time it did not raise interest, but it does now: note that most of the teachers were entitled "Miss". Was that a requisite for teaching school in the pre-WWII era?

5

Grade School Stories

Christmas was always an uplifting time of the year. We'd decorate the house and Ma would bake a variety of cookies and cakes. Redeemer Lutheran Church would have special services during Advent and was nicely decorated with a huge Christmas tree in the sanctuary. Christmas Eve was extraordinary for kids because the church would have gifts for all. Usually there was a bag for each containing an apple, orange and candy. For the younger kids it was a magic night!

Christmas, 1939 was really special for Bob and me. Our brothers had pooled resources and bought an electric Lionel train and set it up under the tree. The train along with our other gifts, usually clothing, made it our best Christmas. It was wonderful!

Our class had several top-notch students. John McC, Carol Amstutz, and Jean R were among the elite. But, we had many other good students such as Beverly S, Faye C, Don H, Wally B, George C and Bud G, to name a few. I was not an outstanding student in grade school but I did manage to earn acceptable grades. There was a boy in our class named Jimmy B who was scholastically impaired (there were no Special Education classes in the 1930s). Some boys would goad Jimmy into doing or saying things that were supposed to be funny, but more often were not. I don't know how some found fun in inciting Jimmy – he was a good boy.

Seventh and eighth grades students would walk (no busses!) to North School, a hearty half-mile from Glen Flora, for classes in shop and home economics. Boys were taught how to use shop tools and had to complete projects before graduating. I still have a sturdy pine footstool that I made under the guidance of teacher Max Busewitz. Girls learned how to cook and bake in their classes.

In all of my school days, I can only recall having gotten into one fist fight. Bob A, for some unknown reason, kept calling me names, egging me on to fight. Well, one day it had gone too far and we met outside on the north side of Glen Flora School among the many oak trees. There was a gathering of about 10 to 12 students eager to see a fist fight. A little pushing here, a little shoving there and we went at each other with the fists. Midway through the fight, we stopped and put on our gloves – it was pretty cold! The fight ended in a draw, neither of us claiming victory. Afterward, I realized how stupid it was to fight. Nothing significant had been gained. However, Bob stopped with the taunting and later we became pretty good friends.

A badge of distinction for Eighth Grade boys was being named to the Crossing Guard Group. We wore a white webbed belt and monitored student crossings at the Jackson Street and Glen Flora Avenue intersection. While only an alternate, I was called upon for duty a number of times. It's interesting to note that only boys were named to the group. Would that stand up in today's world? Elementary school days were good days, happy days in Waukegan. And yes, there were some bitter cold winter days during school years. We walked to school, no bussing, many times through 2 to 3 foot snowdrifts. Snow shoes or boots were unheard of in our family. There were times I wore shoes with cardboard covering holes in the soles. Fortunately, Jackson Street and Glen Flora Avenue were plowed on snow days and some sidewalks had been cleared by the time school was finished for the day and we were able to easily walk home.

Packed snow and ice often covered the streets in the winter around our home on Jackson Street. With a short run we could flop onto our sleds and coast for a ways on the ice and packed snow. I miscalculated one day as I ran and flopped on my sled, not seeing the cleared concrete ahead of me. When the sled hit the concrete, it suddenly stopped but I kept going. My face hit the street and I ground one of my front teeth on the concrete, taking off about one-third of the tooth. Later at the dentist, the missing portion was treated and filled in with gold! Apparently our family dentist had not heard about caps. He did not use an anesthetic while working on the tooth and I swear I saw smoke coming out of my mouth at times while he was drilling away! I had the gold filling for more than twenty years before replacing it with a cap.

Sometimes we would stop on the way home from school at Bale's Drug Store for a five cent Coke or at Kelly's Hardware Store for a hobby item. If we chose to have a milkshake (20 cents!) at the drug store, the pharmacist would always give us a small pack of two cookies. There was a slogan on the package: "Nibble a Nab for a Nickel". They sure tasted good with the malt or milkshake!

Greenwood and Glen Flora Elementary Schools had done a good job preparing us for high school. We were ready to move on in the world! Prior to starting high school, the summer of 1942 was spent lazing about going to Lake Michigan to swim or fish. I had a bad case of acne in high school which I'm sure contributed to my shyness. Dr. Keller advised me to get out in the sun to help clear up the acne. Taking him at his word, I spent a lot of time each summer sunbathing at the beach to the point that I always had a dark tan down to my waist. It may have helped with the acne but I suffer today with skin cancer as a result of the high exposure to sun. No one spoke of the dangers of UV exposure from the sun, including Dr. Keller. If you could afford it, you'd buy a small bottle of sun tan lotion to get the "bronze look". It did little to protect the skin from the sun's radiation.

As a group we'd also play Monopoly on Pat Jones' screened porch during the war. Pat, Carol Amstutz, Jean Derreberry, Lois S, Joan DuB, sometimes Russell H, and I often played for hours at the game. It was good clean fun. Carol introduced us to tennis and we'd play on Atlantic Avenue (without a net) in front of our homes. The same street served as a softball diamond. Once in a while we would play "kick the can".

Of course, we were all concerned about the war. News was not good and our forces were taking a beating in the Pacific and in Europe. My three brothers, Erve, George and Bill had completed basic training and all were serving in combat areas in 1942. We didn't hear from them often because of their engagements and that only increased our concern. We displayed a small rectangular red and white flag with three blue stars in a front window indicating three servicemen from our home were in the war.

President Roosevelt tried to instill courage and a positive attitude in all Americans with his radio broadcasted fireside chats, but it was hard to think of the fighting that our troops were undergoing. The only real photos and movies showing battles were seen at the theaters that featured Pathe News. The *Waukegan News-Sun* newspaper kept us informed of the fighting against Herr Hitler of Germany, Mussolini of Italy and Premier Tojo of Japan. US Forces took a lot of hits in the first years of the war while we at home geared up for manufacturing war materials such as guns, tanks, airplanes and trucks.

Pat Jones' father was appointed as "Civil Defense Warden" of our neighborhood and he asked me to assist. At times we would walk our neighborhood on Atlantic Avenue during a blackout exercise to check homes for any light being seen. We wore an armband indicating our official status and carried flashlights. We never saw a home with light shining through windows or doors. If the city was ever attacked from the air, Atlantic Avenue was secure!

I clearly remember looking up at the sky one day after hearing an unusually loud airplane overhead, to discover the first B-29 bomber flying low over Waukegan. It was monstrous! I'd seen B-17s fly over several times. But seeing the B-29 was a thrill. I knew our air force and military were protecting us from any homeland attack.

6
Waukegan Township High School

My first impression of Waukegan Township High School (WTHS) in the fall of 1942 was feeling overwhelmed! In spite of orientation classes it was still awesome. We were the future graduation class of 1946! Huge buildings, so many students and where were the class rooms I needed to get to? Finding the school office and the cafeteria was easy, but English, Math, Shop, and Science classrooms were tough to find, especially since there were two floors to the school. And Study Room, wow! Then, to find a class assigned to the old, senior high building was almost too much to handle, especially with only ten minutes between assigned classes. But, two weeks after school had started it was a piece of cake. Teenagers are so adaptable!

I was very shy and had difficulty fitting in with groups at high school. To this day I do not know why I was so withdrawn. All of my brothers were outgoing. My mother, however, was a quiet type of person, while my father was a definite extrovert. In classes, I never volunteered to provide answers and spoke only when called upon. In an English class one day, when asked to recite, I ended my answer with 'more or less'. Well, the teacher, Miss Weiss, made quite a production of my response (which was correct incidentally) really embarrassing me. It only served to increase my shyness.

On very cold or snowy days Ma would give me a dime for bus fare. The old bus ran from Greenwood Avenue along Jackson Street to the high school stopping only when a student was standing on a corner. When I say old bus, I mean *OLD*. The bus was not very warm with the opening and closing of the front door but it beat walking in the cold and snow. As the bus crossed Grand Avenue and headed down the hill to Low Street the driver would floor it to increase speed. The engine would be screaming – I thought for sure a piston would come flying through the hood! We had to increase speed so that the bus could make it up the side of the hill, which it always slowly managed to do. It was a thrill riding that bus to high school!

I fit in nicely in shop classes, taking Print Shop, Machine Shop and Auto Mechanics. The instructors seemed less intimidating and helped me to fit in. Mr. Swan in Print Shop was very helpful and encouraging. I excelled in all of the shop classes. In other, more academic classes I did only favorably. One teacher, Miss Grady, took me beyond my borders of thinking in the plane geometry class and helped me realize that I could accomplish much more than I had anticipated. She had the ability to project mathematical principles and get students to accept and understand how to use them. I greatly respect her for helping me to *THINK*! School for me had been mostly learning by rote. She helped me realize that education was much more than memorization of facts. That was the most important thing I learned in high school. I will never forget how she got and maintained order in her classes. She would glare at a student and simply say, "I'm watching you young man!" No one ever questioned her technique.

It was in the summer of 1943 that our gymnasium quietly underwent a major renovation. It had been painted a light golden color with purple trim and large purple letters spelling out BULLDOGS were placed at the east end high up on the wall. No one was allowed in the gym until students were called for assembly and introduced to the new basketball coach, Wilbur 'Strings' Allen. We were in awe! It was as if the entire school had been transformed. Suddenly WTHS had a new coach, a bulldog mascot, an organized pep squad and new vitality. We could follow our teams and yell and cheer and be happy. There was a war going on but we now had the opportunity to have some fun.

One of the most memorable basketball games in the history of WTHS was played in Evanston in 1945. Many students traveled from Waukegan on the North Shore RR to see the game. Most of the game was played with our team merely standing on the floor, one player holding the basketball. It was a new strategy employed by our coach, one that had never been used before. The Evanston team was completely befuddled and could not counter. Waukegan won the game by a score of 5 to 3, the lowest scoring basketball game ever played in our conference. It was a game never to be forgotten. The celebration that night was unbelievable! Many years later, I met a man (John P) at a party in Phoenix who I recognized as one of the WTHS basketball players. We had a delightful conversation recalling the event in Evanston.

In my sophomore year I was required to take two years of Reserve Officers Training Class (ROTC). I kind of liked the marching in order, learning about rifles and military strategy and wearing a uniform. A friend, Bob A, approached me one day and asked if I would like to serve on the ROTC Color Guard. I'd seen the group of five cadets present the flags at games and special school events. He told me I could be a rifle carrying guard (I was only 5 feet 6 inches tall, weighed 120 pounds and could not handle the weight of a flag!). However, the color guard got in free to all athletic events and that convinced me to say yes. I served on the color guard during my junior year in high school.

ROTC sponsored a rifle team of five cadets with several backups that engaged in matches with other ROTC teams in northern Illinois. The object of each member of the team, after sighting in a 22 caliber rifle, was to get as many shots as possible into the bull's eye on an 8 X 12 paper target some 50 feet away. I joined the team and while I did not qualify as a full fledged team member, I did get to be a backup. What I learned in ROTC and rifle marksmanship training served a most important function when I entered the US Army in 1947.

I went out for baseball hoping to make the WTHS team. There was a varsity team and a junior varsity team. I opted to play second base because that was the position my brother Bill played. Bill was an excellent baseball player and easily made the varsity team when he was in high school. He had a falling out with Coach Al Grosche because he played semi-pro ball one summer. Coach wouldn't let him play high school ball after that and there must have been a scene. When I tried out for the team eight years later, Coach obviously remembered my brother because he often called me "Bill" and often found fault with my efforts at fielding and batting. He got so worked up one day during batting practice that he threw a "bean ball" at me. I should have known then I would never be awarded a "W" letter for playing baseball. When I asked him at the end of the season why I didn't get the coveted gold "W" he replied I didn't play enough innings – as if it was my decision when to play in a game.

During the summer of 1943 I found a job at Hansen's bake shop on Glen Flora Avenue. Pay was a paltry 25 cents an hour and I worked three or four hours a day. My work consisted of cleaning bake trays and 'icing' the sweet rolls and arranging them for sale in the front shop. One day leaving work I helped myself to a chocolate covered cream puff. It was delicious! Next day Mr. Hansen informed me if I ever did that again he would fire me. How did he find out that I had hooked it?

The acappella choir sang at most student body meetings in the gym. I enjoyed their singing and decided to join the group. Walking to the top floor of the Senior building I entered the room and told Mr. Schuman that I'd like to sing. He asked me to sing a few bars of a song and told me I would be a tenor. A year later we were told that Mr. Schuman had moved from town and the choir was left without a director. That ended my career as a choir member.

The big entertainment event for us was to see a movie at the Genesee or Academy Theaters. There were two other movie theaters on south Genesee Street: the Rialto and Times. I think I only saw one or two movies at either place. It cost a dime to see one movie at the Genesee and two movies at the Academy. The Academy did not have first run movies and one movie was always a western with Tom Mix, the Lone Ranger, Roy Rogers or Rin Tin Tin. Western movies were not my favorite. The Genesee Theater had a really nice snack bar. When I had an extra dime I would always buy a pack of Walnettos, a walnut flavored caramel. A good movie and caramels - that was hard to beat! Just to the left of the main entrance to the Genesee was a shop that made fresh caramel popcorn. I loved it but most often could not afford to buy any.

That same summer Bob A. invited me to join him in Sunday School at Redeemer Lutheran Church on Grove Avenue. I enjoyed the classes and new found friends. I began going to church and joined a youth group called the Walther League. That invitation by Bob was instrumental in lighting the flame of Christianity in me and was a major turning point in my life. What is most interesting is that Bob stopped going to Sunday School soon after I started and never returned to church after that. My parents had stopped going to church many years prior to my going to Sunday School.

In 1944 brother Bob and I joined the catechism class at Redeemer. Rev. Henry Heise was our pastor and instructor. Initially we met three times a week: Tuesday and Thursday after school and Saturday morning. Later, classes were cut to two times a week so that the church could reduce heating expenses and save coal. We were at war and rationing was mandated by the government. Not only were we expected to maintain good grades in school but also learn about the Lutheran Church and its creed. Rev. Heise was a good but tough teacher and tolerated no nonsense in class. The hardest part for me was memorizing bible passages and parts of Luther's Catechism. Bob and I had no one in the family to help us with explanations for the Lutheran beliefs and we struggled at times. I worried about passing Catechism class until one student, Steve B, told me, "No one fails to pass Catechism!"

We joined the Walther League, a group of Lutheran teenagers who met regularly for fun. I enjoyed the gatherings and became very close to some of the kids in the group. It was there that I met Howard Heyer and we became very close friends. Of course, there were girls and it was challenging for me to talk and be at ease with them. I do remember having an eye for Shirley S – she was a cute blonde. There were no couples. We went for bike rides and picnics and meals as a group. There was a lot of teasing though and laughing and good times – even during war time.

In four years of high school I attended only one dance, sponsored by my aviation mechanics class. We had contracted for a five piece orchestra and even managed to bring in a Piper Cub airplane to grace the floor. I handled the cloak room, hanging up coats and jackets for the dancers. I was so shy that I could not conceive of my going up to the auditorium and asking a girl to dance. I didn't even know how! The dance was a huge success, however.

One of the biggest joys of high school for me was the end of war in Europe in May and the end of war with Japan in August of 1945. Of course, those were happy days for all citizens of the USA! Bob A and I decided to celebrate and caught the North Shore RR in Waukegan and rode to downtown Chicago on VJ Day. The train was packed with civilians and naval personnel all heading to the Loop for a victory celebration. Downtown Chicago was a mass of people, yelling, whooping and even crying. It was literally shoulder to shoulder in the streets and sidewalks with men and women dancing, singing and kissing. There were some folks who had obviously started drinking early on in the day and were, as my father used to say, schnockered. But, who cared? WWII was done – finished! Our boys would be coming home. It was a memorable time!

Graduation from WTHS in June, 1946, was, for the most part, a nonevent. No one from my family attended the ceremony held in the school gymnasium. In our high school class of 356 students, I ranked 65th, putting me in the top quarter percentile. While not a top student, I still did pretty well. I was concerned about grades, of course, but I just did not have a goal in my life. Some of my friends knew they were going on to college after graduation while I didn't even think about a college life at that time. After receiving our diplomas, Bob A and I headed for Chicago to celebrate. Bob had arranged a date for me. Mary E was an attractive girl but had a somewhat shaky reputation. Bob had decided that we should go to the Blackhawk Hotel in Chicago for dinner. I took one look at the menu and nearly fell off the chair! I did not have that kind of money to pay for a full blown dinner. We ended up ordering a sandwich (expensive!). The evening turned out to be very tiring for me, trying to keep conversation going on the trip to and from the city. The relationship died after the second date with Mary. We had little in common and I was a real drag for her.

My parents did not encourage me to further my education. In fact my father talked about "getting a job" upon graduation. And he even helped me find one at Johns-Manville Corporation. I was trained to be a timekeeper in a manufacturing department. Each week I would tally work hours for each man using his punched timecard, calculate production and any bonus made by each and post the results out in the work area. Sometimes I was confronted by a worker who was unhappy about his bonus and I would have to explain the numbers. The job became extremely boring after several weeks – there was no real challenge to it. I would walk around the plant killing time just to avoid boredom. I soon made up my mind that I could not go on working in a factory to make a living. The realization came that there was not a great future for me in doing mind-numbing number crunching.

Things I Learned Completing High School

Think things through – use your feelings and intellect to determine what is right for oneself.

Listen to your elders. Watch what they do. Reflect on what they say.

Make choices in daily life carefully because they determine what your tomorrows will be.

Work is an essential part of life – you gotta have money to live!

7
WWII Stories

It was after dinner on Sunday noon, December 7, 1941, that we moved to the living room and turned on the radio (a Philco console). The news came in loud and clear. Japan had attacked Pearl Harbor, Hawaii. Unbelievable! We just sat and listened, mesmerized by the WGN news broadcaster. We couldn't believe what was happening. More importantly, where were brothers Erve and Bill? We had no idea if they were still in the USA or had been moved overseas. It was a frightening day, a "day of infamy", not only for our family but for the entire country. The next day, December 8, President Roosevelt asked for and got a declaration of war from Congress against Japan and Germany. We were at war!

George had enlisted in the US Air Force right after the New Year's holiday. All three brothers were now engaged. War was tough for us, especially since all my brothers were overseas. Erve and Bill had been sent to the South Pacific Theater of Operations and were serving with Army units in the New Guinea and Philippine Island campaigns. Erve was in the 41st Infantry Division and Bill was in the 40th Infantry Division. George was in the European Theater with the 8th Air Force flying over Germany and Africa in a B-24 Liberator airplane. Letters from the boys were few and far between.

World War II taught us the value of conserving. Everything was in short supply. In our house we saved tin cans and newspapers. Any kind of metal was saved and turned in for use in making weapons. We saved grease from cooking food and took it to the meat market for reclamation. My father sold his car because gasoline was rationed and we, like many families, could only get an "A" card, which allowed two gallons of gas a week. Even shoes were rationed. So I rode my bike or walked. If we wanted to go downtown to see a movie at the Genesee Theater or at the Academy, we rode the streetcar, usually one way, so that we could pay a dime to get into the show.

A War Bond Rally was held in fall, 1944 at the Genesee Theater. Jack Benny, Eddie Anderson (Rochester) and Cesar Romero were notables coming to Waukegan to help sell bonds. There was a parade along Genesee Street ending at the theater. The rally was held inside and featured Jack Benny doing his comedic routine with Rochester followed by Cesar Romero's speech urging us to buy US war bonds and stamps (we could buy 10 cent war stamps at school!). The WTHS Color Guard had presented the flag and colors prior to the ceremony. After the rally, I met briefly with Benny and Romero and shook hands with Cesar. He had enormous hands and they dwarfed mine in the handshake. It was an event I'll never forget.

Weekends in Waukegan found hundreds of sailors from Great Lakes Naval Training Center in town. There was usually a mass of white uniforms downtown in the summer, all looking for an outlet to get rid of pent up emotions. At times it was not safe to go to a movie with a date because of comments from sailors, many very suggestive and sexual. We found Sunday evenings the best time to see a movie. Most servicemen were back at base at that time.

I asked Jean Derreberry one summer day for a date to go to Riverside Park in Chicago. We rode the North Shore Train and got off near the Park. I had less than $25 to spend on rides and activities so I wanted to be careful. I foolishly stopped at an arcade when the attendant challenged me to pop balloons on a board using darts. Next thing I knew I was throwing darts, never quite making enough hits to get a prize. I blew ten bucks very quickly before I came to my senses. Jean and I had a good time that day in spite of my errant dart throwing. Jean was the first girl I ever kissed on a date! In the life of a teenager that is a milestone and for me it was a thrill. OK, I had kissed a distant cousin years before, but she was family and that didn't count.

August, 1943 was particularly difficult. Late in the afternoon with a knock on the door, a Western Union man delivered a telegram from the U.S. War Department. It read, "We regret to inform you that T/Sgt. George F. Scheske has been injured in the course of duty"......! We had no idea how seriously he was injured. It was the only time I ever saw my father cry. My mother was equally upset. It was months before we learned that he had been transferred to a hospital in Florida and then to a Veterans Administration Hospital in San Antonio, Texas. And even then his injury was not made known! Months later he was transferred to a hospital in Madison, Wisconsin. Only then did we find out that he had had a serious head injury.

We learned that while on a mission over Frederickshaven, Germany, George had been hit in the head with a 50 mm shell from a German airplane and had lain injured for hours while his plane completed its bombing mission and returned to England. Protocol determined that planes with injured crewmen landed first to get medical help. Planes ejected a red flare denoting injured personnel aboard. Each of my brothers was injured during the war, George the most severely, and all received the Purple Heart Medal among others awards. And each suffered the emotional injuries associated with war. We were thankful that all three men returned home after the war's end in 1945. Each carried the scars of war long after their service ended.

I respected all of my older brothers for having served under combat conditions. While I only served for a short period under peace time conditions, I did my duty for my country. Brother Bob enlisted and served the longest of anyone in the family. I think all of the boys made our parents proud!

8
From High School to US Army Basic Training

My answer to finding a challenging job in 1946 was to join the Army Air Force – I was absolutely sure of it. My parents were not happy with my decision, but the recruiting sergeant convinced them that enlisting in the service was an excellent choice. I had to have parental permission to join since I was only 17. The written tests were a piece of cake and then it was on to the physical examination in Chicago. Turns out I did not pass the physical because of a hernia. Back to Waukegan, crestfallen, and into Victory Memorial Hospital for repair surgery by Dr. Samuel Keller, our family doctor.

After recuperating and with the help of Brother Bill, I found another factory job, this time at Johnson Outboard Motors. In my second week at Johnsons' I was confronted by a Union Shop Steward trying to get me to join the union – which I refused to do. He spat some choice words when I refused the second time. I have no quarrel with unions. They have, for the most part, served workers well. I just did not see myself as a union member. I felt I could negotiate my salary and work conditions on my own. I did not need to pay someone to do it for me.

Again, I made up my mind to get out of this dead end work. I went to the US Post Office on Genesee Street and enlisted in the US Army. Written tests were a repeat of the Air Force tests – no problem. After passing the physical in Chicago on January 7, 1947, I was sworn in as Private Frederick Albert Scheske, Jr., RA16242787. The group of enlistees, mostly Chicagoans, was whisked off by train to Fort Lewis, Washington. We rode for three days in a Pullman car and ate meals in the dining car. None of us had a clue what we were getting into. Language I overheard on that trip was gross and mind boggling. I had never heard such street language before and it was an education I hadn't anticipated.

A thirty minute stopover in Cheyenne, Wyoming was eventful. Leaving the train, I ran down the main street to a grocery store and bought a pound of black cherries – I love cherries. I handed the clerk a ten dollar bill and he gave me change in silver dollars! Eight silver dollars and loose change in my pocket and I was leaning to the side on my run back to the train. Boy, those cherries were good!

I had never seen scenery like Wyoming, Idaho and Washington offered. The mountains, trees and streams were magnificent. I often stood in awe in the entry way of our rail car taking in the picturesque landscape. They were impressions I shall never forget.

Upon arrival to Fort Lewis, we were quickly assimilated into two platoons, assigned to barracks and beds and led into a building for clothing and bedding issuance. In less than two hours time we were clothed and set, ready for army life. And then it started! Two drill sergeants began by informing us what was in store for us. Our days were to start with roll call at 6 am, breakfast (chow), immediately followed with drills at 8:00 am. Uniforms and schedule of training activities for each day were posted on a bulletin board. It was a full day often ending about 5 pm, followed by mess (dinner/chow).

Drill sergeants mode of operation was to shout out orders,

many times using foul language and fear as motivation. I understood their task of trying to make soldiers out of young men in a limited time period but I believe much more could have been achieved using positive reinforcement. Any screw ups during the day were usually awarded some kind of extra training activity, such as KP, cleaning the latrine or mess hall thoroughly after dinner. And drill sergeants seemed to be able to find something wrong each day. Our particular sergeant took great pleasure in finding fault with someone's performance. Maybe it was marching out of step, or talking when we were told to shut up, or not doing the manual of arms correctly. His finding an infraction and yelling at a soldier only made all of us aware of what kind of screw-ups we had in our platoon. I'm not sure how several men in my platoon passed the written tests to even qualify for acceptance as a soldier.

One evening after two weeks of this turmoil, sad, tired, and dispirited, I sat on my footlocker and wondered what I'd gotten myself into. I knew I couldn't back out of my contract. I'd taken the oath to serve and defend my country! I was really disheartened and homesick. Just suck it up (as they told us to do) and get through basic training. It was a hard lesson in life.

Meals were served family style by KPs (Kitchen Police) in a mess hall while we sat at picnic type tables. That is, trays and bowls of food were placed on each table and we took a portion and passed it on to the next person. Sometimes the guy on the end of the line didn't get a fair portion. For the most part though, we had enough to eat. I gained ten pounds during eight week's basic training!

Acne was again having a field day with me as the food was greasy and fattening. One day during a "personal inspection" by our company's First Lieutenant (who was almost always a couple of sheets to the wind), I along with eleven other soldiers, were ordered to go on sick call the next day. I was to get something for my acne. After a long wait for a doctor and some medicine, we got back from sick call about 2:30 pm and had to sit around the barracks waiting for our company to come in from training exercises.

All hell broke loose when our platoon returned. Our drill sergeant seemed to go berserk because we had not attended training, even though he knew we were ordered to go on sick call. All twelve of us were ordered to clean the mess hall after eating dinner and to stay at it until he found it clean enough. We failed his inspection for minuscule infractions three times. It wasn't until the fourth inspection at 10 p.m. that we passed. Then we had to go back to the barracks and prepare for next day's training. Lights were turned off at ten – we worked quietly in the dark before getting into bed, completely exhausted!

One of the trainees had a radio and he turned it on each morning at wake-up call (6:00 am). Today, whenever I hear the song "Heartache" (played by Ted Weems' orchestra), it reminds me of the times the radio played that song in our barracks. The Seattle station played it every morning, I think. It was nice music to wake up to, I must admit.

One of the Chicagoans, a very short Greek fellow slow of mind, refused to take a shower and after two weeks smelled badly. No one wanted to be near him or sit next to him during mess. One evening four men who bunked near him grabbed him and dragged him screaming into the shower for a GI cleaning. Using a scrub brush and GI soap, they cleansed him thoroughly and forced him to agree to take showers in the future. We never had a personal cleanliness problem with him again.

I could never get oriented in Fort Lewis. Even with Mount Rainier in the distance I could not distinguish east from west or north from south. I took a walk one Sunday afternoon away from the barracks with a fellow soldier and hiked miles from our place. We came upon a lovely lake and across the way was a small village. It was a beautiful scene. Thank goodness the other man knew how to get back, which we did just before mess was served.

One month after basic training began, we were granted a weekend pass to go into Seattle. Our company commander called a meeting before we left and talked to us about sexual activity. We were advised to keep our pants zipped up and to stay out of trouble. I buddied up with a guy of Japanese descent (I cannot recall his name) in my platoon and we headed into town. We got a hotel room in downtown Seattle and set out to see the sights and get some decent food. It was great fun to relax and enjoy the sights with civilians. Sunday he asked if I wanted to go bowling and I agreed. He took me into a part of town that he apparently knew and we walked into a bowling alley. People stopped to stare at me. I was the only Caucasian in a Japanese bowling alley! We had great fun bowling and I thoroughly enjoyed the afternoon. Then, we headed back to the Fort for another month of masochistic training.

Classroom sessions and field training finally brought us to firing a rifle. We rode in trucks to the firing range and were divided into groups of two. One trainee was to fire a rifle while the other acted as a coach. My partner had obviously never handled a rifle and was very nervous. I was first and after sighting-in the rifle began firing at the bulls-eye target some fifty feet away. The firing range officer came over to us and asked about my experience in shooting. I had hit into and very close to the bulls-eye for all of my shots. We assumed three positions while firing: standing, sitting and prone. I wasn't aware at the time but I had qualified as an expert in all positions. High school ROTC Rifle Team experience had paid off handsomely. As my partner and I switched places I had just laid down next to him when he fired the rifle, before getting the order by the range office. My left ear was very close to the rifle when he fired and I suddenly lost hearing in that ear. The range officer had a few words with the trainee who was very nervous. He barely qualified for the firing exercises.

All trainees were trained to drive a 6X6 Army truck. Having to "double clutch" while shifting gears was an adventure. It was tough for some and we heard a lot of gears grinding when shifting. Our First Lieutenant had a field day screaming at drivers who failed to use hand signals when making turns on the training track (no turn signals on those trucks). In the end we all earned US Army driver licenses.

One day while our platoon formed up for more training, a platoon in an adjoining barracks was also assembling. I looked over and saw a man I thought I recognized. Sure enough, Chuck "Eggo" Schroeder was standing there, a big grin on his face. He and I were in the same graduating class at WTHS. We only had a few minutes to talk but he told me he had just returned from the hospital after contracting pneumonia. We both said let's get together, but I never saw him again. I was told he had lost several weeks of training and had been assigned to another platoon.

A big event in basic training is called "bivouac", a term meaning campout. Ours was a three day event that included carrying a rifle and a complete 30 pound backpack with tools, mess kit, blanket and half of a pup tent. Food was served from a little trailer that arrived each day at meal time and was eaten out of an aluminum mess kit. The weather was sunny but very cold, dipping down into the low 30s at night. Each night we would join-up with our buddy, connect the tent halves, drive stakes into the ground and erect the tent. We slept in our clothes on the ground with one thin Army blanket to keep us warm. The first morning I woke up with one foot sticking out of the tent flap, sure that I had frozen it. The hot food we were served cooled very quickly in the metal mess kits, so we ate very quickly. The toilet was a trench in the ground and we didn't take long with that task either. Personal hygiene was forgotten. We marched that day for miles heading I had no idea where. Late afternoon I was very tired and as we approached an inlet of water off Puget Sound, I could not stop running down a steep slope and crashed into a tree, which stopped me cold!

The second night of bivouac was to be training in the use of a compass. We received little training and were sent off with scant directions on how to reach our objective. You talk about a bunch of goofballs, all of us walking about in pitch darkness in the woods with flashlights looking for an object which most did not find. To this day I do not know how to use a compass to guide me in finding a destination! We did manage to find our way back to the tent area, check in and go to sleep. We marched back to our barracks the next day tired, smelly and thankful it was over with. Showers and our bunks never felt so good. Later, I thought about what we had done on bivouac and realized that many thousands of soldiers had done that under combat conditions and how fortunate we were.

I was invited one Friday evening to go along with three other trainees to a beer garden on the main Fort. I did not do much beer drinking but one of the privates, Lenny, proceeded to get pretty smashed. Heading back to the barracks he had difficulty walking and we had to help him along. We spotted an MP Jeep coming down the street and told Lenny to straighten up so he wouldn't get arrested. He assumed a ramrod stance and walked a straight line until the Jeep was well past us. We finally got him into our barracks and his top bunk. Ten minutes later we heard a thud and discovered he had rolled out of his bed onto the floor. We put him back to bed again. He was a sad looking soldier the next day.

In our company's first session of guard duty we were taken to an empty barracks and assigned times and areas of duty. It was a rainy night when I reported for my tour of duty and I took my raincoat with me. I was driven to a location and told to continually circle the fenced area. It was dark, no lights and it was drizzling rain. I had absolutely no idea where I was or what I was guarding within the fence. Of course, I had my rifle and bayonet, but no bullets. My tour ended uneventfully when I was relieved two hours later. My next tour was in the early morning hours just as dawn was breaking. I looked for my raincoat, but it was missing. I reported it missing to the guard duty sergeant. When I got to my area to be guarded, there was sufficient light to see what was inside the fence. The area was about one city block in size and sitting in the middle of this expanse were two pallets of lumber! I had been guarding two stacks of lumber. I couldn't help but chuckle.

Next morning we reported for training and our illustrious drill sergeant held up a raincoat and shouted out the "laundry number" inscribed on it: S-2787. It was, of course, my raincoat and he started belittling me for losing it. I told him it had been taken while on guard duty and he should check with the sergeant to whom I had reported it missing. I got a look that would have frozen water but he did stop with the smart aleck remarks.

In our eleventh week of basic training, five of us were called out of formation and taken to the office. We were informed that due to our high entrance examination grades we were eligible for additional training in a GI School. I was offered two choices: one in a truck maintenance school and the other in an administration school. My brothers, freshly out of the service, had advised me to get into any GI school offered. I'm no dummy! I'd had enough mechanics classes in high school to know that there was little future in that, and I chose administration school in Camp Lee, Virginia (one of the best and wisest decisions I ever made).

For our "graduation" from basic training our company, along with several other training companies, paraded before Fort Lewis' 2nd Army Division top brass. The March day was cloudy and very cold and the ground was covered with snow and ice. Our learned drill sergeant ordered us to fix bayonets to our rifles for the parade. The Fort Lewis Army Band was playing and as our platoon marched in order before the inspection team, one man in the front slipped on the ice and went down. It was like dominoes – men were falling, narrowly missing others in formation with their drawn bayonets! We were ordered to halt and then told to withdraw our bayonets. It was a miracle no one was injured by the bayonets. One did not have to be a college professor to know that fixing bayonets was a lousy idea for a parade on icy roads. It was indeed a thrill for me and the four others destined for further training to pack and leave Fort Lewis the next day.

As we left Fort Lewis in March, 1947, I learned our training company was scheduled to ship out for Germany the following week. Germany was where I wanted to go since my father had been born there and my mother had been conceived there. But, I reasoned there would be an equally interesting place for assignment after administration training at Camp Lee, Virginia.

9
On to Administration School

My assigned group arrived by train in Washington, DC several days after leaving Ft. Lewis. It was snowing the largest snowflakes I had ever seen! Our car was the last in the train and we had to walk at least one block in the snow to get under cover at the station. We stowed our duffel bags in lockers in the station and set out to see our nation's capitol. As we left the train station a cab driver offered to show us the sights for five bucks. What a deal! He took us all over pointing out monuments and points of interest. Our last stop was at the Senate Building where we entered the chamber's visitor section and listened to senators discuss "portal-to-portal" pay legislation (it never passed into law). In about four hours we had gotten a wonderful snapshot tour of Washington and then had to head back to the train station for a ride to Camp Lee.

The first impression of Camp Lee was of wonderment. Buildings were cleaner, much newer and personnel were very friendly. Our first sergeant greeted us, gave us our building assignments and informed us we could pick up our Class A pass any day after completing class. Class A pass? No restrictions? We could leave the Camp any time we wanted after class? Holy Moley! This was the US Army? It felt like a college campus. Then we were led to the mess hall and found out it was part of the Army's Cooks and Bakers School! Food was excellent, far and away better than anything we had experienced in basic training. We had a choice of several meat dishes and vegetables, salads and freshly baked deserts every day. I had to pinch myself to ensure I wasn't dreaming.

Classes were held each day from 8:00 am to 4:00 pm with an hour off for lunch. I learned to type on an old, heavily used Underwood manual typewriter and reached a speed of 33 words (corrected) a minute going full bore, just two words less than the 35 wpm rating of a Typist Class A. But, I was happy to have learned to type. Thirty years later while working in the semiconductor industry the typing training bore productive results when computers became part of the workplace. I was amazed I recalled how to type and easily acquired the skills needed to be constructive in the use of computers when entering data or preparing reports.

Each class day in administrative school we had an exercise to fill out a form called a Daily Report that noted who was present and who was missing for duty. It was a complex report and for some odd reason I had trouble getting the hang of it. Fortunately I was never required to fill one out after being assigned to my permanent unit.

Going off base for leave one Saturday, I rode a city bus into downtown Fredericksburg, VA. I didn't have a lot of money to shop so I walked around taking in the sights. A man in our group had talked about a very beautiful woman working in a drug store and I wanted to see her. She was indeed beautiful – and very nice. About noon I realized I needed something to eat so I walked to a restaurant and checked out the menu. Real life hit when I saw the food prices. I decided quickly to head back to Camp Lee and eat in the mess hall.

I boarded a city bus, noted there was only one seat open and it was in the back row of the bus. Taking the seat, I rode into base. I pulled the cord indicating that I wanted off at the next stop while standing at the side door. The bus came to a stop but the door didn't open. I looked at the driver and he motioned me to come to the front door. As I approached the front of the bus the driver turned to me and said loudly, "Boy (emphasized), you don't sit in the back of the bus here. Those seats are for Negros!" I looked at him and said, "Where I come from it doesn't matter where we sit on the bus or streetcar." Again loudly, he replied, "Boy, you are in the South and it does matter here!" With that he forcefully opened the door as much to say, now get off my bus! It was my first experience with segregation and it was unnerving.

Graduation from Administration School, completed in early May, 1947, was uneventful. We sat around in Camp Lee for two days waiting for orders. I was assigned to a group that was to report to Camp Stoneman, California. I had no idea where I would be stationed, but going to California definitely appealed to me.

10
Shipment Overseas to Guam

The layover in Camp Stoneman waiting for orders was short lived. The group I was temporarily assigned to was only told we would ship out soon for overseas duty. We could only guess where that would be. Most guesses named Japan. Boy, were we wrong! It was not until we boarded an Army transport ship in Oakland that I finally learned we were being sent to APO 246, Guam. Guam? Where in the world was Guam? Most of us had never even heard of it. Later we were told it was an island in the Pacific Ocean in the Marianas Group. Of course, no one had a map, and even if we did, I'm not sure we could have located it.

The day the transport ship left Oakland was cool and slightly overcast. We had been up since 4:00 am, having had a quick breakfast and then moving onto a small ferry boat carrying us to the ship in Oakland. We boarded ship at about 2:00 pm, without having had lunch. Bunk assignment was chaotic. I wound up three decks below in the rear of the ship, quite possibly the worst location on the ship. We set sail about 4:00 pm and began our overseas journey. I got up on deck to see the Golden Gate Bridge and cast a long look at San Francisco and California. We were called to mess about 5:00 pm and were offered hot dogs and Sauer Kraut for supper – not the best meal, but we were extremely hungry and it was OK.

I raced back on deck to catch a last glimpse of California and noted that the ship was beginning to roll with the ocean swells. And the swells started getting bigger and bigger and the ship began pitching and rolling more and more. Suddenly someone at the front of the ship regurgitated his supper and I, among all others on that side of the ship, got splattered. That did it! From then on the night only got worse. We caught the tail end of a storm and the seas were running high. Being at the rear of the ship I could hear the whup-whup-whup sound of the propeller periodically coming out of the ocean water. To say I was frightened was putting it mildly. About midnight some clown repeatedly shouted down the passageway, "All hands on deck!" Fearing the ship was sinking, hundreds of sea sick soldiers ran up on deck only to find out it was a hoax. Somewhere the perpetrators were having a good laugh I'm sure. It was a night of hell all of us were to remember.

Days following were somewhat better but it took a long while for my stomach to calm down. Some men could not move out of their bunks for days because of sea sickness. Some were actually green from their illness. About the third day out I finally managed to eat something and keep it down. Going to the latrine was very difficult because all of them were dirty and smelled from men being sick. It was quick in and quick out. I found the PX on board ship and bought a box of Hydrox chocolate cookies. I ate the whole box in one day and my stomach finally settled back to normalcy.

I took but one shower during the four day trip to Hawaii. We used a special bar of salt water soap, showering in warm salt water. The soap did not lather; in fact it made me feel slimy. But the shower helped in making me feel somewhat cleaner. And putting on clean underwear made me feel better, too. The trip smoothed out and became routine after the third day. During the day there was not much to do but talk to one another and watch for flying fish. Evenings we would watch a movie under the stars and then head back to our bunks. There were always several groups of five to six men playing Poker on deck. If you had any money you could always get into one of the groups. I met one soldier who obviously had some money and who offered loans for collateral, mostly watches. Paul arrived on Guam with at least ten watches forfeited by Poker losers. I bought one from him for ten bucks. Financially, Paul did extremely well on the trip to Guam.

As the ship pulled into Honolulu's harbor the smell of pineapple became very strong. We passed very close to the Dole Pineapple canning plant. We also saw the remains of the battleship Arizona with its mast still protruding above the water.

The ship had a two day layover in Honolulu, dropping off personnel, acquiring more soldiers and replenishing supplies. I was given a six hour pass and immediately walked to downtown Honolulu just gawking at the sights and people. Remember, Hawaii was a territory, still a United States possession in 1947. I bought a flowered sport shirt for brother Bob and arranged for it to be shipped to Illinois. Only later did I discover that the shirt had been made in San Francisco, shipped to Honolulu, bought and then shipped to Illinois. What a trip that shirt had! That evening before heading back to the ship, I wandered around taking in the beach scene, Diamond Head and all the beautiful women in bathing suits.

Following were three more days on board the troop transport before reaching Guam. Part of the Marianas-Bonin group of islands, Guam was discovered by Magellan in 1521. It became part of Spain legally in 1565, but was ceded to the United Sates as a possession in 1898. Guam was invaded and taken over by Japanese forces in 1941. The island was regained by US forces in 1944. It is a key Pacific base for Army, Navy and Air Force personnel.

The Island of Guam is absolutely fascinating. It is 32 miles long and 10 miles wide. Lush vegetation with coconut palm trees, beautiful sandy beaches, and blue skies, it is blessed with semi-tropical temperatures year round and also high humidity. How could I be so lucky to get assigned to this place?

Only about 60 personnel were unloaded from the ship docked in Agana, the capital city (now called Hagatma). We boarded 6X6 Army trucks and were transported to the MARBO Replacement Depot (MARBO is a contraction of the names of Marianas-Bonin chain of islands). Along the way I saw heavily damaged buildings scarred from rifle and mortar shelling. Beside the main road was a rusting, inoperative Japanese Army tank. It was then the realities of war struck me. Here was an island that had been liberated from Japanese forces less than three years before. Remnants of battles were everywhere on the island.

11

Finally! A Job Assignment

When the trucks arrived at the Replacement Center I was struck by the plain Jane buildings. Constructed of unpainted plywood with windows open like awnings, the barracks were raised off the ground and had steel cables over the roofs embedded in concrete. The buildings were anchored to prevent them from being blown away by typhoon winds which we were told did not occur often. Less than a year later we did experience a typhoon with very high winds – and the buildings did not get blown away! But that's another story.

Eight names were called out as we got out of the trucks and were taken aside. The rest were moved into a building to be taken to a different location later. We found out that the Replacement Depot officers had hand picked the eight soldiers, of which I was one, to be assigned to the depot as operational personnel. We were taken to our barracks nearby and told to pick out an empty bunk. We got a quickie orientation telling us what we were to be doing in our jobs and were shown the mess hall. The depot was based in a corner portion of the Army Base Hospital buildings and we would be eating in their mess hall. The buildings were all alike – plywood structures with a covered walkway connecting all to the mess hall. I wondered about the covered walkways and soon discovered why they were built that way. It rains a lot on Guam!

An interesting event happened several months after our arrival on Guam. A nearby Army unit caught two ragged Japanese soldiers attempting to get into their mess hall. They had somehow survived in the rugged jungle not realizing that the war had ended three years earlier. After being given new clothing and a check-up, both were shipped off to Japan. Can you imagine their wonderment going back to their families, probably after being listed as missing or dead?

Our mess hall served decent food but occasionally it would deviate to the point where someone would call the Inspector General (IG) to complain about the lousy meals. You always knew when the IG was about to make an unannounced visit to the mess hall. The food was wonderful for a week or two and then the quality would start to slip. The question in everyone's mind was, how did the food change from bad to great before the IG even appeared? Someone was alerting the mess personnel the IG was coming, maybe?

I always enjoyed going to breakfast on Sunday morning. We were allowed to walk into the kitchen and tell the cook what we wanted to eat. We could call for anything we wanted – eggs, bacon, sausage, toast, pancakes, hot cereal, all made to order. The only thing I did not like was that we were served reconstituted milk. Our company served with units of the Philippine Army and their regulations stated that they must be served rice twice each day. There were times we were served rice three times a day! I did not particularly like rice but I found a way to make it palatable. Mixed with reconstituted milk and adding sugar, it made a kind of rice pudding.

My first assignment was as a general orders clerk. This meant typing a copy of an original order for manpower distribution and sending it to appropriate units and personnel. To say it was boring is putting it mildly. The nice part of the job was that being in the semi-tropics meant that our work day was finished at 2 pm. We were free to do as we pleased after that.

I was soon taken off the orders distribution job and assigned to the mail clerk's job. While being trained for the job by Albert L, we went to the motor pool to pick up a Jeep. It was being serviced so the Pool Sergeant gave us a 4X4 Personnel Carrier, a bigger vehicle than a Jeep. For some reason, I put the packet of communications for Army Island Headquarters in the glove compartment. We drove to HQ, made our rounds of collecting items and headed back to our unit. The next day the Motor Pool Sergeant found the packet of communications in the 4X4 and brought them to our CO. Soon Al and I were brought before Major Palozzi, our Commanding Officer, and were confronted with the undelivered items.

We stood trembling at attention. Al tried to excuse our mistake, making the Major even angrier while I kept my mouth shut. I believe in the words of Will Rogers, "Never miss a chance to shut up!" We were each given a butt reaming that I will never forget. After what felt like five minutes of being chewed out, we were ordered to leave his office and return to work. I knew it was my fault for putting the items in the glove compartment, but Al was the trainer and should have realized we had nothing to deliver to HQ. Both of us waited for the next shoe to drop, a written reprimand, but it never came. We were very fortunate. And, I had changed. That five minute disciplinary incident with the CO had transformed me from a teenage boy to a man! I had grown up in a matter of minutes. Responsibility was something I had to take seriously, realizing that my reputation was on the line.

The first thing I inherited as mail clerk was a GI foot locker full of undelivered mail. Service Personnel having gone through the Replacement Depot to their assigned units often gave the Replacement Depot as their mailing address. I then had to ascertain where they had been shipped to and forward the letter(s). It sounds easy but it wasn't. Personnel moved around, sometimes to adjoining Marianas Islands and it was difficult to track them down. When all else failed I had to stamp the letter: *Address Unknown, Return to Sender.* It took almost a month to clear out all of the letters.

That was only part of the job. I also had to collect orders, communiqués and other sensitive materials to deliver to Army Headquarters on the island. At HQ I picked up any materials for delivery to our unit, including mail. It involved two trips each day, once in the morning and again just after lunch with my Jeep. One day while returning with my materials I was caught in a very heavy rainstorm. The jeep had a canvas roof, but no side covering. I was drenched on the driver side, but there was no rain on the passenger side. In fact, the sun was shining on that side of the Jeep!

Our first sergeant was a 16 year Army veteran who had served in several overseas assignments. A North Carolinian, he was likable and easy to work for. We got the impression, however, that "he was a little light on his feet", if you know what I mean. Others in the group confirmed that he was gay (unfortunately, we called them queers then). It was my first encounter working with a gay man. In spite of it, he was a good leader. We liked him and got along well. After I left MARBO to return to the States I was told that he had been caught in his quarters with another man and had been discharged from the Army. It was sad, because his 16+ years of service meant nothing. He lost his retirement and all benefits. Even in today's Army, being gay brings serious problems.

A very embarrassing event occurred one day when I jumped into my Jeep, put it in reverse and started to back out of my parking slot. BAM! I hit a truck parked in back of me. There were no serious damages to the vehicles, just some scratched lettering on the bumpers, but my ego was affected especially when several soldiers ran to the door to see what had happened. It taught me to look carefully before I began to move my Jeep.

Across the road about a block away from our unit was the MARBO Stockade, a prison for soldiers who had committed crimes. It was bounded by two very high barbed wire fences and was completely lighted at night. I thought it odd that every day, even in the heat of the day, you could see prisoners digging what appeared to be latrines just inside the fence. They just kept moving the trenches. Apparently this was their punishment for committing their crimes.

A much sought after job in our unit was transferring Army and Air Force personnel to a transport ship for movement to the US for reassignment or discharge from the service. Several of our Repl Depo men would truck them to the Agana dock for placement on a ship, often a US Navy vessel. They had to ensure personnel did actually board the ship and were entrusted to the naval officers. After loading, our men would be allowed to eat in the ship's mess. Navy food was always better than Army food – or so they said.

On one occasion they confiscated a monkey from a soldier who was trying to slip it into the US. Of course, they brought it back to our barracks and got the CO's permission to keep it. It was an adult female whom we quickly named "Mabel". My first encounter with her was after coming back from seeing a movie and walking into our tiny recreation room for a Coke, Mabel leaped from the overhead trusses onto my back, grabbing my ears for support. I was shocked, not knowing what had just happened. Obviously, everyone else got a big laugh out of it.

Mabel became our pet and provided a lot of laughs for us. Her "owner" felt she needed a bath one day and washed her with hair shampoo. Mabel did not like it one bit and promptly went out and rolled in the dirt. Later we adopted a stray dog, naming him MARBO. He, too, was a great pet and provided a lot of comfort for us. Still later, our men confiscated another monkey and brought him back to our barracks. We named him "Butch". Butch immediately took to Mabel and often tried to show his affection for her. Mabel would haul off and belt him whenever he made any amorous moves on her and knock him on his butt. But Butch was never to be denied and kept up his efforts to make Mabel his girlfriend.

MARBO, in one of his excursions at night, apparently met up with some Army folks who intended to make a meal of him. We were told that Filipinos often ate dog meat. He had had his throat slit. We immediately took him to the only Veterinarian in the Army fold and he stitched him up, putting a stiff shield around his neck to prevent him from scratching his wound. That lasted less than a week before he tore off the shield and opened the wound. It was left to me to take him back to the Vet and have him euthanized. It was a sad day for all of us.

One Saturday morning while standing in line waiting for the Army PX to open, the fellow in front of me turned sideways and I recognized him. It was Jim Bente, an old school buddy from Waukegan. We chatted for a few minutes before the PX opened. I never saw him again.

The closest friend I had was Dave L from Dundee, Illinois. He and I had become friends in Admin School in Camp Lee, VA. Dave was stationed in a Signal Corps unit a mile or two from my base. We would, at his urging, attend church once in a while at a nearby chapel. It was an old Quonset hut made over into a church. He and I were both Lutheran and the service was a generic Christian format. The Chaplain was not the most inspiring speaker but the service did fill a need. Occasionally Dave and I would attend a movie in the evening. The theater was also a Quonset hut with old folding chairs. Whenever it rained, and it did rain frequently, it was like sitting in a drum. The noise from the rain on the roof drowned out the movie sound system. It certainly was not Waukegan's Genesee Theater!

After much grousing, several of the privates in our unit were promoted to private first class, including me. We'd been in the Army nine months and deserved the promotion. And for that we got a three dollar a month pay raise! Big time stuff. We were now paid 28 dollars a month! In January, 1948, four of us were promoted to Corporal with a four dollar a month raise. I was given rank equal to Corporal, but called a Technician Fifth Grade since I was Mail Clerk. I never did figure out what was technical about being a mail clerk. However, I was now a noncommissioned officer, earning 32 dollars a month!

Every payday on the first of each month the Army's Payroll Officer would come to our unit in the morning with cash for payment to the troops. We would step up to the table, salute and give our name and serial number. He would dole out the cash, we would sign the sheet, step back, salute, do an about face, and leave. We had the rest of the day off. Inevitably, a dice game would break out as soon as the officer left. I watched as one player seemed to be winning so I pitched in two bucks, only to lose on his roll of the dice. Long story short, I lost ten bucks so fast I couldn't believe it. Almost one third of my monthly pay gone in a flash! I learned from that event – stay away from games of chance.

We had a varied group of men, mostly teens, in our unit. A 24 year old Sergeant transferred into our group from an Army airborne unit. In his many jumps as a paratrooper he had broken one of his legs or arms. The Army flushed him out of the airborne and sent him to us. He was a big Texan and each payday he and a man from Georgia bought a bottle of whiskey – no one knew where or how they got it. They proceeded to get

63

drunk and in the process would start talking about the Civil War and how the South should have won the war. I foolishly started talking with them about how the North did win the war, no question about it. They turned on me and it was all I could do to get away from the two drunks. If I had continued the discussion I probably would have gotten my clock cleaned. Next day after sobering up they were friendly again.

Our barracks had an inoperative water heater – which meant we had to take cold water showers. We complained bitterly for weeks before the executive officer ordered a repair job. There were no plumbers on call on Guam. We had two men in the group who served as carpenters, but we needed a plumber. They managed to find information about the heater and ordered parts to repair it. Weeks later the parts arrived from the US and they went to work rebuilding the boiler. It took them a week, but finally after months of cold water we were able to shower as real men with hot water.

Periodically, all personnel in our unit drew Charge of Quarters (CQ) duty. Our work offices closed at 2:00 pm each day. One Officer and one Enlisted Man took over duty until 8 a.m. the next day. The officer usually retreated to his room in the Bachelor Officer Quarters (BOQ). The EM was expected to stay alert throughout the entire shift in the office until relieved the next morning. The officer occasionally called the office to check on the EM.

On my CQ shift one day it was quiet, nothing happening until just after evening chow. I was at the desk reading a book when I heard the door close quietly. I looked up to see a 3-Star General in front of the desk. To say I was taken aback would be mild. I shot up out of the chair, saluted and asked if I could help. The General almost smiled and asked to see the Duty Officer. I didn't even ask him to have a seat – I just ran over to the BOQ and stammered that a General was in the office and wanted to see the CQ Officer. Needless to say, he jumped off his bed, quickly put on some clothes and ran to the office. The two officers then went to a separate area and discussed business. The CQ Officer did not tell me what was discussed. I was relieved to see the General leave. The rest of my shift was quiet, but my encounter was a hot topic the next day. Rarely did we see a general officer in any unit office.

12
Fun Stories While on Guam

We could sign out a truck or a Jeep and go to a beach or into the boonies (jungle) any day after our work period ended. We went swimming often. A particularly beautiful beach was located about a 30 minute drive from our base to a former Navy submarine personnel recuperation site. It had been closed after the war ended and was vacant. However, the Marines claimed it was "their beach" and Army personnel were not to use the facilities. Well, Marines did not get off duty until 4 pm so if we hurried we could use it for an hour or more and then get the hell out of there. One day we cut it too close and encountered a truck full of Marines as we were leaving. Neither truck stopped, thank goodness, but there was a lot of shouting going on. They barked like dogs as we passed and we yelled "jarheads" at them. We never saw them again.

One Sunday we signed out a Personnel Carrier 4-wheel drive vehicle and four of us drove out into the boonies. We saw evidence of battles in the jungle such as telephone lines and shell casings. The most interesting part though came when we found a house and what appeared to be a little farm with vehicles parked all over the place. Of course we stopped and were invited into the yard. Out back where most of the people were we found a cock fight in process. Men were in a big circle betting on the outcome, some with large rolls of dollar bills in hand. I watched for a minute and left – cock fighting is not to my liking. I found it to be cruel and disgusting.

Later we ascended a very steep hill with the 4X4 and I was sure we would tip over backwards. I am deathly afraid of snakes and will avoid them at all cost. I just knew the jungle was loaded with snakes but strangely we did not see any. We were informed later by "someone who knew about snakes" that Guam did not have any snakes. That was reassuring! I was told recently, however, that some type of snake had been introduced into the island and there are many there now.

We swam many times in Tumon Bay, a beautiful half-moon shaped inlet not far from our base with coconut palm trees everywhere. It was there that I contracted Impetigo, a skin disease that develops large, watery blisters. It is caused by microorganisms in the sea water. I had the malady in the crotch area and it was extremely irritating. On sick call I was given potassium permanganate, a purple liquid that had to be applied to the affected area. Imagine the comments whenever I took a shower: the guy with the purple thingies! I couldn't swim for a long time and eventually the "purple liquid" conquered the Impetigo.

Swimming in warm sea water was very different for me. I'd only been in fresh water before (cold Lake Michigan). It was fascinating in that there were many creatures to be found in sea water. I stepped on one very strange thing that was about 16 inches long, one inch in diameter and brown in color. At first I thought it to be a human deposit but then I saw a bunch of them. It gave me the willies. Entirely harmless, it didn't sting or bite, it just laid there on the ocean floor. One fellow in our unit tried spear fishing without proper equipment and was not at all successful. But, we had fun at the beach.

MARBO officers threw a picnic for the entire unit one Saturday at a beach near Anderson Air Force Base. Of course there was beer for all and lots of food. Several officers brought their wives along and most of us ogled them in bathing suits. Commissioned officers were allowed to have their wives live on the island in off-base housing. Non-coms and enlisted men lived in barracks – no wives allowed. The picnic was a nice outing.

13
A Memorable Trip to Japan

Soon after being promoted to Tec-5, I was granted a 7-day rest leave to Japan. Several men in our unit were being awarded leave. In early February, 1948, I received orders to fly to Osaka, Japan and then ride on to Gamigori. I hadn't a clue where Gamagori was, but I was happy to know I was going on leave. Of course, I had to dig out my winter issue clothing (OD's) and pack for the trip. On transport day I was taken by truck to Anderson Air Force Base. The four engine airplane was GI standard with bucket seats along each side of the plane – pretty bare bones. We took off early morning and flew the eight hour flight to Osaka Air Force Base. Mid flight we were given a box lunch which consisted of a dry sandwich and cookie. Real Army food!

It was early evening when we approached the US air base at Osaka. As we started to descend we encountered very rough air and the plane began bouncing around. I was soon air sick and headed for the john to relieve myself. Wedged in the small toilet, I vomited just as we touched down. As soon as the plane's door was opened and I inhaled fresh air I was miraculously OK. We were directed to the Operations Office to get dinner. After eating, our group was led to a train that took us to the Army hotel in Gamagori. We arrived at the hotel about 11:00 pm and were given rooms. My room was pretty sparse and colder than a well diggers butt. My roommate and I were awakened later for breakfast and we went to the dining area for a hearty breakfast. We were advised by Army personnel managing the hotel to not eat any foods offered outside the hotel. Flu-like symptoms were sure to result if we did.

At lunch each day we were served a broth-like soup that was absolutely delicious. I am not a soup fan but I looked forward each day to the serving. Evenings we would sit around a charcoal burner in the center of a large circular table on cushions, no chairs. Our shoes were left at the door of the room. Each table had a Japanese hostess, dressed in native attire, who prepared our meal, usually meat with vegetables. Every meal was a delicious treat.

Our stay in Gamagori was interesting and eventful. Tours were arranged each day. The first day the Army hostess took us to visit a nearby sake distillery, not much more than a large garage, but the vats were cooking. The sake was sold in large blue, 2-liter glass bottles. Several of the drinkers in the group bought bottles to take back to the hotel. Sake tasted like a mix of beer and white wine, not my cup of tea.

Another tour took us to the Noritake China factory in Osaka. I was shocked to see workers in large unheated rooms, all wearing only a coat to keep warm with sandals on their feet. I bought a few small pieces of china to give to my mother and father. Osaka was still a war torn city in 1948 with bombed out buildings still in evidence. Bicycles and motorcycles were everywhere on the streets with few autos around. I saw children playing on sidewalks lightly clothed with only sandals on their feet without socks, and feet blue from the cold. The high temperature that day was probably around 40 degrees.

One morning walking away from the hotel, I noticed a bridge over a small inlet. A man standing at the bridge had a camera and offered to take my picture for five dollars. "And how do

I know I'll get my photos," I asked? He assured me in broken English, "You pay when I give you photos." He took two pictures of me, one on the bridge and one nearby. Two days later he showed up at the hotel with my 4X6 black and white photos. They were excellent! I have the photos today, the only really decent photos of my duty in the Army.

A new-found friend from Brooklyn and I took bicycles one day to ride out in the countryside. There weren't many roads outside the hotel, mostly pathways between rice paddies. We saw several men carrying two "honey buckets" on a bracket on their shoulders. We had to stop, get off of our bikes and step to the edge of the path to allow them to pass. We found out the buckets contained a mixture of human poop and water, used to fertilize their crops. We gave them wide passage. I found the countryside to be interesting and, occasionally, beautiful. There were statues of Buddha in small, picturesque spots along pathways and roads.

At one point in our bicycle trip we came upon four Catholic Nuns walking along the path. Of course, we met them at the narrowest point in the path, stopped our bikes, got off and I promptly slipped down the side of the path into the muck of the rice paddy. I was well beyond my ankles in the mess — remember, farmers used diluted poop to fertilize. I had a nice job cleaning my boots when we got back to the hotel.

14
Back to Work

Too soon the rest leave in Japan ended and we were flown back to Guam. The heat and humidity of the island were in sharp contrast to the cold weather in Japan and it took a few days to become re-acclimated.

Work each day was at a humdrum pace again. In March, 1948 rumors began about cycling men back to the US. Many of us had enlisted for an 18 month tour of duty and we were due for discharge in June. Unbeknown to us, the Army was undergoing a reduction in manpower and a list of about five men in our unit, including me, were due to be sent back home before the end of our enlistment. In early April, an Army transport ship was scheduled to load personnel at Agana, going to Manila, PI, before heading back to San Francisco. At first we heard the rumor that we were on the list for shipment. Next we heard that the Executive Officer of our unit, a member of the Filipino Army, had refused to allow us to leave citing a shortage of personnel. Well, that went over like a dark object floating in a punch bowl! A final decision came from our Commanding Officer, Major Palozzi, that we were not going to be released. More grumbling from the troops!

We'd gotten word that a huge storm, called a typhoon, was forming in the Pacific Ocean and Guam was in its path. We readied for the storm by removing canvas tops from trucks and parking them away from our buildings. Building window coverings were locked into place and doors were prepared for locking. Office equipment was covered and files were locked and covered. As the storm approached the sky turned a light green and rain began falling. The storm intensified, the sky became very dark, high winds and rain became unbelievably heavy to the point we began to wonder if the buildings would stand. It lasted for several hours and finally began to dissipate to our relief. We found later that we had not incurred the full wrath of the typhoon. The steel cables did their job by holding the buildings in place. Cleanup took a day, mostly working on the trucks and jeeps to remove mud and debris. Our offices remained unscathed. The typhoon was a memorable event, but one I'd rather not experience again.

Two weeks later, another rumor spread that we were going to be released for shipment back to U.S. on another transport ship with a stopover in Honolulu. This time five of us were going to be assigned as guards for five general prisoners. A general prisoner is a soldier that has been court martialed for a crime: an assault, rape, murder, grand theft or other major crime! The prisoners were to be taken to San Francisco, transferred to Army MPs and then taken to a U.S. Army prison. And, we were to guard them all the way to the transfer in California! Not one of us knew beans about guarding a prisoner. Nevertheless, we were given brief instructions on what to do and were issued a 45 caliber pistol to be worn in a holster when with the prisoners – but, no bullets!

Orders were cut in late April to release us from MARBO Replacement Depot. We packed our duffel bags, said our goodbyes and were ready to ship out. Trucks took us to the ship in Agana and we waited for the prisoners to arrive, our 45s securely belted at our sides. Soon MPs rode up with the five prisoners, took them aboard ship and locked them in the brig. We signed a transfer document, were given cell keys and instructed on how to give each prisoner two fifteen minute breaks on deck each day. We each had an assigned prisoner to "escort and guard" while on deck and then return to the brig.

On the fifth day of our voyage, one of the prisoners "disappeared" on deck. How could this have possibly happened? There was an alert issued and all five guards went nuts searching for the prisoner. After a 30 minute frantic hunt we found the man playing poker with a group who didn't even realize he was a general prisoner! One guard got a real butt chewing for not being alert and we were extremely careful after the incident. I shudder to think what would have happened to us if the man had escaped – but where could he have escaped to?

Upon arrival in San Francisco, five husky Army MPs boarded ship and went to the brig to accept the prisoners. We surrendered our 45s and signed the prisoners over to the MPs – guard duty was finished. We were back home safe in the good old USA!

We were trucked into Camp Stoneman and unloaded our duffel bags near the supply room. A cocky, loud mouthed Supply Sergeant shouted for each of us to dump the contents of our bags onto the ground and wait for an inspection. Inspection for what? I soon found out. He and a crony looked at each heap, looking for contraband. They stopped before me and picked through my belongings. I had purchased an old style army field jacket (no longer standard issue) while at school in Camp Lee, Virginia, from a soldier who needed some money. While on Guam, I paid an artist in our unit to paint an emblem of Guam on the breast of the jacket. The eyes of the Sergeant lit up when he saw the jacket and he asked me where I had gotten it. I told him and he asked me to show him the sales receipt. I had none, of course, and he wouldn't accept my explanation – so he confiscated it. I was angry but I had no recourse. That was the Army's way of doing things. The next day a friend told me he'd seen the jerk wearing my jacket in the supply room.

Each day we were herded into a room and given lectures on what to do to receive our discharge benefits, back pay, payments for travel back home, etc. They also had an officer address us three times on the benefits of re-enlistment. Are you kidding? All most wanted was to get back home. Believe it or not, several men did re-enlist. Three days of listening to windbags and we were finally given our discharge papers, some cash and told to leave the base.

15
Reflections On Army Service

I'd been in Army service for just over sixteen months, but that time had changed me from a teen aged boy into a man. The experience proved to be invaluable. I had seen and done things that an eighteen year old could only have dreamed about. Not only had I been trained to manage a job but also to think and plan how to do it efficiently. I had seen Hawaii and Guam, "vacationed" in Japan and "cruised" the Pacific Ocean. I had learned to talk when I should and to shut up when I shouldn't. I learned to take an order and to report progress in following the order. I learned the importance of being neat and orderly and of taking care of my body and personal equipment. I learned that responsibility was important and that it could affect my reputation and status. It was a wonderful learning and growing experience. I had earned the distinction of becoming an Army veteran and I was proud and honored to have served my country.

Other Things I Learned in the Army:

Take orders seriously and follow them. There is no room for interpretation.

Commissioned and non-commissioned officers are to be respected, like them or not.

Cleanliness is next to godliness.

Discipline and orderliness are very important (and not just in military life).

Don't gamble with money if you don't understand risk in games of chance.

The best part of my service in the Army was that I had earned two years of fully paid college work. After being honorably discharged I was classified with a student status which exempted me from further service, that is, as long as I remained in college. The draft started in 1949 to secure men for the Army and Navy due to the threatening situation in Korea. That threat turned into a nasty war with Korea in 1951 while I was attending the University of Nebraska in Lincoln. I remained exempt and did not have to serve in that conflict.

16
On to Civilian Life in Waukegan

My first move after discharge was to go to San Leandro, California. A former neighbor and friend from Waukegan, Pat Jones, lived there and I wanted to see her. She and I had exchanged letters while I was on Guam and she had invited me to stop and see her and her parents before I traveled back home. A bus dropped me off in downtown San Leandro and I phoned Pat. She and her father picked me up and took me to their home. For several days I lived like a king at their home, was given meals, a room and tours of the city. I loved California! Its beauty was spectacular. But, after two days I knew I had to get on home to attend my brother Erve's wedding. I said goodbye to the Jones', thanking them for their wonderful California hospitality.

I hopped a Greyhound bus in San Leandro and headed for Chicago and then Waukegan. A stopover in Hastings, Nebraska, proved to be interesting. I got off the bus to stretch my legs and came face-to-face with two Army MPs. What in the world were they doing in Hastings? Apparently there was an Army base nearby. Well, I did not have my jacket buttoned and I did not wear a cap. I did have the gold "ruptured duck" sewn onto my jacket so they could easily see I'd been discharged. That didn't slow them down one bit. "Button up your jacket, soldier!" one of the MPs said loudly. I'd have liked to have given him the single digit salute, but decided to just button up and shut up. Having done their duty, the MPs walked away. Just another reason I was happy to be a civilian again.

Three very long, boring days on a Greyhound bus convinced me never to do that again! Buses of the 1940 vintage did not have a restroom as they do now. And they were not at all quiet, having very loud diesel engines. I arrived in Chicago on a Friday afternoon, extremely tired and needing a shower badly. It was early May and the weather was cool and clear. I took a cab to the North Shore electric train station and boarded for the ride to Waukegan. It took an hour to reach the station in Waukegan and by then I was exhausted from the trip. A cab took me to my parent's home at 613 Atlantic Avenue – and no one was home!

My parents had gone to the JM Club for dinner and drinks. Apparently a neighbor saw me and contacted them, letting them know a soldier was sitting on the front porch in the dark. My mother rushed home (note: not my father) and after a quick hug, let me into the house. I just wanted to go to bed and sleep. She had my old bed ready for me, knowing that I was on my way home from California. She made a quick supper and I was off to bed. Somewhere around midnight I was awakened by my brother Bob and Bob A. They wanted me to get dressed and head out for some carousing. I did give them the single finger salute and told them to bug off – I needed sleep.

Saturday morning I awoke, still somewhat tired but ready for the day. My brother Erve was getting married to Edna Marchinowski that day and I was happy that I had made the trip in time to attend the wedding. The day went by quickly after talking with my parents and brothers. I had no civilian clothes to wear so I had to tidy up my uniform and wear that to the ceremony. It was a nice wedding, held in the chapel at St. Anastasia Catholic Church on Glen Flora Avenue. Erve was not Catholic and the priest would not marry them within the church.

After the wedding we all went to the party held at a facility in downtown Waukegan. Erve immediately introduced me to Edna's sister, an attractive young lady whose name I cannot recall, suggesting we dance and spend the evening together. Well, she had other ideas, one being that she wanted nothing to do with a soldier, an ex-soldier at that. In spite of her beauty, I wasn't particularly attracted to her either. I spent very little time with her that evening which met with her approval, I'm sure. Eventually the party ended and I headed back home very tired. The trip from Camp Stoneman to San Leandro to Chicago to Waukegan with little sleep had caught up with me.

Over the next several weeks I re-established friendship with former buddies. The first person I called was Dean Keller just home from school at the University of Nebraska at Lincoln. His father, Dr. Sam Keller, had graduated from the School of Pharmacy there and it was only natural that his son attend the U of N. I was to find out that Dean was on scholastic probation for low grades – this came to light later (as you will see). Other friends were Howard Heyer, Ron Gilbert, and Ron Short. Evenings spent together included going to movies, "hanging out", going to sporting events and church functions. We'd often drive up and down Genesee Street or Washington Street looking for "girls" to take for rides – we never were successful! Usually there was a stop at Sander's hamburger shop on Washington. They had the best burgers, fries and milkshakes in town. There was always chatter going on between cars and "girls" were always to be seen.

Discharge from the Army had put $500 into my wallet, including my last month's pay of $32 and travel expenses. I was rich! Thinking about a car, I asked Pa if he would help pay for one if I put in my $500. He readily agreed and we headed off to look at used cars. We found a dark blue 1941 Ford 4-door sedan that had a reconditioned V8 engine. We agreed to the price of $800 and signed papers for a $300 loan. The car was in pretty good shape with new tires, having been given a thorough going over by mechanics at Reed-Randle Ford. It was a pretty "hot" car and I beat a number of contestants roaring away from red stop lights. Of course, I never told my parents about those events.

After lying around the house for a week, my father led me back to reality with the question, "When are you going to get a job?" I told him I was going to college in the fall since I had earned two years of the GI Bill. He looked at me like I was joking and I affirmed that I was going to go to college. Well, I got his message and applied for a job at Johnson Motors, where I had worked before enlisting in the Army. Post WWII law stated that employers must rehire employees who had gone off to the service. The Johnson Motor Personnel manager was not too happy to see me come back but I was offered a menial job in a storeroom, stocking bins of materials and sweeping the floor. Talk about a drag – I hated that job! Storeroom employees were not at all friendly and it was a real chore to work there. I was happy to end each workday at 3:30 pm.

During the summer months we talked about going to college. I applied for admission to Lake Forest College and was accepted. The town of Lake Forest is an idyllic community south of Waukegan on the shores of Lake Michigan, having many large estate type homes with a lovely English style town square. The liberal arts college is small having less than 2000 students and was founded by officials of the Presbyterian Church. It was full to the brim with students when I enrolled with many veterans taking advantage of the GI Bill. Orientation at LFC opened my eyes to a much different world. Students were eager to begin classes and conversation centered on the classes each was signing up for.

I entered the world of business administration based on an aptitude test taken at a VA Center, indicating I would excel in accounting and economics. Boy, was that test misleading! I barely passed the accounting class. The instructor, a woman, just couldn't get the principles of accounting into my head. And, Economics 101 just wouldn't fit within my intellect. Who cared what Adam Smith espoused a century ago about business and economics? I received a D for my effort in that class. This was an eye opener for me. I had never received a below average grade in any of my high school classes.

In English 100 - 101 classes, most of the work centered on writing essays. I did okay on most projects but one in particular stands out in my mind. I'd written a paper about Adolph Hitler and what he had done to spur the economy in Germany in the 1930s amidst a terrible depression. The teacher, again a woman, tore the piece apart, partly I believe, because she must have thought I was supporting Hitler. I certainly was not, but to her my writing apparently looked like it. There were red marks all over the paper – it looked like someone had bled on it! During Christmas break, the teacher quit her job and we had a replacement for the rest of the semester. I got a big C grade for the class.

Some classes were interesting but I questioned the value. The Freshman Art Appreciation class left doubt about how it would enrich my life. Why would being able to identify a particular musical instrument help me in the world of business? Religion 101 was equally questionable. I was Lutheran and I knew, or thought I knew, what the church stood for. I gained little useful knowledge from that class as well.

I was required to take a foreign language and chose German, thinking that my parents could help me if I had trouble learning. Both parents took one look at the text book and shook their head. They could not help me. They spoke what is called Platt Deutsch (low German) while the text taught Hoch Deutsch (high German). I struggled through that class. As it turns out, I earned a 'C' average for all freshman classes (except Accounting) that year at Lake Forest College. Not bad, but I certainly should have done better.

Having owned a car, I was able to get paying riders to class. Each would pay $2.00 a week to ride Monday, Wednesday, and Friday. All but one paid every week – one fellow still owes me $10 for his rides. The income paid for my gasoline and car maintenance.

Being commuter students we did not participate in campus activities. Dating college campus girls just didn't happen. One of the riders encouraged me to ask a mutual friend, a girl from Waukegan, for a date. She was a nice girl I knew from high school who was attending vocational school. After much encouragement from my riders I called "Mousie" B and asked if she would like to see a movie. To my amazement (remember I was pretty shy around women) she agreed. We did attend a movie at the Genesee and we had a very nice evening. We hugged at her front door. She was my first date as a college student!

17

Lake Forest College to University of Nebraska

During spring break, several LFC students and friends began discussing going to another college, preferably out of state. My friends consisted mainly of Dean Keller, Norm Gilbert, and Howard Heyer. Dean was particularly adamant about attending the University of Nebraska in Lincoln. We agreed that is where we would go to college. I applied for my second year of GI Bill assisted schooling at the U of N, was accepted and asked Lake Forest to transfer my credits! Other students, and principally Dean, kept giving me excuses about enrolling at Nebraska. Come the fall, I was the only one going to Lincoln. I was on my own. Nice guys! Dean (on scholastic probation from U of N) and I drove to Lincoln before school started and I found a private room to stay in, not wanting to get into a dorm. The rent was $20 a month, which left me $55 for food and extras. I received an allotment of $75 each month from the VA. The landlady was very nice and happy to rent the room, obviously needing the income.

I traveled by Greyhound bus from Chicago to Omaha, Nebraska, and had to transfer there for the bus trip to Lincoln. There was a six hour layover in Omaha for the bus to Lincoln. While waiting in the terminal for the 5:00 am bus, I noticed a man walking about looking for someone. He sat down near me and began talking, saying that his friend had not shown up and he would have to leave for Lincoln without him (in retrospect, a likely story, right?). He asked where I was going and when I told him to the university in Lincoln, he asked if I wanted a ride. I hesitated but then thought it would be better than sitting in the terminal for five more hours. I agreed and walked with him to his truck. It had started to rain and he carefully drove out of Omaha.

Outside of town it started to pour, the wipers barely able to clear the windshield. About that time the driver placed his hand on my left leg and moved it about. Fred, I thought, you should not have accepted the ride! I couldn't get out of the truck it was raining so hard. Carefully reaching into my travel bag, I found a roll of dimes inside and grasped them in my right fist. If he made one more move on me I would hit him full force in the face with the roll of coins in my fist. At least he would know that he had been hit, I thought. I think he got the message that I would not play his game. It took over an hour to reach Lincoln and I thanked God for getting me there without further incident. The rain had stopped and the sun was about to come up when I reached my rooming house. It was my second encounter with a gay man and I'd learned a valuable lesson: Check out every "situation" carefully and think about what could happen.

The room turned out to be a major drag. The landlady made it clear we were not to prepare meals there. I shared a bathroom with another student who was recluse and uncommunicative. The room was about two miles from campus and I had to walk to and from school. I'd scheduled classes for Monday, Wednesday and Friday, leaving Tuesday and Thursday for studying in my room. It became wearisome walking to school, finding a place to eat each day, returning and studying in a bleak room.

Attending a football game one Saturday after a month of this lonesome routine, it was good to get out with other students and let off steam at the game. We played Oklahoma that Saturday and the Cornhuskers got their clock cleaned. After the game I headed out of the stadium for my "rented space" at the house. I was dreading the evening alone.

Deciding to take another route, I walked down an unfamiliar street and noticed a sign on the sidewalk inviting Lutheran students into an adjacent building. The sign also said there was food. That was enough for me, so I went into the building. I was greeted by a rotund pastor, Rev. Erb and his wife. We talked for a while and then he steered me to a group of men and introduced me. They were all from the Lutheran Fraternity, Beta Sigma Psi (βΣΨ). Their fraternity house was just a few blocks away. It was nice to talk to friendly students and eat some snacks. One of the students approached me later and asked, "Would you come to the Frat House for dinner next Wednesday evening and meet other Lutheran students?" "Uh, Yeah" I nearly shouted!

As I walked back to my room that evening, I reflected on what had just happened. What had prompted me to take a different route back to my room? How had I come to stop and read the sign and then decide to go into the building? Later in life I became convinced that God was guiding me that day. My decision that Saturday evening turned out to be very beneficial.

On Wednesday evening I entered the Beta Sig fraternity house and was greeted by several members. I quickly felt at ease and engaged in friendly chit-chat. Soon we went to the dining room for supper, we said Grace, and I was amazed at what was served. It was a delicious meal, something I had not had in quite some time. Again, there was a lot of interesting talk at the table. After dinner I was invited to the living room where two of the members began talking to me about joining the fraternity.

Being Lutheran, we had a lot in common and I found the offer very appealing. The great thing about joining was that I would share a flat with a bathroom next door in the Annex with four others, have three meals each day and be right across the street from the campus, all of this for $50 a month! That would leave me with $25 for spending. Wunderbar! I agreed to join. I moved, with the help of two members, the next Saturday. My landlady was very distraught. I explained I couldn't continue living so far away from campus and eat meals at restaurants. I was quickly running out of money.

Life at the fraternity house was eventful and being a "pledge" I had duties to perform each day. Since our furnace was coal fired it was my job each day to remove the ashes and take them outside. I also had to attend a class once a week to learn about the fraternity. The rest of my spare time was devoted to study and attending classes. I quickly fell into a pattern I enjoyed.

Friday was a day of celebration after classes each week and many went to a bar nearby for a few beers. I was not one for drinking but I was persuaded to go along for the fun. We sat at the bar until several others joined us and we were going to move to a table. I picked up my glass of beer and suddenly felt a hand clasp my shoulder. The waitress informed me I could not move the beer from the bar to the table and that she would have to do it. What kind of stupid rule was that? Apparently it was Nebraska State law.

Pledge night was a free-for-all. All pledges left the house for an evening of fun and celebration. We didn't realize that the house and annex had been locked up after we left and we couldn't get in if we tried. The group I was with decided to drive to Omaha to get beer. I never understood why we had to drive to Omaha. Why couldn't we buy beer in Lincoln?

Anyway, I along with four others in the car drank far too much beer and we headed back to Lincoln.

After unsuccessfully trying to gain entrance to the house, we walked along the street in front looking for something to do. Carl H, feeling no pain, took a running leap at a Buick dealer's sign hanging above the sidewalk (It was about10 feet off the ground). Carl missed the sign completely and fell face first onto the sidewalk – splat! We helped him up onto his feet, groggy and shaken. But, he started walking and shook it off.

Someone suggested we get something to eat and named a place near the airport. I ordered a hamburger and immediately left the restaurant before eating, being very sick to my stomach. I walked miles sobering up to get back to the frat house only to find the doors were still locked and couldn't get in. Someone finally unlocked the main door just before daybreak and I was able to get into the living room to sleep it off on a couch. What a night that was!

18
My Life Was About to Change

Saturday night was date night but for those of us who didn't have a girlfriend it was a night playing cards, studying or going to bed early. I did not have a date so I stayed in the flat reading or studying. Bob B, one of my roommates, said he could "fix me up" with a date if I OK'd it. Well, yeah! It was no thrill sitting in an empty flat at night (no TV, no radio). Bob arranged a date for me the next Saturday when three couples were going to take in a movie. Dressing up for the impending date left me a little concerned. Would I look OK? Could I make a good impression on the girl? Was she a nice girl?

Saturday evening the three frat boys jumped into Gil G's car and drove off to pick up the girls. My date was the last one to be picked up and Bob escorted me to the door of an imposing house in Lincoln. He introduced me to a lovely girl, Marlene R, who was employed as a Nanny for two children in a banker's family. Wow! I was just taken aback. Marlene was a real chick, very attractive and very nice.

I kind of stumbled and fumbled conversation-wise but did manage to not act like a complete fool. With six people in the car, guess who sat on my lap in the back seat? Mmm, Mmm, good! The movie was great and the evening turned out very nicely. When I walked Marlene to the door, I asked, "Can I see you again?" She replied, "Yes!" I was ecstatic and fairly ran back to the car. The boys kidded me all the way back to the House. Wonderful, wonderful evening!

Of course, I wanted to see Marlene every day, but couldn't. Studies kept me very busy, but she was often on my mind. I'd use the frat house phone to call her, but it was not private and anyone could hear conversations. Our house mother's apartment was next to the phone and she always kept her door open. Marlene and I began dating. She invited me to her work home where we often had long talks, and of course, kissing events. I couldn't see enough of this lady! Well, the inevitable happened. My grades started going downhill to the point I was assigned to a study hall every evening at the house. Horrors! That left Saturday evenings my only chance to see Marlene. I had to bum Carl H's car when possible to drive out to see her.

In February while playing intramural basketball for the Beta Sigs, I was kicked in the right leg by an opponent. At first I thought it was just a bruise but soon found out it was a major injury. The throbbing pain became unbearable. Student Health diagnosed the serious injury as torn ligaments and I was admitted to their small campus hospital. Hot water therapy and massages helped but didn't completely stop the painful throbbing in my leg so after four days in bed a plaster cast was applied and I was released to go back to school. I hobbled about on crutches for three weeks with the cast and saw Marlene only a few times. We missed seeing each other. By now it was apparent that we were a couple.

With removal of the cast my leg was OK, no pain, all gain. Bob B suggested we all go to Wilbur, Nebraska for a good old fashioned dance one Sunday night. Nebraska farmers worked hard all week, shopped on Saturday, went to church Sunday morning and raised hell Sunday evening with dancing and drinking. Marlene and I joined the group and we were off to Wilbur. I was a poor dancer at best but Marlene loved to dance. So I submitted to her dancing with some of her old high school classmates since she had visited the dance hall many times in the past. I was not thrilled with it, but I knew better than to keep her from dancing. We had a good evening anyway and then drove back to Lincoln.

All of our cuddling, kissing and personal talk inevitably led to the ultimate intimacy. Our first encounter was in her Nanny quarters. It was wonderful, passionate, fulfilling love making! It was very gratifying for both of us. Marlene and I developed a very close, intimate relationship after that. There was no question in my mind that she and I would marry one day. I was very much in love with her and I believed she loved me.

She invited me to her parent's home in Plymouth, Nebraska for a weekend. It was a slightly tense but interesting time talking with her father and mother. I had the feeling I did not score many points with either of them. I tend to be quiet when in a new encounter and didn't contribute a lot to conversation. I don't mean I didn't talk. I just listened more than talk. Her parents were cordial and checked me out carefully, I'm sure. Anyway, it was good to return to Lincoln. Her brother, Arlen R and his wife who lived in Lincoln, invited me to dinner several times. We hit it off immediately and each visit to their home was pleasant and enjoyable. I felt to be part of her family.

Marlene and I dated as often as possible given my need for study and classes. I had asked Marlene to come to my home in Waukegan for spring break at Easter and she agreed. We hitched a ride with Fred C and his girlfriend who were driving to Indiana for the holiday. We were dropped off in Chicago and headed to my home. Marlene was welcomed by my parents, brothers and sisters-in-law. It was quickly obvious to me that she had been accepted into the family. She was at ease with all of them and I was beaming with pride. Could life get any better? I introduced her to several of my friends and they were impressed. Break was soon over and we headed back to Lincoln. My father let me take the 1941 Ford to drive back to school. This would make it easy for me to pack up and return home at the end of the semester.

The semester ended early June, 1950 and I made preparations to go home. Leaving Marlene was very difficult for me and I think for her also. I promised to call and write letters. My first phone call to her, however, left me with an uneasy feeling. I couldn't put my finger on it but I detected a sense of detachment in Marlene. The feelings only grew through the summer. While I had sent several letters to Marlene, she sent none to me.

I worked at Johns-Manville the entire summer on construction. How I, a skinny, 125 pound kid, ever got hired to do that kind of work I'll never understand. I'm sure my father had a lot to do with it. The work did a lot in building my physique. I developed muscles I never knew I had. I had saved enough money working during the summer and bought brother Erve's 1941 Mercury coupe. It was a good car but it had a lot of mileage on it.

19
On My Own at U of N - No GI Bill

Summer over I headed back to Lincoln to continue college work. I had no GI Bill to pay for tuition or books, so I was on my own. The fraternity offered to let me stay in the flat conditional upon my staying in school. I was to work during the day and attend school in the evenings. I enrolled in two classes and set out to find a job. My first job was in a small grocery store as a stock boy. It was a dead end job, and I continued looking.

I was offered a job at the University in Inventory Control. Mr. Lamb, my manager, oversaw my work locating and tagging new equipment and furniture. He and I hit it off from the start and we became good friends even as I was his subordinate. His secretary, an attractive married woman, began making remarks to me about how her marriage was heading for separation because of her macho husband. I began to see how suggestive some of her remarks were and became very careful in my association with her. I refused to become involved with a married woman.

After several dates I sensed that Marlene was no longer committed to our relationship. She had left her job as a Nanny and was enrolled in a business school. She had gotten an apartment with a girl friend and was off to a new direction in life. I'd asked her out to dinner one evening and when I knocked on her apartment door her roommate answered. She informed me that Marlene no longer wished to see me. I was absolutely stunned! The door closed and I just stood there. She wouldn't even tell me to my face that our relationship was over? I couldn't believe what I had just heard. I returned to my flat and was devastated. How could she treat me like that? Her rebuff was so much out of character, it floored me. Naive me, I never expected anything like that.

I really hit the dumps. Depression set in quickly. My school work went south and the job was completely meaningless. I'd learned in the Army that real men suck it up in troubled times and get on with life. Yeah, well, it wasn't working for me! Frat brothers knew that we'd broken up and offered well meaning remarks. Christmas break was coming and I decided to head back to Waukegan and try to get my life back in order. I told Mr. Lamb that I would not return to the job after the holidays and he tried to talk me out of it by offering more pay. I did not explain my personal situation with him. He was a great boss, but I just wanted to get out of town. Before leaving Lincoln I talked to the Registrar's Office explaining that I would not complete my college work and accepted an incomplete for the two courses I was taking.

20
Back to Waukegan!

Fred C hooked a ride home with me, offering to help pay for gas. We packed and left four days before Christmas. Midway into Iowa, Fred was driving and accelerated to pass a car. We heard an unusual sound from the engine and I knew that it was not a good sign. The sound only got louder as we approached the Mississippi River and the Illinois state line. By the time we reached Rockford, the engine was screeching. I knew we had thrown a piston rod and had torn apart one of the cylinders. What to do? Fred and I looked about, saw a covered garage next to a downtown hotel and drove the shrieking car into it. I explained to the attendant that I would have to leave the car and return for it later. He wanted up-front money for parking and I paid him ten dollars. It was very cold as we extracted our bags and headed for the bus stop. Greyhound bus took us to downtown Chicago and Fred and I parted ways. I rode the North Shore RR to Waukegan, a really depressed twenty-two year old man. What else could possibly go wrong?

I spoke with my friend, Dean Keller, about my disabled car parked in Rockford. He offered, "Let's go get it!" "How do you propose to do that?" I asked. We talked a while and agreed the best way to get the car back to Waukegan was to tow it. Dean had a 1951 Studebaker with a four cylinder engine. Could it pull the heavier Mercury? He checked around and found it could be done using a tow chain. We tried Sears, Montgomery-Ward, and hardware stores and couldn't find a heavy duty chain for towing. We finally found a local store that carried tow chains and I bought one for the trip. Dean and I started out early one morning with the temperature in the 30s. The trip took about two hours to get to Rockford.

Trying to push the Mercury into position for towing was not easy. I finally started the engine and amid the screeching backed it into the street. People stopped to see what we were doing. We had to explain several times that we were going to tow the car. It suddenly dawned on me that there would be no heat in the car and it was going to be a frigid cold ride back. Dean and I solved that problem by switching cars every 30 minutes. It took us more than five hours to reach my home, cold and very tired. Dean and I had performed a miracle, at least I think so. We got the hulk into the garage and gave a sigh of relief. Who else but twenty year olds would attempt such a thing in frigid winter?

I began searching for a garage to repair or replace the engine, and learned quickly that no garage would attempt to repair it. Noticing an ad in the *Waukegan News-Sun*, I called a repair shop in Zion, Illinois who told me they would replace the engine if a rebuilt was bought from Sears-Roebuck. Better, they would also tow the car to their shop. I bought a rebuilt engine from the Sears store but had to get credit approval from their finance department. Filling out the pages of paperwork for credit, the clerk informed me that Sears would not approve the credit request because I had not held a job long enough. In spite of the fact I was a veteran, she would not approve the application unless I had someone co-sign the papers. Would this debacle never end?

I talked to my parents and my mother agreed to co-sign the note. It was back to Sears for final approval of the credit. Next day the shop picked up the disabled car and hauled it away for the rebuilt engine replacement. One week later the car was up and running and back in the garage. I was back in business. Working at Johnson Motors, I was able to pay off the $350 loan in three months. That required some scrimping, but I did not want to put my parents at risk for the loan. Completing college was on the back burner. Now I had to concentrate on earning a living.

Reflecting on what had happened in my life the past year, I knew I had hit bottom. My parents had provided a lot of help. Without them I don't know where I'd have ended up. I was humbled. But then it dawned on me – I was convinced God had let me hit rock bottom, was planning a new chapter in my life and would open new doors.

Things I learned going to college:

Use your intellect to plan life and solve problems

Set a goal: finish all school work satisfactorily

Minimize 'social' activities – school must be the first priority

Seek help when in scholastic trouble

Focus on graduation!

I had set out to complete four years of college work. Unfortunately, I did not have a viable plan in place to financially handle the third and fourth year of school. Consequently, my desire to graduate flopped! Would I have been better off staying at Lake Forest College? I have asked myself that question many times and I still haven't found an answer. I know I grew as a man while at Lincoln, but had failed as a student.

21
Life in Waukegan and Abbott Laboratories

I returned to Redeemer Sunday School teaching a class. The kids were great and it was a joy working with them. Mr. Elmer Kreuger, the Sunday School principal, needed help and asked me one day to count contributions from all kids, tally it up and record the amount for the Church's Financial Secretary. It meant giving up my teacher's role but I agreed. I did this task for several weeks when Mr. Krueger asked if I would be interested in a job at Abbott Laboratories, where he was a department manager.

Would I? Oh, Yeah! The next day after work I drove to Abbotts and interviewed with the Director of Research Operations, then with Mr. Kreuger, Manager of the Control Department and finally with his Assistant Manager. I apologized for appearing in my not-too-clean factory clothes, but they seemed to understand. I didn't apprehend what the job entailed but I told each that I was willing to learn.

Mr. Krueger called me the next evening and offered me the job! It involved assaying samples of liter solutions produced in the plant and in Abbott's foreign plants. Simple chemical tests checked for sodium and potassium, and visual inspection checked for foreign materials in the solutions. A more complicated test, using sodium light, revealed the percentage of dextrose content in the liquid. I was kept very busy and the days flew by. Abbott supplied all personnel in the department with clean white shirts and pants to be worn in the work place. Wages paid were 75 cents an hour – not too bad in 1950. We also had access to a wonderful cafeteria serviced mostly by gray haired ladies. The food was outstanding and very reasonably priced. I found work in the Control Department to be challenging and enjoyable. It was a clean, professional environment with skilled, qualified employees. I was slowly getting back on my feet and life was starting to be good again!

Abbott Laboratories is a leading pharmaceutical manufacturing company with headquarters in North Chicago, Illinois. It is a staid, conservative company with excellent management. Leaders are chosen from employees who have proven themselves over the years. I was impressed with the organization and managers. Jobs are very well defined and carefully monitored. Deviate from the job standards and you are out on the street! I saw two employees in the Control Group fired because they had fudged results on drug assays. Legal and ethical issues were too important to overlook or turn aside. My supervisor, Fred Ferguson, checked on me regularly. I'm sure somewhere along the line he had given me liter samples that had been altered to check my assay. I called them as I tested them. Fortunately I passed such tests.

Fred informed me one day that I would be moving to my own lab located in the Liter Manufacturing area. He took me over to see the place, a huge lab across the aisle from manufacturing. It was about four times larger than my workplace in the Control Dept! I was thrilled. Weeks later I moved what little equipment I used into the new lab and set up my workplace next door to the manufacturing office (where my sister-in-law Gladys Scheske, Brother George's wife, worked as the department secretary). I quickly made friends with manufacturing personnel who were happy to see me working close by. Bob Flint was the department's manufacturing manager and the lead foreman was Bill Harju. Bill and I formed a close working relationship. Mr. Ferguson would come by at least once a week to see how things were going. But I had little interface with other people from the Control Dept.

Being just across the hall from the manufacturing area, I became very interested in how liter solutions were made. I was allowed to step into the production area and watch personnel mix de-ionized water and dextrose (sugar) or sodium chloride (salt) in huge 500 or 1000 gallon vats. Smaller quantities of specialized chemicals, such as potassium chloride mixed with drugs, were made in 250 gallon tanks. Several samples of a solution were taken while mixing and sent to my lab where I would assay them. When a solution met standard it was OK'd for packaging. After being thoroughly mixed by large electric powered blades, the solution was piped through special ceramic filters and into sterile glass bottles. All of the packaging was done by machine in a restricted, super clean room. The sealed bottles were then labeled and sent to shipping. Packaging has since changed from glass bottles to soft plastic containers.

22
I Meet My Future Wife

I was still grieving to some extent the breakup with Marlene, but making progress and slowly moving on. She still came to mind occasionally. Bill H came into my lab one day and asked if I was seeing anyone. Strange question I thought, and replied "I'm not currently dating if that's what you mean". Bill told me that he knew a "nice lady" working for the Manager of International Shipping. "Would you like to meet her?" "Well, yeah. Who is she?" I asked. Bill said, "You'll meet her soon." He set up a lunch date with the lady and I met her in the cafeteria a few days later. Lo and behold, I knew her from high school! Margaret Crawford and I were in the same class at WTHS and had graduated in 1946. She was a beautiful lady and very personable. I stammered my way through lunch but I did manage to ask her for a date the following Saturday night. We seemed to hit it off from the start. Saturday night arrived and I drove to Margaret's apartment to pick her up. We'd had snow a few days before and there were still spots of snow and ice everywhere. On the way to the car I slipped on a patch of ice and nearly went down (old Mr. Klutz!), save for Margaret's grasp on my arm. The movie was good, the evening went along beautifully, and our first date was a success. Life was suddenly getting much better!

We began dating twice a week, sometimes three times a week,

and always on Saturday nights. Movies and dinners were the most frequent outcomes but often we met to just talk and exchange ideas about what we wanted to do with our lives. It quickly became obvious that we wanted to share our lives and get married. I thought at length about this and decided that Margaret (who was Catholic) and I had to reach some important decisions.

We were on a Sunday night date to see a movie at the Genesee Theater. I had parked across the street from the theater and said we needed to talk. I explained that I could not change religions and become a Catholic, the reason being that I would not agree to have children brought up with the Catholic Church's philosophy. We discussed it at length and Margaret told me that she would change to become a member of the Lutheran Church! I was taken aback and thrilled at the same time. What I had anticipated to be a lengthy, perhaps heated discussion turned out to be reasonable and decisive. We kissed and began making more concrete plans from that moment on. This was in April and we began looking at diamond rings for our engagement. We found just the right one at a jewelry store in beautiful downtown Waukegan and I signed for a payment plan that I could afford. Life was getting even better!

In late May, 1952, I asked Margaret to marry me and she said yes. Did I have any doubts she would say that? Well, perhaps a few but she didn't disappoint me. I presented the diamond ring to her, we kissed and it was official! To make our statement to the world, well, to Waukegan at least, I knew where my brothers and their wives would be that Friday evening. We drove to the Bally Muck Tavern on Grand Avenue and there they were. No one noticed Margaret's ring except the owner/bartender George Beschel, an old friend of the family. He kept setting me up with Seven and Seven drinks and I was downing them way too fast. Finally one of my sisters-in-law spotted the ring and then the party started. I was already three sheets to the wind and about to bow out. We stayed a short while longer and then I begged off before I got really sick. I drove to South Beach on Lake Michigan where I tried to sober up. After a while I took Margaret home and quickly drove home myself. It took three days for me to feel human again. From that time on I rarely had more than two alcoholic drinks at any event. To this day I cannot handle alcohol very well.

Margaret had joined our Lutheran Church's informational class, similar to a catechism class, and after several months of study was accepted into the congregation as a communicant member. Later, she sent a letter to her father, Tom Crawford, telling him of her upcoming marriage and he exploded! She mentioned in her letter that I was Lutheran, that she had become a Lutheran and we were to be married in Redeemer Lutheran Church in Waukegan. Tom was a devout Catholic and he could not envision his daughter marrying outside the Catholic Church. He flew into town bent on changing her mind. Understand he had never even met me. There was an intense meeting with Margaret and her mother in which he tried to convince her to come with him to see a Priest. She refused and Tom was incensed! I met Tom at dinner a day later and he was cold and impersonal. He left town the next day, still insisting that Margaret see a Priest. It was a tense weekend for all of us. She was set on having our upcoming marriage proceed as planned.

Margaret had applied for an Abbott owned apartment across the street from the plant in North Chicago. She had intended to get the place for herself and her mother. Now it became apparent that it would serve as an ideal home for us after we married. We had not yet set a date for marriage. Margaret inquired from her boss about the availability of an apartment. There were three in the building on the second floor above Abbott service offices. One was a studio, another had one bedroom and the third was a two bedroom apartment. Obviously we would have preferred the one bedroom but the choice was not ours to make. Her boss looked into it and found the one bedroom would be available in late August. Unbelievable! With a little pull from her boss, Margaret's name came to the top of the list and she was awarded the one bedroom lease. Many people wanted any one of the apartments and we were fortunate to have gotten the OK. We asked for paint to color the place and they gladly supplied the colors we wanted. So, now it was up to me to belly up and start renovating the apartment. In mid-September the painting was finished and the apartment looked terrific!

Meanwhile, we looked for furniture for our apartment. There were not a lot of furniture stores in Waukegan but we settled on a place across the street from the high school. It was a husband and wife operation and they were kind and patient with us. We bought living room, dining room and bedroom furniture all in one evening and they set up a payment plan that we knew we could handle. Since we could not put the furniture into the apartment before a given date, they stored it for us. Weeks later we walked in to visit the couple and only the husband greeted us. Asking for his wife, the man replied sheepishly that she was not there anymore. Why? He told us that he had walked into the storeroom one day to find his wife in the arms of another woman, kissing each other. What a shock! We had not even heard about Lesbians then. The husband was really torn up about the dissolution of his marriage. But, true to form, he delivered our furniture on the agreed upon date and our empty apartment became our home.

23
Wedding in Waukegan

Our marriage in Redeemer Lutheran Church took place on Saturday, September 20, 1952. It was a beautiful fall day, sunny and cool. Pastor Otto Eifert performed the ceremony that afternoon and pronounced us Man and Wife: Mr. and Mrs. Frederick Scheske. My brother, Bob, served as Best Man and had flown in on leave from the Air Force. Bob, for some reason, was very nervous during the ceremony and I could hear him breathing loudly, almost snorting. All of my family attended: mother, father, brothers and sisters-in-law. Margaret's Mother, Pearl, and Aunt, Alice Hanselman, were also there. Notably absent was her father Tom. Howard Heyer and Harold Francke served as ushers. Howie also offered to chauffer us to the reception in his Dad's shiny black Buick. Margaret and I felt like King and Queen. Life was very, very good.

Our reception was held at Bonnie Brook Country Club in Waukegan thanks to Margaret's mother and aunt. Being a city facility, liquor or beer could not be served within the clubhouse. We had arranged for a huge fountain of punch for the guests. A friend sneaked in a bottle of Vodka and spiked the punch, making everyone happy. The reception was a pleasant event. Our friends were animated with a lot of conversation and laughter. The realization that I was now a husband and had a wife finally hit home. We were very happy!

Brother Bill invited some friends to his "bar" at the close of the reception. Bill had converted part of his basement into a recreation room, complete with a bar. There were about twenty-five family members and friends there and the party got pretty vocal with lots of stories and jokes being told. Margaret's friend, Florence Turner, introduced us to her friend, Frank Z. Frank was an immaculate dresser, friendly and very outgoing. He was all over the place telling stories to my family. No one knew who he was but they loved his stories. Later, Frank insisted on asking me where we were going to stay for the night. I just blew him off, not telling him where we were staying. Margaret finally let him know that we were going to a hotel in Highland Park, Illinois. Frank and Florence insisted on following us to the hotel to offer a toast. When we got to the hotel we found they did not have a bar, but they did have a "closet" that contained an amazing number of liquors and champagnes. Frank bought a bottle of fine French champagne and toasted our marriage. It was a fitting close to our marriage day celebration. Several months later we found out that Frank had been sentenced to a term in Wisconsin State Prison. He was a member of the Mafia in Kenosha, Wisconsin! We never saw Frank again.

Our honeymoon started in Indiana at a lovely state-owned lodge. It was in a pleasant park area and we enjoyed walking about the place for three days. The first night Margaret felt the urge to celebrate and get loaded on champagne. I still had memories of our engagement night and limited my intake. She, however, got smashed and soon found herself ill – really ill. At ten o'clock at night I was on the road trying to find a restaurant for some soup. I did find a small roadside place that had some chicken soup and I bought a container to take back to the lodge. Margaret was still hurting when I got back but managed to take a little of the soup and crackers and eventually fell asleep. Next morning she suffered what I had gone through after our engagement party and was very subdued for most of the day. We talked and walked and loved and treasured our first three days of marriage in Turkey Run State Park. Then it was off to Virginia to visit our friends Dean and Judy Keller. The trip was especially enjoyable for both of us, seeing parts of the U.S. we'd never visited before.

Kentucky was enchanting seeing the many horse farms with acres of green grass surrounded by white fences. The horses were magnificent, beautiful creatures. We drove on through, stopping in West Virginia for the night. The motel was not the greatest but it was clean and served a purpose. The manager signed me in and gave me keys to the room with a leer on his face. I wasn't able to figure out what was on his mind – he was weird. Next morning, we were up and at 'em early and back on the road. We stopped for lunch in Charleston, West Virginia. It was a lovely Southern style hotel with an overhanging balcony situated on the main street. It was after 1:00 pm when we were seated in the dining room and it became obvious we were late for lunch. Our waiter made it clear by his attitude and actions that we were holding up his rest time. We ordered a Virginia ham sandwich with iced tea and it was superb! As we leisurely ate our food the waiter became more and more fidgety, asking if there was anything else he could get for us. He hovered close by, watching as we ate trying to hurry us. We finished our meal, paid the bill and left the hotel, much I'm sure, to the waiter's relief.

We arrived in Richmond, Virginia in late afternoon and quickly found Dean and Judy's home. Judy informed us that Dean was stuck on base with duty and would not be home for the next day, at least. We had only planned on staying in Richmond for two days. I could not leave without at least seeing him for one day. Judy had graciously prepared a room for us to stay over. We were at dinner with Judy when Margaret began to suffer severe pain in her private parts. I took her to a nearby clinic that turned out to be a place for pregnant women.

The doctor quickly diagnosed her problem as being Cystitis, an infection that was treated by a drug he prescribed. I was told to refrain from "sexual activity" for a few days. Dean arrived home from base and we spent a day reminiscing and talking about the future. Then it was back on the road again.

I had arranged for two weeks of vacation with my boss for our marriage and honeymoon. I knew that we would not make it back to work in time with the extra time spent in Richmond. So I sent a telegram to Mr. Krueger telling him I'd be late returning and asking for several extra days off. How could he possibly respond when we were on the road? I was sure he would grant me the time without any penalties, and he did. He chuckled when I got back to work and explained what had happened. We travelled the Pennsylvania Turnpike on the way home. It was one of the first superhighways in the U.S. and it was a marvel. We happily paid our tolls as we drove along to get into Ohio. Stopping for lunch at a store we purchased bread, some lunch meat and cheese and Margaret made sandwiches in the car. We'd gotten about twenty miles beyond the store before we realized the Swiss cheese was excellent and with the ham, we had wonderful sandwiches. We'd gone too far to go back and buy more.

Arriving back in North Chicago, we were tired but very happy. We'd had a terrific wedding and a wonderfully fulfilling honeymoon. The trip served us memories we'd never forget. And our little 1950 Studebaker Starlight Coupe had made the trip without one problem!

24
Our First Home

Our apartment was an ideal setting for us. It was located across the street from Abbott's at the intersection of Sheridan Road and 14th Street, one block away from a grocery store and next door to Levandusky's Bar and Grill. The one disadvantage was that we had no garage. Illinois winters can be tough on cars parked outside. A company parking lot was across the street from the apartment, just 50 feet from our door. I soon found a garage for rent a block away so that solved that problem. One winter day as I got into the car and started up the engine, I heard a big clunk and quickly turned it off. When I lifted the hood of the car, I found a big rat dead on the engine! It had crawled up there to keep warm and when I started the engine it had gotten caught in the fan blade. From that time on I always made sure the car windows were closed when I parked it.

Margaret and I found an easy way to manage meals. We would eat lunch together in the company cafeteria. It served excellent meals every day and we'd made them our dinner. After work we'd make a sandwich at home – it helped cut our grocery bills. Margaret had a great business sense and we agreed she would set up a budget. I'd never even heard of a budget! She laid everything out including envelopes for us to put money in to pay our bills. I marveled at her savvy! My budget would have been to carry the money around in my pocket and when it ran out I simply couldn't spend any more. But I quickly found out that married life didn't allow that. She had learned living with her Mother through the Great Depression that you had to have a plan and a system in place to cope. We managed to pay our bills and put money aside into savings. Life was good!

We'd made friends with several couples from Abbotts. George and Marion Marquis, Bill and Wanda Barker became very close. Dean and Judy Keller returned to Waukegan after his discharge from the Army and they too became close friends. My brothers encouraged me to join the VFW bowling league and that entered into our social network as well. Margaret fit in beautifully with my family and they included her in many activities, such as card playing and shopping. I was very proud of her and loved her very much. I know she cared a great deal for me too. Now, her mother Pearl was another matter. I know she respected me as a son-in-law but I was the one who had taken her daughter from mother's nest. We tried to include her as often as we could in parties and get-togethers. But, she still spent many days and nights alone and it affected her.

Abbott Labs was employee oriented and offered many benefits besides good wages, health insurance and a retirement plan. It sponsored intramural athletic activities such as golf and softball. I had played in the golf league and was not a winner in any sense. I won my holes but never really was a top golfer. I enjoyed playing until one match with a young man from the research group. As we were about to tee off one evening, he announced he was going to, and I quote, "Whip my ass!" I looked at him and saw he was dead serious. Psychologically, he was playing a game with my mind – and he won! I lost every hole except one that evening, having played the worst game I could remember. I soon quit playing golf after that incident. It just wasn't fun anymore.

Abbott also sponsored a group called the "Study Club". It was a group of about 75 employees who volunteered to take drugs for a test – check to see what effect it had on blood pressure or other body function. It was always a safe test. There were never any ill effects suffered. As a reward for volunteering for a test, Abbott would provide tickets to live theater in Chicago and dinner at a famous restaurant. Margaret and I loved being volunteers!

Each spring Abbott would sponsor an entertaining event for employees. I remember one major event in particular. Merv Griffin performed with his orchestra in the auditorium. It was a marvelous show with music, singing and comedy. The company provided a lot of perks for its employees.

One afternoon at break, several Control Group men were complaining about not being able to play softball. There were five teams in the Abbott league, and none offered new players an opportunity to join. We talked about forming our own team. It would be just a bunch of guys who wanted to get out, exercise and play some ball. Guess who got elected to go to Personnel and get the paperwork necessary to from a team? Me! Long story short, we formed our team, lost most of our games that first season, but had a lot of fun. After every game we'd head out to a local watering hole and poke fun at one another, laugh about our errors and losses and drink a few beers.

Next season, two "hot players" from other teams came to me and wanted to join our team, citing our fun atmosphere. Well, we won a lot more games that year and came to be recognized as a contender. The third season we were the premier team, not only having fun but winning first place in our league. We qualified and entered the Lake County softball tournament and advanced all the way to the winner's championship game. We were up against a young bunch of men, some former professional ball players and they were impressive. As manager

I was told about their long ball hitting and was implored to change our normal style of placing outfielders. Normally we would play with a short fielder, a roamer who would position himself for individual left or right handed batters. I reluctantly changed our defense to four long outfielders with misgivings. The other team saw our mistake and capitalized by hitting short bloopers into the outfield, quickly scoring three runs which we were not able to overcome in the game. We lost the championship game by a few runs due, in part, to my error in judgment. But, our team still had a terrific celebration that evening! Second place was not bad for our bunch of happy misfits!

Margaret and I loved out little apartment on 14th Street and Sheridan Road in North Chicago, but we were getting itchy feet after four years. George and Marion Marquis had bought a nice house in Waukegan, Bill and Wanda Barker had bought a lovely home in the Bonnie Brook subdivision in Waukegan and Dean and Judy Keller had accepted a beauty of a home in Buckley Hills in Waukegan, a gift from Dr. Keller. Talking with Brother Bill, he convinced me that building or buying a house was the only way to go. Besides building equity, it offered tax advantages as well. I had gone to college for two years in business administration and couldn't figure that out for myself (man was I a dolt!). The more Margaret and I talked about it the more firmly we believed that we needed to build, or buy, a house. We decided to build.

We first needed to find a lot on which to build. The north side of Waukegan was the place to live – or so many folks thought. We couldn't find anything reasonably priced on that side of town. Then we found an ad in the *Waukegan News-Sun* announcing lots for sale on the southwest side of town. We hurried over to look at the lots and found one that fit into our budget, meaning we could afford to buy this piece of land with a little help. We had about half the price saved in the bank, but needed more to buy the lot. I spoke with my parents and they agreed to loan us $900 so that we could purchase it. I guaranteed them we would have their loan paid back in less than a year. We purchased the lot from Jerry Drobnick and reveled in our piece of land. Only later did I learn that we had a problem with the downward slope to the back of the property.

We began looking for house plans and after weeks of searching we finally found "our dream house". It was a one and a half story Cape Cod Style with a one car attached garage, two bedrooms, kitchen/dinette, living room and bath over a full basement. I bought the plans and submitted a set to Jerry Drobnick for approval. Two weeks later the plans were approved and we set out to find a building contractor. We showed plans to D. Johnson and to Bob Runyan for an estimate. Bob came in a little lower than Johnson and we found his construction work more favorable, so we signed a contract with him for $14,500. Now we were in real debt! Abbott's originally secured the loan (but later transferred it to North Shore Savings and Loan in North Chicago). After a thorough investigation Abbott's agreed to give us a 30 year, 5% loan with a 20% down payment. Most home loans at that time were averaging over 6%. Working at Abbotts definitely had its advantages. Such a deal!

The first problem we encountered was the lot. Digging the basement clearly showed that the slope of the lot provided not enough dirt to cover the backside basement wall. Bob solved it by telling us he could have dirt trucked in to provide the needed coverage. We drove to the building site at 2301 Ninth Parkway every evening after work. I worried about everything. When the walls were framed I noted a window sill in the back bedroom was cockeyed. I called Bob complaining about the shoddy work and he explained he would check it out the next day and fix it. He slowed me down telling me, "Fred, it is just a house. It can be corrected!" I came back with, "Yeah, Bob, but it is my money that is paying for it!" We both laughed and went on from there.

An option that Bob gave us was to choose what kind of woodwork we wanted in the house. We could have stained pine or natural Mahogany. We opted for Mahogany. Turned out it was a great choice. It just seemed to make the house a little nicer. He installed mahogany kitchen cabinets and beautiful oak flooring. Brother Bill and I bought vinyl tiles in a cork design for the kitchen. He helped me install the tile, and we did a magnificent job if I say so myself. Margaret and I did a lot of sanding and cleaning while the house was being built. We wanted it to be the perfect home. Well, that idea soon lost favor as we got more and more tired trying to keep up with the builders.

Our neighbor to the east, Joe M, became a real thorn in our side. The first encounter came when the builder began putting up redwood siding on our house. Joe went bananas! He shouted at me that I had to have brick veneer on the house. I told him that Drobnick had approved the house plans that called for siding. He was absolutely incensed! I understand he went to Drobnick's office and screamed, to no avail. Later I planted a hedge on the side of the patio in back to create privacy. Joe didn't like the hedge and complained bitterly about it, again to no avail. It seemed that no matter what I did in the yard or with the house, Joe did not like it. He was a bitter, vocal man. I'm sure his family lived in great fear of him.

When I attempted to plant grass in the front yard I was foiled by the hardness of the soil. Since we lived on an eastward sloping street, most of the top soil had long since been washed down toward Lewis Avenue. I couldn't budge the dry clay, even with a pick axe. A friend told me to get some sludge from the city waste treatment plant, mix it in with the clay soil and I would have success in growing grass. After getting permission,

I was able to get four large trailer loads from a dormant sludge bay at Waukegan's sewage treatment plant. It was a long day hauling the stuff to our home, but it was finally deposited on the front yard (and I smelled!). My neighbor to the west, Bill S, became upset when he got a whiff of the stuff. The odor was pretty ripe! His main concern was the possibility of his kids getting an infection or contracting a disease from the sludge. I assured him that I would as quickly as possible have it mixed with the soil to stop the odor. For three days I roto-tilled the stuff into the soil – and it still smelled! Finally a drenching rain came to help stop the smell and enrich the soil. The following year I had the thickest, most beautiful Kentucky Blue Grass yard in the city! Well, I thought so anyway.

Our friends, Dean and Judy K talked about getting out of town for a weekend and invited us to go with them to a resort in Rock River, Illinois. The resort was a series of rustic buildings with lovely bedrooms and suites, a four star restaurant, a lounge and bar and a greenhouse enclosed swimming pool. The restaurant featured outstanding food with a superb violinist who moved from table to table playing songs on request. Another couple, friends of Dean and Judy, met us at the resort. Margaret and I soon realized we were odd couple out. You know the old saying: two's company, three's a crowd. While it was a pleasant outing for us, it was also an eye opener to be treated like a third hand. Margaret and I just did not fit in. We learned to inquire before making future trips like that again.

Mother and Father on their wedding day,
September 27, 1912

Our home at 1703 N. Jackson Street.
It was a cold house in winter!

Bob and Me after his release from
Milwaukee hospital, 1937.

Ma and me in front of our home, 613 Atlantic Ave.

"And how was the food and living conditions . . ?"
—Cpl. Ervin Scheske

Erve's prize winning cartoon in 1943 YANK Magazine

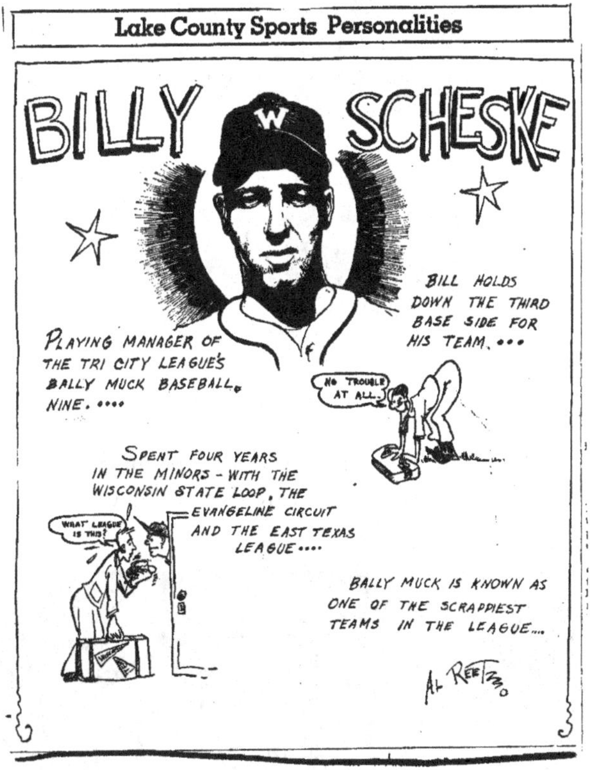

A 1947 clip from the Waukegan News-Sun

PARENTAL PRIDE—Mr. and Mrs. Fred Scheske, 1703 N. Jackson st., have the distinction of contributing three sons to Uncle Sam's peacetime army. The sons are (left to right) William, 23; George, 24, and Ervin, 26. William and Ervin will be inducted Sept. 23 from Waukegan selective service district No. 2. George is expecting to be called in December. William has just finished playing baseball with Wisconsin Rapids in the Wisconsin State league. Ervin and George are employed at the Johns-Manville plant.
—Waukegan Post Staff photo; engraved in The Post plant

A clip from the Waukegan Post, September, 1941.
Peacetime Army? Who are they trying to kid?

John Hall, Jim Bente, George Chandler, and Me on our
way to Ringling Brothers Circus, 1937

WTHS Junior Building (top) and Senior Building (bottom)

I was a serious ROTC cadet, 1944

The Genesee Theater in beautiful downtown
Waukegan – my favorite movie theater.

"Butch" and me outside MARBO
Offices. 1948

Outside our hotel in Gamigori, Japan, 1948

A Sukiyaki dinner served Japanese style, 1948

Our wedding reception in Bonnie Brook CC, 1952

Family portrait after Dan's adoption in 1967

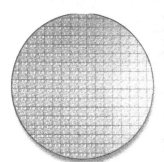 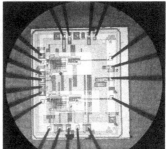

A finished silicon wafer with 180 Integrated Circuits
(left), microscopic view of one circuit wired to
leads (right), and a typical plastic encapsulated
integrated circuit ready for testing (below).

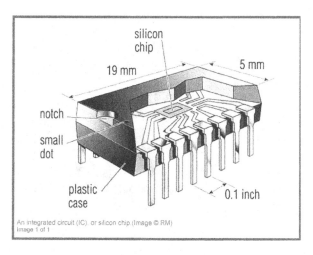

silicon chip

19 mm

5 mm

notch

small dot

plastic case

0.1 inch

An integrated circuit (IC), or silicon chip.(Image © RM)
Image 1 of 1

The last gathering of the remaining "Scheske Boys"
In Mesa, Arizona, 1982
Fred, Erve, Bill, Bob

Fab 6 in Chandler, the first Intel factory in Arizona, 1980

Celebration of Cathy's graduation from
University of Texas-Dallas, 1996
Dan, Cathy, Margaret and Fred

Michelle and me at our wedding in Chapel of the Flowers,
Las Vegas, NV, June 2007

Fred and Michelle with our dogs: Sparkle, Sugar and Sammy

Michelle, Fred and Karenlin Madoff

25
Time to Expand Our Family

Margaret and Wanda Barker worked in the same office and often talked about having a family. Neither had become pregnant and each wanted a baby. Well, it was fun trying but after two years it became clear that Margaret and I could not produce a pregnancy. We were advised by a Gynecologist and tested repeatedly – nothing. It appeared that I could not produce what was needed to induce a pregnancy. And, it looked like Bill and Wanda were in the same boat. It was Wanda who came up with the idea of adopting a baby and Margaret jumped on it. Unbeknownst to me, Margaret called the Illinois Home and Aid Society in Chicago looking for help. The first word I got was finding out we had an appointment with a case worker. I wasn't against adopting a child. It was that I just didn't feel ready to be a father. However after several meetings with the case worker I'd bridged the gap and felt I could handle fatherhood. She told us it would take about nine months to complete the checks and prepare us for the adoption.

Lo and behold, after many interviews and nine months we got a phone call from the Aid Society telling us that a baby was available for adoption. We were to go to Chicago to view the baby and make a decision about accepting the child. Even though we had said we wanted a child, the realization that one was waiting for our acceptance hit us between the eyes.

Margaret literally stuttered talking to me about picking up the baby. She wasn't sure if she was ready to be a mother. I tried to assure her I thought we'd be able to handle it.

Of course, we drove to Chicago anticipating the viewing. We were led into a reception area and given information about the baby, including medical data. Finally the case worker led us into a small room with a bassinette. Inside was a beautiful seven day old baby girl who had a spot of dried milk on her upper lip. I was speechless. Margaret began to tear up. We just stood there taking in her beauty. A question popped into mind: How could a mother give up this lovely baby for adoption? The caseworker watched us for a few minutes and then told us we did not have to make decision just then. "Take a little time, go get a cup of coffee and then decide if you want to adopt her." We quietly left the office and crossed the street to a coffee shop. We'd regained our composure by then and talked about the baby. After less than five minutes she asked, "What are we waiting for? Let's sign the papers and take her home!" I quickly agreed.

We rushed back to the Society's Office and told the caseworker, "Yes, we want the baby!" I think she knew all along that we'd want the child as our own. We signed the papers, got a quick review of the baby's feeding schedule and actually picked her up and held her. We were in absolute awe. After receiving documents and congratulations, we headed out to our VW Bug and the drive back to Waukegan. I cannot remember why, but we decided that Margaret should drive the car while I held our baby on my lap. Meanwhile, baby Scheske had not uttered one cry the entire time! And she did not cry for the entire ride back to Waukegan. We were impressed with this lovely, tiny baby!

Margaret and I had discussed a name for the baby and had tentatively agreed on Catherine Alice. Margaret's Aunt, Alice

Catherine Hanselman, was instrumental in raising her during childhood and we felt reversing the first and middle name would be appropriate. The adoption papers were submitted to the state of Illinois and Catherine Alice Scheske became a part of our family. Pearl Crawford was thrilled to have a granddaughter. So were my parents. We settled into our newly directed life. Margaret had resigned her job with Abbotts with her boss's blessing and I assumed the new role of sole breadwinner for our family.

The first night with little Catherine in our bedroom was nearly sleepless for Margaret and me. She was so quiet that we were afraid she had stopped breathing! We kept checking her to make sure she was alright. We soon found a schedule for feeding her at night and getting a reasonably good night's sleep. Baby Catherine wanted to be fed only once at night – unbelievable! She was the quietest baby we'd ever heard. It was years later that we realized that Catherine had never, ever barfed (much to my relief)! This kid had an iron stomach.

One month after we adopted our baby we had a surprise visit from my parents and sisters-in-law, bringing presents for her. It was a pleasant evening. My mother held Cathy for a while and beamed. The first adopted baby in Scheske family history was grandly accepted within its circle. Margaret and I were very proud parents.

26
First Experience With Death in the Family

A week and a half after the party, about 9 a.m. on Saturday, August 30, 1961, I received a call from Bill telling me to get to the house. Our mother had suddenly died! I felt like I had been slapped! My father had gone to phone the doctor after she had complained of having chest pains. When he finished calling he found her dead on the couch. Suddenly my world came crashing down. All of us were in shock. No one had an inkling she was having that kind of problem. We knew she had been seeing Dr. Keller but she seemed to be OK. My father was traumatized. Dr. Keller was called and he confirmed her death. We waited for the agents to come and transport her to the funeral parlor. Next came the difficult part of making arrangements for her funeral. That evening my father and all of the boys drove to the funeral parlor to select a casket and make final arrangements. On the way an unusual, warming feeling came over me – it was hard to describe. I realized later that God was speaking quietly to me, telling me I was not alone and that He would grant me strength to get through this. I have often thought about that evening and what it meant to me.

At the funeral parlor, we had a spirited discussion about selection of the casket. I was the only one who wanted a wooden casket while the others wanted a metal one. I felt that wood was more appropriate – I didn't like cold steel caskets. To end the arguing, we finally agreed on a beautiful oak wood model and the arrangements were completed. Since I was the only one who attended church regularly it was up to me to speak with Pastor Otto Eifert to arrange a church service. My mother did not attend services regularly, but pastor was kind to agree to hold a funeral service in Redeemer Lutheran Church. Many things were going on and it became a blur from then on.

The viewing and church funeral service was very emotional. The final part in North Shore Garden of Memories brought the event to a poignant close. The Wake (Lutherans really don't celebrate death with a Wake but the after event is much the same) was held at Brother Bill's house. I did not feel like celebrating and after a while Margaret, Cathy, Pearl and I left to return home. I had lost my mother but just as importantly, my friend. Ma and I always seemed able to talk about anything. I never felt able to do that with Pa – or with my brothers either. Sharing grief with my family was very difficult. Emotions were held within and talking about feelings was shunned. Thank goodness I had Margaret to share my feelings and emotions. She was a blessing.

Soon after we married, I had begun attending night school at Lake Forest College, continuing into my junior year with 300 number classes. I usually took two classes a semester but with the addition of a baby, I cut back to only one class. It became increasingly difficult to study and go to class, a drive of about 25-30 minutes one way. By the time I finished class and drove home, it was usually close to 10 p.m. I completed my junior year and had signed up for a 400 number class when I realized I could not keep up the pace. I completed one Literature 400 class and called it quits. I was physically drained. I have regretted not completing my college work ever since. However, I am pleased that I did complete as much as I did. I was the first in my family to go to college and it paid off handsomely for me in later life. I have not since worked in a factory although I did work in a super-clean "semiconductor fabrication facility" for many years. That is a far cry from the dirty, poorly lighted factories I worked in prior to my going to college. I don't mean to denigrate factories or factory workers. I had determined early on that I did not want to spend my working life in such a facility.

After nearly twelve years my job at Abbott Laboratories had become tedious. I then worked in a highly respected section, Infrared Spectroscopy in the Quality Control Department. We routinely received chemicals and materials from other departments for analysis. My work consisted primarily of properly preparing a chemical sample, running it through the infrared spectroscopy system for analysis and giving the resulting printed graphic display to a chemist for interpretation. Over time I began to understand and could identify some of the major constituents in a sample. But the report still had to be finalized by a chemist. My supervisor had designated me as the technician to write procedures in our section to achieve standardization of sampling procedures. In a way I was the trainer for our small group.

My Supervisor, Bill Washburn, was a good man. I admired him for his knowledge of chemistry and IR spectroscopy, but he had a way of letting me know that I was low man on the totem pole. For example, one of the men in the group with a degree in chemistry from Michigan State University complained about having to take time to clean his lab glassware each day. Bill took me aside and "asked" me to wash the guy's dirty glassware. What could I say? So, I usually spent the last hour of work each day washing not only my glassware but also his. It was a little thing, yes, but demeaning.

The winter of 1961-1962 was one of the worst the Midwest had ever experienced. Not only was it very cold but it snowed a great deal. In fact by January, 1962 the snow piled on the sides of the driveway was so high that I could not throw it up to the top of the pile! The only way we could get into our car was to enter it in the garage or out in the street. You could not open the car doors in the driveway! While backing out of the drive one day after the city had plowed the street, I got stuck in the pile left in my driveway entrance. The little VW Bug simply rose up in the back and the wheels couldn't get any traction. About the same time I heard the plow returning on my side of the street. The snow thrown curb side by the plow forced my car forward and back into the cleared drive. Fortunately, the plow did not hit the car.

While returning home from a chemistry night class at Lake Forest College during a monstrous snow storm, I approached an intersection, noting that I had a green light. Just as I entered the intersection I saw a huge state highway snow plow coming at me from the right – and it was not about to stop for the red light! How he missed hitting my car I will never know, but he did. By this time I had had enough of snow and cold weather. Having been in the Army stationed in a place with very mild weather I realized that there were more pleasant places to live in the world.

The crowning blow came in early February, 1962 after yet another snow storm. I had gone out to clear the sidewalk and driveway and while shoveling, the handle broke off of the shovel. I threw the handle into the snow bank, walked into the house and told Margaret, "We are out of here and moving to a warmer climate!" Miraculously, we had gotten the Sunday edition of the *Chicago Tribune* and featured that day was a section on Arizona. Margaret pointed to the paper and said, "Read this." I did read it and was convinced we needed to check out Arizona. Subsequently we talked a lot about moving. We were still in the process of adopting Catherine and weren't sure when the process would be finalized. But, we agreed to pursue exploring Arizona for relocation.

Opportunity presented itself in late February, 1962. Pa was still grieving the death of my mother and did very little to help himself. He sat in his chair, smoked cigarettes and ate only when Brother Bill or his wife Norma made something for him. He simply was not coping. I talked with him one day and asked if he would like to visit Bob who was stationed at Manzano Air Base in Albuquerque, New Mexico. I saw a spark in his eyes and I agreed to arrange the trip for the two of us. What I didn't tell him was that I planned on continuing to Phoenix, Arizona after arriving in Albuquerque. I planned to seek a job while in Phoenix and arranged a three day stay there. I had earned three weeks of vacation and spoke to my boss about taking one week off, not explaining why I needed time off in cold February.

We travelled to New Mexico on an AMTRAK train. It was a day and a half in hell! Two couples with three small children in our car created havoc the entire trip. The children continually ran up and down the aisle, either crying or yelling while the parents did little to curb their activity. Worse, all the kids smelled badly, obviously from dirty diapers. Pa and I were very happy reaching our destination, departing from the train. Bob and his family met us at the station and drove us to their house on base. It was good to see my brother and his family and to see Pa actually laugh and talk at length. The weather was ideal – sunny and cool with daytime temperatures in the high 60s. We spent a lot of time out in yard. The trip was just what Pa, and I, needed!

Only then did I explain that I was going on to Phoenix and would be back in four days. Pa was taken aback, not understanding that I was seeking a different job. Bob took it in stride and wished me success. It was back on an AMTRAK train for the trip to Flagstaff, Arizona and then a transfer to Phoenix. Arriving early morning I checked into the hotel where I had reservations and readied myself for a job search. First stop was at the Arizona Department of Economic Services, just a few blocks from the hotel.

After a short questioning period, the clerk wrote two addresses on a 3 X 5 card. The first was for Motorola Semiconductor and the second was for an architectural firm. I never got beyond Motorola. I was interviewed and re-interviewed for two and a half days by several electrical engineers. I explained my current job with Abbott Labs time and again. For the final interview, the manager of the Research and Development Group, Jack H, took me into a separate room, told me to diagram my job on the white board and explain what it meant while questioning me. That went on for almost two hours! I explained that I had booked a flight to Albuquerque for 3 o'clock and I had to get to the airport. Still no offer – but no rejection either! Another engineer took me aside as I was leaving and asked me to call him from the airport and he would let me know about the job opening. Talk about suspense!

I held my breath as I phoned the engineer. He congratulated me and said that I would receive a job offer by mail from Motorola. Wow, success! To say I was happy would be trivializing my feelings. Fatigue hit big time waiting for the plane boarding announcement. I was absolutely wiped out. I had called Bob earlier and he said he would meet me at the ABQ airport. I then called Margaret and told her the good news. She was thrilled – and then started asking questions. When would we move? What about salary? Where would we live? Enough, already! Let me get back to Waukegan and we can start making plans. Arriving in ABQ I just wanted to go to bed and sleep. But Pa had other ideas. He asked, "Why are you looking for work in Arizona?" He couldn't understand why I wanted to leave our family in Waukegan. It was difficult to explain to someone who had worked forty-two years for the same company why I wanted to start another career.

Back at my job at Abbotts I was queried about "my vacation". One of the technicians had a fifth sense that I had been interviewing and began questioning me more closely. I could not reveal at that time that I had been offered a job at Motorola since the adoption still was not officially completed. We spoke with Illinois Home and Aid Society about the timeline for completion and I think she began to wonder why we were pushing for the court order. Cathy had been with us for seven months and it was clear, I believe, that we were fit parents. Mid March I received the job offer from Motorola, detailing salary and moving allowances. I responded immediately, accepting the offer with the caveat that we were still waiting for the adoption completion order from the court. A letter from Motorola followed stating that I was to notify them when the order came through with the expectation, I think, that it would occur soon.

We waited, and we waited, for the final order, getting more and more antsy about the job offer. Motorola was being very patient with me, but I was beginning to feel that they were not going to let the job offer drag on forever. Finally, in July, 1962 the court order came through and the adoption was complete. Now we could move! But wait, was the job still open? I called Motorola to confirm the court order and let them know I was ready to move to Phoenix. After some checking, they noted that the original job that I had been offered was now filled. Oh, great! But after a pause, they had another job with a different engineer in the same group and I could fill that opening. Talk about relief! So, the move to Phoenix was on.

When we told Margaret's mother Pearl that we were moving to Phoenix she went into hysterics. I listened to her complaints for several days about our leaving Waukegan and finally, at dinner one evening, I leveled with her. She had a choice. She could stay in Waukegan and we would find an apartment for her or she could move to Phoenix with us – period. She looked stunned and was very quiet for a long while. Finally she said she would like to move with us.

I broke the news to my boss, Bill Washburn that I would be leaving Abbotts for a job with Motorola. He was taken aback and began asking questions about the job. He then informed the department manager, Elmer Kreuger, of my resignation. I suddenly felt the cold shoulder from my colleagues and from management. Only a few department colleagues came to me and offered congratulations. On my last day at work I asked to see Mr. Krueger to thank him for the opportunities he had provided me and to say goodbye. He coldly shook my hand, told me he hoped I liked the 120 degree temperatures in Phoenix and sat back down at his desk. The meeting was over! I left Abbotts that day with empty feelings. We didn't get many wishes for happiness from my family, either. It was like a slap in the face. I did not understand their feelings about our leaving town. Later I was told most thought we'd be back in Waukegan within six months.

Previously, we advertised our house on Ninth Parkway for sale on a Friday and had an offer within several days. A young couple fell in love with the house and wanted it. They had been pre-approved for a loan and were ready to move in. We sold many items in a yard sale, paring household items as much as we could for the transfer. A national moving company just happened to have a van available the last week in July and the deal was made. Leaving Waukegan was happening very quickly. We packed our 1961 Studebaker sedan after the moving van was loaded, turned over the keys to the new owners and were on our way to Arizona.

27
Arizona, Here We Come!

The trip was not without incidents. We got as far as Elgin, Illinois the first day – a total of about 60 miles on route 66. It was a hot and muggy August day and traveling in a car without air conditioning was not pleasant. In addition to Margaret, Cathy and Pearl, we had two tranquilized dogs. Unfortunately the medication given us by the veterinarian made the dogs very agitated and they even began fighting at one point. Pearl was in the middle of the fray and we had to stop, separate Fritzie and Mittens and calm them down. We didn't use the medication again.

Early next day we were on the road again hoping to make it to St Louis, Missouri by evening. The day only got hotter and more humid as we approached the city. The temperature was 95 degrees and the humidity was 98%! Talk about discomfort. We found a nice motel with air conditioning that would accept dogs. We spent a cool, relaxed night resting up for the next foray. The third day was spent driving in rain but with much cooler temperatures, arriving in Oklahoma City. We were becoming acclimated to travel and each motel arrival and departure was easier and faster. Eating at restaurants posed a problem because of the dogs so we would eat in shifts, one eating while the other fed and watched the dogs.

Our next stop was on the outskirts of Albuquerque where we met Bob and his family for a short get-together. Next morning, we were up early for the final leg to Phoenix. Coming near Phoenix, we stopped in Globe, Arizona to fill up on gas. It was cool, but the air smelled like sulfur. Globe is a mining town and the smell is consistent with mining. Happily leaving Globe, we descended into the Valley of the Sun toward Phoenix. Temperatures rose into the low 100s and we were gagging (but it was a dry heat!). I actually had to turn on the heater in the car to keep the engine from boiling over! It was brutal! Toward evening we found a sleepy little motel in downtown Tempe and literally ran inside to cool off. Air conditioning is wonderful. We were finally home – or what would become our home town.

The trip to Arizona was interesting and fun in spite of three adults, a baby, two dogs and luggage being in a cramped car. We marveled at the scenery along the way and enjoyed meeting and talking with folks at our stops. Margaret would initiate talking to strangers in restaurants and at motels. She loved to talk – but then so did Pearl. People would often ask about our baby or dogs and the talking would begin. Seeing pine trees and then wide open spaces and huge saguaro cacti in Arizona was dazzling. We even saw a black bear sitting on a hill next to the highway! The contrast in environment was almost unbelievable. I had tried to explain what the scenery looked like as we neared the state but the actual sight overwhelmed Margaret and Pearl. Baby Cathy just smiled, loving the ride in a car. The dogs took it in great stride as long as we stopped regularly.

28

Our New Arizona Home

We quickly found an apartment above a garage across the street from Arizona State University in Tempe. Not the greatest apartment but the owners were happy to rent it to us. We soon found out why. The air cooler had not been serviced in years and the fiber pads were old, dirty and inefficient. The very day we moved in there was a huge dust storm in the evening that overwhelmed us. We'd never seen anything like it. The storm went on for nearly an hour and before it subsided had deposited a fine layer of red dust throughout the apartment. The cooler was next to useless in providing cool air for us. In speaking to the owners they said to turn up the cooler water supply and it would be fine. Well, it wasn't fine. The "cooled" temperature in the apartment hovered around 90 degrees every day and didn't reach 80 until late in the evening. We slept uncovered the whole time we lived there. We decided that we had to find other living quarters quickly.

Each morning after I had left for work, Margaret and Pearl would take Cathy for a walk in the stroller. Across the street from our apartment was an open area of the ASU campus and the marching band would practice there. It was an enjoyable walk each day for them. Two blocks down the street was a small shopping center and the three would often wind up in a restaurant having coffee before returning to the apartment.

Walks had to be taken pretty early in the morning to avoid the hot temperatures.

In our travels driving about the area to get oriented, we found two homebuilders within two miles of our apartment. Visiting the new homes and talking with the sales people we narrowed our search to north Tempe, adjoining Scottsdale. Kaufman and Broad Homes had several spec homes nearly finished and ready for sale. We settled on one home and talked business with a sales rep. He could have the home ready in two weeks if we wanted it, complete with our choice of cabinets, carpet and tile – and it had air conditioning! Margaret and I huddled and decided to buy the home. A bonus was that the nearest elementary school was in the very highly rated Scottsdale School District. We had money in the bank so financing was not a problem. The cost of the home was slightly less than the sale of our home in Waukegan. We were in fat city!

29

My New Job as a Process Technician

Motorola Semiconductor Products Division had been formed on the recommendation of a member of the Board of Directors from Chicago Headquarters who vacationed in Phoenix each winter. He'd convinced board members that starting a transistor manufacturing division in Arizona would be a good business decision. Low real estate prices, low taxes and an ample supply of labor were deciding factors. The site started in a small building on 56th Street in Scottsdale while a larger facility was being built on the corner of 56th Street and McDowell Road in Phoenix. By the time I joined the division (Employee number 1220) all operations were housed in the new facility. The older, leased facility in Scottsdale made digital watches. That money losing operation soon stopped when digital watches were being cheaply made by many companies, including foreign enterprises.

Emphasis was then placed on making transistors largely for computer manufacturers, predominantly IBM Corporation. Transistor manufacturing competition came mostly from U.S. companies such as Texas Instruments (TXN), Fairchild (FCS) and National Semiconductor (NSM). A project I worked on under the direction of my engineer was to "reverse or back engineer" transistor products from competitors. It involved removing one transistor from a "metal package" (a heat sink) and dissecting it layer-by-layer with chemicals to determine how it had been made. It was tedious, often unrewarding work.

Technicians I worked with in my group were generally very uncooperative when it came to explaining the process of building transistors. Most acted like they were afraid to reveal knowledge that they had gained. Find out yourself seemed to be the motto!

My job at Motorola was completely different than what I had expected. Making transistors on thin, 7/8 inch diameter polished slices of round silicon was totally overwhelming. I hadn't a clue initially about what I was supposed to do. I had received no training, had been given minimal job instructions and had no background in electronics. It was a day-by-day learning process with many fumbles and stumbles along the way. Months into the job, my engineer, Dick J, took just a little time each day trying to instruct me in the process of manufacturing semiconductors. I took copious notes which proved to be beneficial later. Little by little I learned the process. I'd been accustomed to going to Abbott's library whenever I had a question about my work there. When I asked where Motorola's library was located I got a laughing response – there wasn't one!

Dick J took it upon himself to teach process technicians an after-hours class on electronics and the processes used in making transistors. Classes were about an hour long and very rewarding for me. I felt I was finally getting a handle on the manufacturing process. The notes that I had been making as I worked became very useful. I began to write a booklet describing how to make semiconductors with the blessing of my engineer. When I completed the work after several months of writing, editing and gaining approval of group management, Dick had the booklet printed and bound. I had finally gained some respect among my colleagues. I found later that the booklet had been disseminated and some even wound up in the University of Utah's library!

30
Our New Tempe Home

We moved from our tiny apartment into our new 1500 square foot air conditioned home in Tempe. It seemed like paradise. Margaret, Cathy and Pearl quickly adapted to the new neighborhood, making friends with our neighbors. After work each day I put muscles to work on landscaping the front and back yards. I didn't know beans about what would grow in the Arizona climate. So, I spent a lot of time at nurseries gleaning information on suitable plants and trees. When I had finished, we had a reasonably good looking landscape. Margaret wanted two clothes poles in the backyard, so I hired a man to do it. We did not have a clothes dryer initially and drying clothes in the outdoors was a quick process. You've heard the phrase I'm sure: It's a dry heat!

Margaret and I joined a Lutheran Church nearby our home in Tempe and made many good friends as a result. Our Pastor, Reverend Eric Hoefer, encouraged small bible study groups and we joined one. For the most part they were educational and uplifting. On one occasion, however, something happened that turned off Margaret and me. While holding hands and praying in a meeting, several members started talking in tongues. We were completely confused as to what they were saying or why they were saying it. After the meeting, two of the members took me aside and told me that the only way one could get to heaven was to be able to speak in tongues! Well, that was completely contrary to what I had learned in Luther's Catechism class or in any pastor's teachings. Speaking in tongues is a gift from the Holy Spirit. It is not criteria for gaining entrance into heaven. I scheduled a meeting with our Pastor and spoke with him about talking in tongues and what had happened in our session the night before. I explained that I had never heard that one must speak in tongues to be assured of going to heaven upon death. Pastor Hoefer kind of beat around the bush, but assured me that one must only believe in Jesus Christ as our Savior to assure a home in heaven. Margaret and I never attended another small group meeting at that church.

In August,1965 Pearl stepped out of the house onto the patio, fell and broke her right hip. She was taken to Scottsdale Memorial Hospital and immediately went into surgery for a hip replacement. After a long wait, a surgeon came out to report her condition. He told us Pearl had a 50-50 chance of surviving the surgery. Margaret was in shock. After several days we were informed she was ready to go home. She was transported to our home and into bed. During the first night she called out to Margaret in pain. Her incision had opened up and she was bleeding! We found later that while in the hospital she had called a nurse to help her with a bed pan and when no one responded she messed her bed. Her incision had become infected and had burst open that night at home. It was back to the hospital. The doctor told us the next day that she should be taken to a nursing facility where she could be closely monitored. We found a small care facility in Scottsdale and she was transferred there. Pearl spent thirty days in that facility, slowly declining in health until her death in September. Our family was falling apart. We had a memorial service for Pearl in the Chapel and she was interred in our sites at Green Acres Memorial Park in Scottsdale.

31
A New Job Role

Meanwhile, my job was changing at Motorola. The small Research and Development Group evolved into a Development Group – no more research. We were charged with making larger quantities of transistors before the product would be given to the main manufacturing group at the plant. I was one of three technicians who were made supervisors, each having about four or five operators to build transistors.

An operator was a person, usually a woman, who operated specialized equipment in processing transistors. The supervisor's role was to schedule a group of wafers (thin silicon slices) through a designated process. The designated process was an engineer's written scheme of how to build a given transistor. Standard processes still had not been instituted. Additionally, the supervisor had to ensure quality work by the operators, often by using a microscope to inspect wafers.

And then there were personnel problems to handle. For example, I found an operator asleep at her station one day. I cautioned her about snoozing on the job. I spoke with my engineer that day when I later found her asleep again. He explained he would handle it and he did so by speaking with her. The next day I found out that she had been sleeping with him while his wife was out of town! This was new found territory for me – I'd never experienced anything like this before.

An engineer explained to me one day that the semiconductor industry should really be called the "sexiconductor industry". It was a new, struggling industry still in the raw beginnings with a lot of work being done by the seat of your pants. Some male managers and supervisors took advantage of the loose operating conditions, using influence and power to beguile and seduce female operators. Work operations were loose and wide open. Product specifications? There were none. We wore latex finger cots to prevent depositing finger prints on wafers. We didn't cover street clothes while working. Often equipment was modified right on the floor to meet needed conditions. Equipment technicians carried less than clean pliers, screwdrivers and even hammers in the manufacturing area. And with this type of operation making tiny semiconductors was to be the next technology revolution?

32
Two Trips to Waukegan

Summer of 1966 I experienced a strange feeling. An inner voice told me I should travel to Waukegan to visit my father. I talked to Margaret about making the trip and she agreed we should drive back. We owned a little '64 Pontiac station wagon and I'd been having trouble with the air conditioning system. I found a mechanic who knew GM cars and felt he could get the AC working again. After an hour's work he had cold air cooling the car! We were ready to hit the road in comfort. Plans were made and we headed out to Illinois.

It took three days to get to Waukegan – and the AC had pooped out on us along the way. We spent two days with Pa and the rest of the family in hot, humid August weather. The last night before leaving a huge thunderstorm moved in and we sweltered in our bed. At three o'clock in the morning we were up, ready to hit the road back to Arizona. We'd said our goodbyes the night before and we left amid the rain, thunder and humidity. It was the last time I saw Pa alive.

The following January, 1967 I received a phone call from Bill telling me that Pa had had an aneurism and had died at Victory Memorial Hospital. I flew into Chicago, got a rental car and drove to Waukegan. The funeral was not as emotional as my mother's. I did not have the same feelings for my father as I did for my mother, being sad of course, but not torn up.

There was a short service in the funeral parlor and then the drive out to North Shore Garden of Memories for interment. Both parents were now gone and I felt their absence. I had seen Pa just months before his death and I was happy about that. After two days I was relieved to leave the cold in Waukegan and head back to Arizona.

33
My Pink Slip – Laid Off!

In 1967 the U.S. economy was tanking and sales of transistors were hitting new lows. In October after more than five years of service, Motorola gave me a pink slip. Human Resources told me that they were sure I could find another job quickly. Turns out you couldn't buy a job in Phoenix! Wherever I went it was the same story: nothing available.

A good Moto friend, Bob, directed me to his wealthy brother-in-law who was building apartments in the Valley. He took me on as a clean-up man, having to clean debris from buildings so that plumbers and electricians could do their jobs more easily. I did that for four days. Then he told me to get up on the roof and help the roofer lay down sheets of plywood on the joists and secure them in place with nails. I did that for two more days. Next he told me to start nailing 1 by 2 inch strips of wood on concrete block walls so that drywall could be attached. At the end of the first day of that operation I was using both hands on the hammer to drive special iron nails into the block, swinging with all that I had in me. It took one whole day for me to "strip out" one apartment while an accomplished carpenter did three apartments. After two weeks on the job I got a paycheck and my walking papers that day – to my unending thanks.

Weekly trips to the Arizona Department of Economic Services had me answer the same question, "Have you been looking for a job?" "Of course, and if you could give me a lead I would appreciate it!" It always produced the same drab look from the agent. Later a check would appear in the mail for $65. How could a man support a family on $65 a week? On the other hand, it was better than a kick in the pants.

A Moto colleague and good friend, Gordon, whom I'd worked with prior to my layoff called me one day at home and told me that he'd heard of an opening in a diode manufacturing group. He knew the engineer in charge and had recommended me for the job. The open requisition called for a technician to help solve technical problems in the production line. How the engineer, John L, had managed to get approval for the position was beyond me. However, he called me and told me the job was mine if I wanted it. If I wanted it? I'd been out of work for nearly two months – of course I wanted it! And I thanked Gordon for helping me get back into the work force.

I reported for work and was introduced to members of the group. My reception was lukewarm at best. It took a while to gain the respect of supervisors and technical personnel. The diode production line had a serious problem with glass packages and yield was not very good. The glass packages were washed in a special wash/rinse system, dried and sent to the production line for assembly. There was a different diode manufacturing group on the other side of the building. I walked over there one day and spoke with the engineer in charge. Discussing the glass packages, which were identical to the ones we used, I found they did not wash or rinse the glass before assembly and had a very high production yield. I whizzed back to our line, spoke with John L about not washing the glass and he agreed to try assembly without the wash. The first batch came through with flying colors. The second group came through equally good. Our yield problem was solved! Why had no one from our production line talked to others about the problem? Non-communication was a common problem at Motorola, I believe. Anyway, it put me in solid with my new group and work life was getting to be good again.

Work conditions at Motorola were always in flux. The whole semiconductor industry was a fast moving, changing business. One company was always charging out front with a new design, always touted better than its competitors. Motorola was a me-too company. By that I mean it never seemed to be first with any design or product. However, any product it manufactured and sold was always top notch. It just couldn't seem to bring out the bestest with the mostest first!

34
Our Family Expands

Margaret had plans to enlarge our family and told me one day that she had called Maricopa County about adopting a child. Did that surprise me? Not really. I knew she had always wanted a boy and a girl in our family. Soon a lady from the Maricopa County Child Services Agency called upon us to begin the adoption process. After many visits we were asked to describe the child we would be happy with. In discussion, the choice came down to a boy, between two and three years of age, preferably blond with blue eyes. She smiled, said she'd talk to us later, and left.

A call several months later told us they had a boy in mind and asked if we would like to meet him. Of course we would! About a week after the call we were told to meet the case worker at a shopping mall in central Phoenix. Margaret and I were very nervous as we approached the meeting site. After waiting a few minutes in the mall the case worker appeared with a boy, blond with blue eyes, dressed in a white shirt and blue shorts. We were told the boy was two and half years old. We couldn't believe our eyes!

Meeting Daniel was awesome and we hit it off right from the introduction. A short visit and we were convinced he belonged in our family. The whole process of visits, telephone inquiries and paperwork completion had taken nine months! Unbelievable! The adoption process was completed with a court order formally naming our new son Daniel Robert Scheske. The foster family that had been caring for Dan initially refused to release him but after a court order was issued, gave him up for adoption. Finally, little Dan moved into our home with one paper bag of clothing, a pair of cowboy boots and several toys. Our family was now complete.

35
Yet Another Motorola Job

I eventually transferred from the diode group to a new unit being formed as a lead supervisor with two junior supervisors reporting to me. The group was charged with making something very new, an MOS (**M**etal **O**xide on **S**ilicon) Integrated Circuit (IC). Individual transistors on a chip had been replaced with IC units which contained several hundred transistors, all on one chip. Our group was headed by Jim G, an electrical engineer who fancied himself as a top notch manager. We quickly set up our work area in a large empty room using recycled equipment, badly in need of repair. With months of tremendous start-up effort we were able to bring a newly designed integrated circuit into production every two weeks. For more than one month I worked seven days a week, twelve hours each day in order to help make the line productive. We'd bring in volunteers on Sundays and treat them to lunch (along with double time pay). At the end of the long month my supervisors and I were so tired we could not think objectively. Secondly, Margaret had had her fill of my not being home. My leaving early in the morning, returning exhausted late at night left her very angry. I was not being a good husband or a good father.

Months into manufacturing, an engineering change of a photo mask set took place. I had not received written notification about the change and we continued using the old procedure.

The engineer refused to assume responsibility for the change saying he had informed me verbally, which he had not. Operating procedure stated any process change was to be initiated with a written order. I had not received the change notice. Our fearless leader, Jim G, took me to lunch one day and stated that I was responsible for the lost product. He would not even listen to my side of the story. Shortly after that incident, Jim gave me my yearly performance review. He informed me with a straight face, "Fred, you are a Jack of all Trades, Master of None!" I very nearly spit in his face. Many months of busting my tail and getting a lousy performance review was more than I could handle.

I thought a lot about the situation and finally decided I'd had enough. After more than six months of constant pressure, I walked into my newly assigned manufacturing manager's office one morning, placed my Motorola ID badge on his desk and said, "I quit!" He was flabbergasted! After some discussion, he told me to go to my desk and wait for him to call me. I did that, waiting and reading journals in my cubicle for five days. He came to me at last and spoke of the need for training, asking me to organize a training group in the department. I agreed, not knowing how to even start up a training organization. It was the beginning of many years of service as a training manager and a training program development specialist.

36

A New Career Path

Within a day of that "promotion" I had two requests from experienced operators wanting to transfer into my training group. They were quickly transferred into our department. To start, we moved forward by documenting equipment operating procedures to form a base for uniform training. In days the group began refreshing operators in the correct procedures of processing wafers using sophisticated equipment. What prompted the need for operator training was incorrect or improper operation of equipment. Semiconductor manufacturing equipment had become increasingly complex and accordingly, very expensive.

When I started in the semiconductor business in 1962, a company could start operations with an outlay of about five to eight hundred thousand dollars for equipment. Less than ten years later the cost of a startup had increased to two million, five hundred thousand to three million dollars or more! This was due mostly in part to computerization of the equipment but also to refinement of the machines. For example, vacuum systems needed for deposition of metals on wafers had become increasingly complex, not only from the operator's viewpoint but also from the maintenance technician's perspective. Without proper training, million dollar pieces of equipment could sit inoperative while repairs were made, costing production time and many dollars in lost product.

Secondly, manufacturing areas had to become super clean to be able to increase and maintain profitable yields. In the course of a few years, engineers, operators and service personnel had to change from wearing street clothes to wearing white nylon coveralls called "bunny suits", safety glasses and latex gloves in manufacturing areas. Training emphasized the need for cleanliness in all operations. This included, for example, smoking only in designated areas outside the production room. Smokers were trained to rinse their mouth with water before reentering production. Believe it or not, cigarette smoke contains particles and contaminants that produce defects on integrated circuits. Clean air systems were installed to provide ultra clean air within the production room. The resultant production area was much cleaner, in fact, than most hospital operating rooms! Learning about "clean room" requirements, proper chemical handling procedures and equipment operations were the equivalent of years of college education for me.

Months later we were informed that the Phoenix MOS operation was being transferred to Austin, Texas where a newly built Motorola fabrication facility (Fab) was ready and waiting. We also learned that our infamous manager, Jim G, had left the company for a new post in Pennsylvania. In the meantime I had been transferred to the Motorola Semiconductor Division Training Group as a training specialist to work for Bob McD. The intent was to have me transfer with manufacturing personnel to Austin. The division training group was mostly comprised of self-centered, college bred elites and I was an outsider from the beginning. I felt like a leper and could not seem to fit in. Only engineers and supervisors were offered jobs in the new Texas plant. I was offered the position of training supervisor and could take one qualified training specialist with me.

37
Orientation Trip to Austin, Texas

Margaret was less than pleased about moving to a strange new city. Motorola had arranged a four day orientation trip, paying for all expenses. Friends agreed to care for Cathy and Dan while we were gone. We travelled to Austin on a chartered flight and were greeted by city officials and realtors. A real estate let-us-show-you-what-we've-got meeting in a local Austin school auditorium led us to a couple who were eager to meet my wife and me. They were distantly related to a Fred A. Scheske, Mayor of Gonzales, Texas and were absolutely sure we were kin. But that is another story.

We were driven about Austin and shown a variety of homes in a price range we could afford. Most were very nice homes with lovely green yards and oak trees. We were impressed. In the evening we were invited to dinner with entertainment, Texas style. In all, it was a very pleasant day. We agreed Austin is a lovely town.

Margaret's opposition to moving to Texas was lessening. I was convinced it was the only way I could make any upward progress in the company. The four days we spent visiting in Austin was educational and enjoyable. Some of the folks from Phoenix, however, were not impressed with Austin or the new facility and openly stated they would not move. I tried to play it cool and not put pressure on Margaret to make a decision. Returning from our trip it was apparent that she had less doubt but still was not ready to say yes to moving. We talked and talked and finally agreed that we would move.

But events were not helping me say yes to my Training Manager, Bob McD. For example, all of the requisitions I had submitted for office equipment and training supplies to be used in Austin had not been processed. When asked about it, Bob told me that they were in the works. When I investigated with Moto Purchasing I found that not to be true. The crowning blow came when I was informed that only I would be funded to move to Austin. That is, I would not be allowed to have a lead trainer accompany me. I told Bob that I would not transfer without a lead trainer, training supplies and office equipment. He was stunned.

38
On Shaky Ground

Bob immediately went to the newly appointed Fab Manager, Frank D, and gave him the news. Frank exploded and told Bob, "Fire that SOB on the spot!" Bob could not do that because He had not provided me with the resources I needed, to which he had originally agreed.

Frank and I were not on the best of terms since his hiring and entry in Motorola Semiconductor and appointment as PMOS (**P**ositive **M**etal **O**xide **S**ilicon) Fab Manager. He was hired from another company, yet another Motorola managerial acquisition from the outside. He was a tough, no nonsense, results oriented engineer who took no excuses. He was respected but not readily liked by engineers or supervisors. In an affable mood during a meeting one day, however, someone asked him about his head cold. Frank, an Italian, had a very large nose and replied, "When I get a head cold I really have a head cold!" It cracked up the whole group. Frank was seldom that funny or warm.

He and I did not click from the beginning. He had a very trifling view of training and training personnel noted by disparaging remarks he made in meetings. After ordering Bob to fire me, I was on very shaky ground. Fortunately, another MOS group was forming and I would be able to move into that slot. Competent training personnel with manufacturing experience were not readily available within Motorola. It couldn't have come at a better time. Bob quickly released me from the Division Training group, which I felt never to be a part of anyway and convinced a division training expert to accept the job in Austin (who had no manufacturing experience). For a short period I did not have a job home.

A meeting was soon called to introduce the NMOS (**N**egative **M**etal **O**xide **S**ilicon) Phoenix manufacturing group's manager, Carmelo S (Carm). He had earned a PhD in electrical engineering from Harvard and was yet another Motorola acquisition outside the company. However, we found him to be the opposite of Frank. Carm was friendly, warm and easy to work with. I liked him and so did engineering and supervisory personnel. Had I just lucked into a better position? The group quickly went about moving into quarters in "P Building" designated for NMOS.

Operators were hired, equipment was installed and put through operational tests. I was provided several competent trainers who had manufacturing experience and we set about to train operators. Even though operators had experience, we had to qualify them to run new, very expensive manufacturing gear. The process used to fabricate NMOS integrated circuits was new and complex, certainly different than what most operators were familiar with in building simple transistors. It was a challenging time for all of us but we managed to get the production line up and running in just over a month. Slowly but surely die yields began to climb and finally reached satisfactory levels. Die, the plural of singular dice, are components on a silicon wafer.

39

A Primer: Semiconductor Manufacturing

The business of semiconductor Integrated Circuit manufacturing is to achieve high product yields, that of getting as many electrically acceptable die as possible on the surface of a highly polished silicon (not silicone) wafer at the lowest cost. Silicon is a non-metallic substance made from sand. Heating silicon to a high temperature in the presence of oxygen produces a layer of glass on the surface. Glass prevents the transmission of electricity, essential to building semiconductors. Integrated circuits are built with six to eight layers on silicon using photolithographic and diffusion processes. Photolithography utilizes a thin layer of light sensitive material (called photo resist) on an oxidized wafer surface, aligning a patterned glass mask over the wafer, and exposing the surface material to Ultra Violet (UV) light. Washing the surface with a chemical removes the unexposed portion of photo resist from the wafer. Immersing the wafer in an acid etches a pattern in the oxidized (glass) surface. The remaining photo sensitive material is removed from the surface using yet another liquid chemical (a solvent).

From there the patterned wafer is moved to a high temperature diffusion furnace where a vaporized chemical is diffused into the exposed patterned silicon. Silicon will actually accept a vaporized chemical into its exposed surface, thereby changing the electrical qualities in specific areas of the device. This process is repeated several times, resulting in several layers of deposited materials and silicon dioxide (glass) on the surface. Finally, a thin layer of aluminum is deposited on the top layer of the device. Each wafer is again patterned in a photolithographic process that provides the electrical wire connections for the device.

The entire wafer fabrication process can take anywhere from a week to ten days to completion. The completed wafer then moves to an electrical testing area where each die (an integrated circuit) undergoes computer evaluation to determine whether it meets electrical specifications or not. The above description is a much simplified version of integrated circuit semiconductor manufacturing.

After each die on the wafer is electrically tested, they are separated in an assembly procedure. Each acceptable die is then bonded to a plastic package and hair thin wires are used to connect pads on the die to leads on the package. The package is then sealed and sent through another computer electrical test. Packages are marked with the company logo and a specific product number, ready for sale.

Computer controlled machines in ultraclean rooms have now replaced most of the previous hand operated equipment. Polished silicon wafer slices have progressed from 7/8 inch size to the twelve inch diameter range accommodating thousands of individual dice. While not being able to design an integrated circuit to perform specific electrical functions, I did know and understand the manufacturing processes. Thirty-two years of service in the semiconductor industry taught me the nuances in fabricating transistors and integrated circuits. It was an experience I shall never forget.

After months of operation in Phoenix, the NMOS group was preparing for the move to Austin, Texas. Called into Carm's office, I was asked if I would make the move with the group. My response was yes. I had not cleared the answer with Margaret, but I was sure that she would agree – little did I know! When I spoke with Margaret and told her of my response to Carm's question, she let me have it. I reiterated that we had spoken about this and I believed she was OK with the move. A very spirited discussion followed. Explaining that I had very little, if any, choice in jobs if I remained in Phoenix, we finally reached consensus and made preparations for the move.

40
Our New Life In Austin, Texas

Margaret was not happy about moving to Texas in spite of the orientation trip that proved to be informative and interesting. Her biggest concern seemed to be uprooting Cathy and Dan and enrolling them in a different school system. She also loved our house in Mesa and did not relish moving into another home. On the other hand, I found the change to be exciting.

Our Austin house hunting trip proved to be rewarding as we found a lovely home located on the Balcones Ridge on the northwest side of Austin. The home had been built and occupied by a law professor at the University of Texas and his family. The reason they wanted to sell the place, we found later, was because their baby girl had suffocated in her crib. Memories were overwhelming and they wanted out. Had we known this when we made the offer to buy, I'm not sure we'd have bought the house. Nevertheless, it was a very nice tan brick, three bedroom house with a fireplace, two car garage and a huge yard with seven oak trees.

The lawyer professor was a misfit when it came to tending the house and yard. The first thing I did, while on a business trip to Austin, was paint the entire house inside. The yard needed much attention and I left that repair 'til our move into the house. Carpeting and window treatment would be left to

Margaret's expertise. My family moved to Austin after school was out for the summer. Furniture arrived a day after we got there and we officially moved into our new residence. Margaret immediately got involved replacing worn carpeting and fixing drapes and window blinds. Close inspection inside cabinets under the sinks revealed real messes. They appeared to have not been cleaned since the day they were built and installed!

Several days after move-in while watching TV in the family room, Dan went into the kitchen for a snack and screamed. On the floor were two roaches mating, fully three inches long! We'd never seen roaches that large. By the time I got there to stomp on them, they'd disappeared into the cabinets. It took us several months to eradicate the roach colony in our kitchen.

The yard posed another problem. Trees and shrubs had not been pruned since their planting. Cutting away excess tree branches and shaping bushes took weeks of work. The house was in need of paint for all of the wood trim, including garage doors. Dan and I set about painting and finished in less than two weeks. Now the house, our home, looked presentable. A few finishing touches such as antiquing the front door, planting a yellow rose bush (The Yellow Rose of Texas) in a large pot at the door and installing large house numbers on a panel near the garage beautified the place.

Meanwhile, Margaret was busy getting the kids registered for school and meeting neighbors. Our neighbors to the west were lovely folks. Jim was a PhD working in electrical science research at the university and his wife, May, took care of their two children. We became fast friends. Neighbors to the east were less than friendly, partly due we were told, because of the poor relationship with the former owners.

While registering the kids for school, Margaret met Alice Floyd, a lady with two boys, and they became very good friends. Cathy and Dan became close buddies with the boys,

Peter and Bobby. Their father was a Major in the US Air Force stationed in nearby Elgin Air Force Base. He had contracted a rare blood disease while stationed in the Middle East and his health was not good. We met only once with the Major. Due to his duties and ill health he spent most of his spare time in his home seldom going out.

Dan was in 6th grade and his teacher challenged students to learn chess during lunch hour. He would teach and play with them. Dan became quite good at chess with tutoring. One day several parents complained about the teacher using up lunch period by teaching chess. Unbelievable! Chess lessons and games stopped immediately. Cathy meanwhile was in middle school and found it to be very challenging. While she was ahead of her class in a few subjects she was much behind in others. Schools in Arizona had differing teaching methods. We joined a Lutheran Church only because it was nearby our home. The pastor was rather cold and haughty and we found it difficult to converse with him.

Life at work was interesting and demanding. Training Texan operators proved to be very challenging. It was much more difficult to teach operators to work with cutting edge equipment than it was in Phoenix. Part of the reason, I think, was due to the fact that all operators were new to semiconductor manufacturing having had no experience with the methods or terminology. Operator learning curves were much longer and shallower than with Phoenix operators. My single trainer was exhausted after work each day due to the stress of working with raw recruits. I spoke with Personnel, hoping to raise their selection process but to no avail. Meanwhile I was documenting procedures trying to achieve repeatability in our training processes. Because of the size of incoming groups of new operators we had to rely on older operators to help in training. It was not working to perfection, that's for sure. Carm and manufacturing managers were not pleased with the training operation. But then, everyone was unhappy with the caliber of operators that were being hired.

It came like a shot out of the blue one day when we were notified that Carm S had been fired as manager and had left the company. We were only into our fourth month of operation and had barely gotten the line up and running. Yield was not good but that is to be expected in any new operation. A highly placed manager from Phoenix Motorola, the "Hatchet Man", broke the news and told us he was going to manage the group for the foreseeable future. Well, he lasted for about a month and during that time near chaos reigned in the group. When he exited, The MOS Group Executive Manager took over to try and stabilize the organizations.

Six weeks later, yet another manager was announced to lead us. He was an engineer, a Canadian, who had been hired in Phoenix as a production line engineer. This man was the driest, most ineffectual manager I have ever worked for. Why he was given the job no one could understand. To give an example of his ineffectiveness, he delivered my yearly performance review. The review said little about my performance and dealt mostly with the role of training in the group. I responded to one of his remarks and while I was speaking the man fell asleep! I was astounded. But it became very clear that he and I were on a collision course. His attitude toward training was much the same as Frank D's: Who really needs it? Any engineer could train operators and do it better!

Interestingly, almost all of the managing and supervisory personnel that transferred from Phoenix became ill with allergies about this time. And, all went to doctors for treatment and all were given prescriptions to treat the allergies. The villain causing the allergy was: blossoming cedar trees. I had no idea cedar trees blossomed, but they do. They have brownish tips on the ends of branches that give off pollen. The pollen is picked up by wind and distributed 20 to 30 miles! And there were thousands of cedar trees in and around Austin. The prescription all of us were given was AFRIN. It affected all of us the same way. We walked around like zombies. We were all out to lunch during work hours. It was difficult to think and perform to the best of our ability.

While on a business visit from Phoenix to the Austin plant, Bob C and Jerry C came to see me. We had worked together several times on different projects at the Phoenix facility. As an aside, I told them that I would like to get out of Austin due to many changes in management (which they were well aware of) and because of my allergy. I was not the only person looking to get out of Dodge. My lead trainer also wanted to leave. My friend in Quality Control was as eager as I to get out. Working conditions under the new manager were abysmal.

Two weeks after my meeting with Bob C, I got a phone call asking if I was really serious about relocating. Of course I was. He had something in mind and said he'd call me later. Now, I'd said nothing to Margaret about moving from Austin. She knew of my discontent with work and about my allergy. Strangely, she nor the kids had a problem with allergies. When I did broach the subject of moving back to Phoenix, Margaret flipped out. She was not thrilled with living in Austin, but she hated the thought of moving again. We were at loggerheads once more.

Taking a ride out of town one Sunday we headed for Gonzales, Texas to meet the other Fred A. Scheske. I had no idea where he lived but I'd been told that all I had to do was ask and we'd be directed to his home. Stopping at a gas station I asked the attendant if he knew Mr. Scheske. He replied, "Of course, he is our mayor." "How can I reach him," I asked. The attendant picked up the phone and called the mayor. I was given the phone and when I heard hello, I asked, "Is this Fred Scheske?" "Yes, it is." "Well, I am Fred Scheske." A long pause and the mayor said, "You must be the man I was told about who lives in Austin. Come on over to our house and let's talk." He provided directions and we were soon in front of his beautiful home.

At the door he greeted Margaret, the kids and myself and invited us inside. His lovely wife offered us Texas iced tea and we began talking. I was amazed at the similarity in Fred's physical stature which I found to be very much like my father's. We talked for two hours and discovered many interesting similarities in families. The one fact that told me we were not related was that his family had emigrated from Germany near the same time my father had but had entered the U.S. in Galveston, Texas. My father and mother had entered the U.S. in New York City.

It is still amazing how many familial characteristics there were. The short stature, large boned physical traits were amazingly similar. At the time I did not know that my father's family had entered the U.S. under the name Olsheski. I'm still not certain when or how Pa changed his name to Scheske. The name Fred A. Scheske appears in the 1920 U.S. Census as having lived in Wauwatosa, Wisconsin where he married my mother. Anyway, it was a most interesting day to meet a person with the same identical name as my father's: Frederick August Scheske. Fred and his wife were gracious hosts to my family, typical of Texas hospitality.

42
Back at the Ranch

I was approached one day about working on the Motorola Austin Picnic committee. Anything to break up the monotony of the trivial work I'd been assigned, I agreed. The group interviewed several caterers, each preparing a lunch to show off their skills. We finally settled on one who made the best beef barbeque I have ever tasted. The picnic was a huge success. How could it not be with beer, barbecued beef and Cole Slaw on a lovely spring day? We received much kudos for our work arranging the picnic.

Soon after the picnic a phone call from Bob C informed me of the job opening in Mesa. He told me he was to manage and set up a small manufacturing group to make the same product as was being made in Austin. Huh? Why? There were some new products coming down and he was going to get them into production. He asked if I wanted to work for him as a lead supervisor. I would have a supervisor, of my choosing, and 12 to 15 operators to work one half of the whole group. I would also have full engineering support. Wow! Yes, if it meant my getting out of Austin, you bet! "OK, I'll start the paper work to transfer you back to Arizona!" I was thrilled.

Then it hit me. How do I tell Margaret that we'd be moving back to Mesa? She'd be happy, right? Wrong! Margaret hit the roof when I told her I'd been offered a new job in Arizona. She wouldn't even talk about it. I was tops on her S--t list! Word came down two weeks later that the transfer was approved and I could move at any time. Well, I had to sell the house first. Bob didn't see it that way. "I need you here now to get this thing rolling," was his reply. Telling Margaret that I had to leave within a week, she just wouldn't talk to me. We'd lived in Austin for just over one year and she couldn't cope with the fact we were moving again.

I tried to prepare everything for the move without much help from Margaret. I explained to Cathy and Dan that I had an opportunity in Mesa and I was going to take it. I didn't get much reaction from them but I could tell they weren't thrilled with moving again. I packed my VW Van and prepared to leave on a Friday. It was raining hard with thunder and lightning that morning and Margaret was in a foul mood – she wouldn't even say good bye. It was not a pleasant day in the Scheske family.

The trip to Arizona was not without incident either. I had purchased a used VW van in Austin and it had a few miles on it, but had given me no problems in the city. On the road, however, it began acting up outside Tucson, Arizona and I barely made it into Mesa that day. I limped into the VW dealer and they checked it out, finding all of the spark plug wires were nearly fried. I was very fortunate to have made it to Mesa. The van's engine needed a lot of work but they finished it in one day. It ran like a top when I drove away from the dealer. I quickly found an efficiency apartment in a complex not far from Motorola's plant. I called Margaret as soon as I could and found her to be very cool. The transfer to Arizona was not turning out as I had hoped.

43

My first order of business on the job was to call a former Phoenix Moto colleague of mine, Mary M, and ask if she would accept the job as my line supervisor. We talked at length and she said she'd call me the next day. Hiring operators and getting the area ready for operation was exciting and fulfilling. Jerry C was my engineer and we worked well together. It was such a contrast to my job in Austin and I was finding happiness in work again. Mary called the next day and said she would like to work as my supervisor – she was an excellent, respected leader and I was extremely fortunate to have her accept the job. Bob and Jerry were equally pleased with my choice.

We began the task of selecting operators, people we felt would be conscientious and reliable. Other manufacturing groups were not pleased when our selections asked to transfer. Personnel let us know that they had gotten many complaints about our tactics. We had enough muscle to make our requests for personnel accepted. When done, we had assembled one of the best groups of operators in the company. Many of the operators had worked for either Mary or me before and knew how we managed a production organization. Some operators wanted to join just because they had heard about us.

Equipment began to be installed and we started qualification tests. We were very busy from start of shift to end. It felt good at the end of each day knowing that we were putting together a top notch manufacturing group. Engineering and manufacturing worked hand in hand to make things right. To boot, we were having fun! Our side of the group, diffusion, assembly and testing was shaping up very nicely. The other side, photolithography, was doing equally well. Bob was in hog heaven! It was weeks before wafers began moving through the line and the kinks were quickly taken care of.

Meanwhile, life for my family in Austin was not going well. I had repaired the kitchen faucet and soon after I left it sprang a big leak. The kitchen floor was flooded with water. Fortunately, Dan was there soon after it happened and knew what to do. He turned off the hot water supply and the leak (translated flood) was stopped. Margaret and I had re-established communication before this happened, but this event put a sharp edge into our relationship. Worse, she had to heat water on the stove in order to wash dishes. I felt very inadequate. My repair job had created a huge mess and I was dejected. My apology was heartfelt and I told her I would make it up to her when she got to Mesa (I assumed she would move at this point).

Our small NMOS manufacturing group was taking off and we began producing wafers on a weekly schedule. Rushing test lots through to completion, we began to see remarkably good die yields. Tweaking processes produced even better results and full scale production started. A month of operation showed very good yields and Bob was poised to start a second shift.

He called me into his office one day and told me that a second shift supervisor was in place and asked me to help get him started. When I asked who the person was, Bob told me he'd been forced to accept a man who he was not pleased with, a person with nearly 17 years of experience with Motorola. He mentioned his name, Dale, and I knew immediately we had a problem. I remembered the fellow from a previous job and he was not a prize in any sense of the word. But, I thought, let's put a positive emphasis on this and work with the man. He was an affable person and not difficult to get along with.

His major problem was he would listen to what I asked him to do and he would nod in agreement – and then go do it the way he thought would be better. I had no problem with finding better ways to process wafers but he was not a quality oriented supervisor. His forte was to stroke (not literally) his operators and not worry about wafer or die yield. He just wanted to get through the shift with acceptable wafer output quantities.

Bob began hearing unusual remarks from Security about our second shift. He told me that Dale was letting operators leave early on Friday nights. Dale was smart enough to let them leave in small groups of two, but they were still leaving 30 to 40 minutes before end of shift. Meanwhile he was signing operator timecards off as having worked the full eight hours. Motorola's policy strictly prohibited falsifying timecards. In meetings with Bob, Dale displayed a haughty, know-it-all attitude which did not earn any points. This went on for two weeks with Security providing written reports of the operators' early exits.

Bob invited me to his office one day, closed the door and told me, "Do whatever it takes to get rid of this guy! Document everything he does and keep me informed." I was taken aback – I'd never done anything like this and it alarmed me. Taking someone's job away was not an easy task. I knew he was a jerky supervisor but firing a person was very difficult at best. I left his office and tried to put this thing in perspective. I had to be very careful and make sure I was not getting myself in a personnel firestorm. I could gather more evidence of operators leaving but it would take time and probably needed photos.

I did have a project that needed to be done. We'd ordered a safe locker for storing pure gold pellets used in manufacturing. It was to be installed in the production area. While not a tough job, it was important in that it required not only the installation but a system to record amounts of gold taken out and returned for storage. Previous experience proved that quantities of gold pellets often "disappeared" from improper storage facilities. I met with Dale and laid out the project for him, giving him three weeks to complete it. He understood what had to be done and said he would do it on time. I carefully documented our meeting and even had him sign off.

At the end of the first week I inquired how the project was going. Dale made a half-hearted excuse that he'd been very busy with production. The second week I asked again how it was going and got the same reply. Meanwhile the safe had arrived and was sitting on the production floor, unattached to floor or wall. Meeting with Bob, I explained Dale had not even started on the project and he was one week away from disciplinary action. Meanwhile I had gone to Personnel and explained what was happening and made them aware of the consequences.

Near the end of the third and final week for project completion Dale reportedly told a Security guard that this was his final week at Motorola. When I asked again about the project, Dale just blew it off and said he wanted to get the "whole thing" over with. I told him that I had no choice but to write him up for disciplinary action and he just smiled. I produced a fully documented report for Personnel and Dale was brought in for termination. He left the plant without further incident. I felt badly for Dale but he had made no effort to complete the project or to modify his supervisory techniques. He knew he was taunting us but refused to change the way he worked. I honestly think he wanted to leave Motorola. I spoke with Bob and told him it was over. We went back to work and second shift worked without a lead supervisor.

Several weeks later the manufacturing manager from the Austin NMOS plant paid us a visit. Our yields and profit margins had proven to be much better than his unit and he wanted to find out what we were doing differently. Actually, we were using the same process and the same photo masks to produce die. Our equipment was older and not quite state-of-the-art as Austin's but we had fine tuned them to perfection. The main difference, we felt, was that we were working with more experienced and capable operators. He was frustrated because he couldn't pinpoint a mechanical or process issue. He returned to Austin, scratching his head.

Months later, an announcement by Motorola's MOS Executive Director to all Mesa personnel threw us for a loop. It was a lightning bolt out of the blue. He told us matter-of-factly that the Mesa NMOS operation was to be shut down within a month and all product was to be transferred to the Austin facility. He expressed no emotion, stating it was just a business decision. I, along with everyone else, was shocked! He indicated that operators would be able to transfer to openings within the Mesa or Phoenix facilities. Supervisors and engineering personnel were on their own to find a job.

My first move after the meeting was to go to Bob and find out what the hell was going on. Bob had found out about the change just an hour before we were notified and he was just as angry as I was. Why had management decided to start the operation in Mesa if they had any thought of closing it down eighteen months later? Secondly, we were beating the pants off of the Austin plant in die yields, lower cost of operation and faster throughput time. What was wrong with these people?

Reflecting on the shutdown notice, I was really fed up with Motorola and its management. Their management practices led to very low morale and low employee job satisfaction. Bob assured me, other supervisors and engineers that he would do everything possible to find suitable positions for all. We were all in a funk.

Mary, my supervisor, and I talked at length about the situation. She, too, was angry and upset. Worse, she had no idea what she could do for a job or where to go in the semiconductor division in Phoenix or Mesa. Positions were not that easy to find at the time. We had assembled a first rate production group, set high yield records and in a flash it was all over! Operators were equally upset.

About a week later Bob called me and told me he had lined up a job for me – in the Industrial Engineering Group. I had absolutely no clue what IE's did or why! And I was going to work as one? I learned that I would be one of two to be trained in IE techniques and would eventually be assigned to a manufacturing group to work with engineering and management in that group. Well, I was grateful for the opportunity but also hesitant about taking the job. When push came to shove, I had no choice. Positions were nonexistent in either facility. How the IE manager, Chuck F, had managed to get two openings was the question of the day. Mary, due to her excellent reputation, was finally able to get a supervisory position in the older Phoenix plant. Operators were picked up by production groups as well. Slowly we shut down our operation and shipped product to Austin. It was over!

Prior to the hullabaloo, we had purchased a nice home in north Mesa with a huge fenced yard on a corner lot. We had our patio extended and a side walk installed and completed landscaping the yard. The neighbors next door were retirees, nice but a little unusual. Directly in back of our homes was a large citrus grove and it harbored many birds, including Gambel Quail. The quail would often walk across our back yard on top of the block fence. We enjoyed watching families of quail walk in single file along the fence led by the Daddy. For some reason our neighbor took offense with the quail walking on his fence. We heard shots one day and found out he was shooting at the quail. We informed him we did not like that, but he just blew us off. It did stop him from more shooting.

Cathy and Dan had fit back into Mesa schools and were happy with life in Arizona. Margaret was somewhat happy to be near our old Mesa haunts and had adjusted to the Arizona lifestyle. I tried not to burden her with my work life but she could see that it was affecting me. When I told her I was in training to be an Industrial Engineer she was baffled. She knew I'd had no college work to support that kind of effort.

Dan had taken on a science project at grade school to make a solar reflector. His intent was to make it cook food. He cut out triangular pieces of cardboard and fastened them together to form a six-foot diameter concave disc. He then covered the inside of the disc with aluminum foil for reflection. The sun's energy was focused on a point about five feet from the center of the disc. It took several weeks to complete the project. To test it, he cooked a hot dog for lunch with the concentrated beam of sunlight – and ate it! The large disc then sat on our patio for a week before he moved it to the side of the house, never to be used again. But, his science project was a success.

44
Introduction to the World of Industrial Engineering

The next week I reported for duty in the IE Group and met with Chuck F. I liked him immediately. He knew what had happened in NMOS and expressed his good fortune in being able to acquire two good employees. He assured both of us that he would personally train us and we would fit in nicely with IE's. Three of the real IE's were accepting of the two of us and even helped assimilate us into the group. About a month into the training I was taken to the manufacturing group I was to eventually work with and got a hearty non-welcome. Boy, this job was going to be fun!

An Industrial Engineer's major job at Moto was to assess work functions, diagram each operator motion in steps of a job, measure time elements and then analyze the entire job to try and make it more productive. Well, most production operators know a given job inside out and do not appreciate some Yahoo coming in to analyze it and tell them there is a better way to do it. I ran into opposition at every turn. Supervisors were reluctant to let me in to even observe a job. I spoke with the real IE's and they assured me I would get used to it. Just keep on doing my job. Three months of this and I had had it! There was no joy in coming to work and trying to do something even I was not sure was necessary. I had built up a real resentment for Motorola and its management. Chuck sensed my feelings and we talked about the job and satisfaction. He was sensitive about subordinate's feelings and job satisfaction.

About this time I began seriously thinking about leaving Motorola. I felt my forte was in manufacturing training and I wanted to get back into it. I opened a Sunday edition of the *Arizona Republic* and noted a large job advertisement for a company in Texas. Voila! They were seeking engineers, supervisors and training personnel for an expansion of their plant in Carrollton, Texas. My heart fluttered! Was this something I should look into? Margaret knew I was very unhappy and discussing the job opportunity with her, she agreed that I should look into it.

Long story short, I met with MOSTEK hiring personnel and hit it off. They were extremely interested and read my resume carefully. The words you love to hear: We will get back with you! I had talked with a Motorola NMOS engineer just a week before and he told me he (I've lost his name) was leaving to join MOSTEK in two weeks. He was excited about going to a small but noteworthy company, one recognized as a leader in MOS design and manufacturing. I, too, became excited about moving to a noted leader in the semiconductor industry. Three weeks after the extensive interview, I had not heard a word from MOSTEK. Now I was getting antsy.

45
The Big Texas Vacation

I proposed a family vacation trip to Texas to check out the company. The kids loved the idea and even Margaret became enthused. We planned the trip just after school was out for the summer. The two day drive to Dallas (Carrollton is a suburb on the northwest side of Dallas) was enjoyable and we had fun. We found a motel just blocks away from the plant. I entered MOSTEK's plant and announced to the receptionist that I would like to meet with the HR person who interviewed me in Phoenix. He was not in but I was shuffled off to another HR person for a meeting. I was told that the position had not been filled but that they were not going to hire for the job right now. Wow! What a letdown.

As I was about to leave the building a sudden thought came to mind: call my friend engineer from Motorola and talk to him. He was called and came immediately to the lobby. We talked and I explained what had happened. He told me, "Let me see what I can do and I will get back to you. Call me tomorrow."

I don't know who he talked to but when I called he told me to come back to the plant the next day to meet with Production and Personnel managers about the training job. I met with several managers who all agreed the need for training was paramount! I laid out what I felt I could do in establishing a training program. Asked about a time line, I replied that it would take at least three months to establish a new hire orientation program, which they felt to be their greatest need. I could feel their enthusiasm! At the end of a three hour interview with several mangers, I was told they would notify me of a decision in a week. I just knew I had the job! We checked out schools, homes and shopping while in Carrollton and came away with a positive impression. Then it was back to Arizona with great expectations.

46
A Bona Fide Training Job Offer – And Decision Time

Sure enough, after getting back home in Mesa, a job offer was extended. It would include a 10% pay increase and moving expenses to Carrollton. Having second thoughts about the offer, I asked if I really wanted to leave Motorola. It was a good company, it had taught me a lot about manufacturing and I had gained a lot of confidence in my ability to lead and organize people in a production entity. But, Moto had a political structure that was difficult to break into and kept outsiders, like me, from moving upward.

Sure, I had gotten decent raises along the way but my pay scale was below what insiders were being paid. How do I know this? Word gets around. Bits and pieces get out and pretty soon you have a good picture of what is actually happening. To break into the inside structure one had to play with the boys. That is, head out at lunch time and drink beer, maybe play some pool. Or, get on your motorcycle and ride to the boonies for a "fun day" with your boss on a Saturday. It wouldn't hurt to play golf with the big boys, either.

I saw mediocre lead supervisors and engineers get promotions and raises they didn't really deserve. How, then, did they survive and move up? They were smart enough to have very good supervisors or technicians (usually women) working for them who did the real work and often got very little in return. None of the "good ol' boy" BS appealed to me. What time I had off the job was spent with Margaret and our children. Consequently, I paid the price. I soon reached the conclusion that if I didn't leave Moto, I'd be stuck in run-of-the-mill jobs, none of which would involve training.

While attending evening business classes at Arizona State University, I learned a simple, valuable technique for reaching a logical solution to a problem. It's called a "T" form. Draw a big "T" on paper, labeling one side as "positives" and the other side as "negatives". List all of the good things about a situation on one side, all of the bad things on the other. For example, concerning the move to another company, some of the positives would be: organize training group, design and implement training procedures, and lead and structure the group. It would be good to include pay increase as well. On the negative side one could put: stagnated job, no structure to work with training, indifferent attitude toward training. Taking time to fully think through the plusses and minuses, one can usually find a relatively easy answer to the problem. I worked through the "T" form and saw that the positives easily outweighed the negatives. Hence, the decision to move was made. Margaret and I talked at length about moving and we finally agreed the best decision was to go.

I announced my resignation to Chuck the following week. He was not at all surprised. He felt my frustration with IE work and gave his blessings. Later that week I bumped into Bob C and he was not as enthused as Chuck about my leaving Motorola. I sensed from his talk he felt I was making a huge mistake. Bob was a very calculating man, always carefully looking for a way to move upward and onward. His manner had gotten him fair rewards with Moto. I didn't share his outlook with this company.

It was a sad moment when I said goodbye to Mary and others that I had worked with.

On the day that I was processed out of Motorola, the Personnel Representative began questioning me about the new job with MOSTEK and repeatedly asked me about salary. I felt it was none of his business, saying only that I had been offered a nice increase. I asked about my 15 year award from Motorola as I was less than two weeks short of 15 years. I knew it wouldn't be given, but I wanted to hassle him a bit. And I got the response I expected. "Well, you haven't been with the company 15 years." I thanked him and left the room, my employment with the company at an end. Motorola Semiconductor had taught me much about technical manufacturing and I was grateful for the experience. But, I was happy to be leaving.

We put the house on the market with a very good real estate company. We dropped off the keys the day we left Mesa. They felt they could sell the home quickly, and in fact, they did.

47
It's Back to Texas!

The move to Carrollton was for the most part uneventful. Margaret and I were each driving a car and almost got separated in El Paso, Texas. She followed me in her car. The highway split for entrance to Mexico and she was very nearly forced to turn off at that point because of heavy traffic. It would have been interesting had she not been able to finally maneuver out of the right turn lane.

Reaching Carrollton, we found a nice motel not far from MOSTEK and set up our home in a suite of rooms. As soon as possible I reported for work and Margaret set about registering the kids in school. Cathy would go to Carrollton High School and Dan to Perry Middle School. Evenings we searched the area for a suitable home. A real estate agent showed us several places but we kept coming back to a red brick, three bedroom home close by the high school. The price was right and we signed papers to buy the place. We had the cash because our home in Mesa sold very quickly. Processing paperwork took several weeks.

Meanwhile we were cooped up in the motel and it got a little touchy. School began and the kids were on their way. Margaret was beginning to feel the effects of the move and was not too happy with events. The move had a negative effect on her and she felt very lonely. We quickly joined Prince of Peace Lutheran Church in Carrollton, admiring the pastor, Stephen Wagner. He was an excellent preacher and we became good friends with him and his wife. Cathy and Dan joined the youth group at the church and began to feel at home. It was here that Cathy met her future husband.

We made arrangements for our furniture to be taken from storage and moved to our new home. While men moved our bedroom chest of drawers into the house I noticed two drawers were missing. I stopped them and asked where the drawers were. I got a "how are we supposed to know" look and a shrug of shoulders. We called the mover's office and were told they were aware of the missing drawers and were looking for them. The next day the mover called and said they had found them and would deliver the drawers later in the day.

We received two empty drawers. Everything had been taken from them. Then it hit me! I had foolishly stashed several family treasures in the drawers before leaving Arizona, including an engraved Johns-Manville Quarter Century pocket watch my father had given me the last time I saw him. Talking to the mover's insurance agent I was asked to estimate the value of all missing items. How can you place a value on an heirloom pocket watch? Days later we settled on a figure to replace the stolen items. But I was heartsick about the loss of my father's watch.

On the work side, I was overwhelmed with what was in front of me. I planned what had to be written and produced in preparing an orientation program, it being the first item on the agenda I had agreed to with manufacturing managers. I then learned that MOSTEK had a turnover ratio of nearly 70 per cent! That meant that 7 out of 10 new hires quit during the first month with the company. I was astonished. I felt very strongly and voiced my opinion that a well prepared new hire orientation program could cut that ratio drastically. Now I had to prove it.

The initial new hire orientation program was designed to use combination audio/photo slide presentations followed with a lecture/question session (this was long before computer slide presentations were available). Each program was designed to last about an hour. Periodic breaks were to be given to allow new hires a breather. An occasional tour of MOSTEK facilities would also be given to break up classroom work. Each classroom program included a rather simple written test to check material understanding and retention. Some sessions included demonstrations such as proper wearing of clean room gear or the effects of contamination on wafer/die yield. Training sessions were designed to begin on Monday and last four days before operators would be taken to their respective work areas on Friday. I intended to spend the fifth day grading and recording orientation test results to be given to manufacturing supervisors. Tests provided an indication of the new hire's capabilities and interest in producing semiconductors.

It took three months of intensive work to produce the orientation programs. Manufacturing managers and supervisors were the first to sit in and review the new hire training program. The first reaction was: "Go for it!" It was rewarding to hear the positive comments. Now it had to be put into action to see how newly hired personnel reacted.

The first new hire program was admittedly demanding and tiring. I'm sure I flubbed delivery on some of the points in the sessions. However comments and reaction I got from the new hires was mostly positive (each was asked to fill out an evaluation of the orientation program at the end). I sent a written evaluation of each new employee to the appropriate supervisor, and got another reaction however. Most wanted to know what they were supposed to do with the evaluation and I sensed negative feelings. I had to explain that it was just an indication of how the person reacted in training sessions and could be used to help in evaluating the performance of the individual. This was new to many shift supervisors who had never been exposed to operator training before. I believe some felt I was horning in on their domain (which I was).

Each week another group of 12 to 15 personnel came into the new hire program and it wasn't long before I began to feel the demanding pressure. In a meeting with both manufacturing managers I explained that I could not continue to meet the demands of weekly training without help from several qualified operators to act as trainers. I laid out a plan that would utilize trainers in teaching new hires and in developing new training procedures. They immediately agreed and said I would have two trainers within a week (turns out I had no input as to who was selected). Sure enough, two manufacturing operators reported to me in days. Both were nice ladies who had worked at length in production. The only problem was that neither had ever trained someone in manufacturing techniques. Now I had the added task of training operators to be trainers. Both took to the tasks of training exceedingly well and worked very hard to be accomplished trainers.

Meanwhile, Margaret had taken a job as a sales solicitor for a heating/air conditioning firm in Carrollton. She had wanted to get into the work force again to earn some spending money. Margaret was very good as a sales person and she was happy with the job. However, after several months she became aware of some faulty record keeping by her supervisor. Keeping very complete files of prospective customers she had talked to about services Margaret discovered that her supervisor was taking credit for some of her calls and receiving compensation for the sales. She was being short changed several times each week. Confronting her supervisor with the evidence there was a scene and Margaret quit the job. She was understandably upset and did not re-enter the work force again.

48
New Hire Orientation Was Paying Off!

New hire orientation continued unabated for months. I began to hear some amazing numbers regarding operator turnover. The rate was dropping dramatically. In fact, in a little over one year the turnover rate had dropped from 70 percent to 24 percent, a 65 percent decline! Consequently, less operators were being hired and new hire orientation was held only every other week. We were still losing operators but at a rate that manufacturing could tolerate and still make product to meet demand.

MOSTEK hired many Vietnamese as operators, finding them to be excellent workers. I found them to be intelligent and eager to learn. I was impressed with their respect for teachers. Often when walking about the company I would see them stop and bow their heads as I passed by. Inquiring about their behavior I was told they greatly respect teachers and I was considered to be one. Very rewarding!

Now we had to concentrate on training operators properly for manufacturing operations. I asked for a qualified trainer to assist in developing programs for training operators on manufacturing equipment and a hiring requisition was made available. A former teacher, Bob K, was hired to help develop the needed training. He fit in very nicely with the small group and began writing programs with help from the two trainers. About this time I was called into a meeting with Human Resources and was told of the need for training supervisors. They asked if I would like to work in a group of three developers to create a program for supervisors. They made an offer I couldn't refuse.

Bob K took over the operation of managing the new hire orientation and operator training when I transferred to the Human Resources group. I joined two HR personnel who had teaching backgrounds and we began to plan the program for teaching supervisors how to be effective leaders. We were constrained in the design of the program(s) in that we could not hire any more developers. This led us to opt for a written program that supervisors would read and hopefully become more proficient. I would have preferred a lecture/discussion series, feeling that student's direct involvement would produce better results. But you go with the flow, management deciding we could not do that type of training program. We asked why but were not given an answer.

Little did we know at the time that negotiations were underway to sell the company.

L. J. Sevin, the founder and driving force behind MOSTEK's success was selling out. Apparently he had had enough and wanted to retire. A small MOSTEK branch in Boston had already been sold. It was the Boston unit that triggered yet another move in my work life.

The Supervisory Training Group continued its work on writing programs. Since I was the only one with manufacturing experience, it was my job to plan and write the programs for the production end of the venture. Previously I had written and published a handy-dandy pocket sized glossary of semiconductor terminology. It was a huge success with non-manufacturing personnel such as assembly/test, human resources, sales, marketing and service personnel. Manufacturing folks felt the glossary was just eh! It was a boon to new hires, however. We had great plans for the supervisory training program and slowly the manuals began to take shape. Experienced supervisors were used to review and edit the drafts that we wrote. We got a lot of complimentary comments and some not so complimentary. But it was all good input and work continued to make the manuals even better.

An announcement from company leaders took everyone by surprise on a Monday morning, late1979. MOSTEK had been sold to United Technologies headquartered in Connecticut. We were told that UT was a leader in helicopter design and production, and was an offshoot of the original Sikorsky helicopter company, the first to build and fly a helicopter. Yeah, well, what did they know about building semiconductors? As it turned out, they knew little to nothing.

It soon became evident that UT had differing ideas on how to run the company. Bean counters came in and started making changes to accounting, sales and marketing procedures. Several key NMOS semiconductor design engineers resigned after a major reorganization in engineering and left for a small company in Colorado. The whole small company aura changed in the matter of a few weeks. You would see managers standing about shaking their heads, obviously discussing the shift in direction. Gradually operations began to settle down but people were not happy. Our little supervisory training team began to falter but our manager, Richard M, a nice guy but one who had zero training experience, kept pushing us to complete our work.

Near the end of our scheduled completion date we all went out to lunch to celebrate. Richard got completely bombed and we literally had to assist him back into the plant against our wishes. We wanted to take him home to sober up but he insisted on going to his office. All of us were feeling the effects of the new management team from UT. With work on the supervisory training manuals completed we wondered, what do we do now? Richard had no clue other than to administer the distribution and record keeping of personnel reading and reviewing the manuals.

It was at that time I got a phone call from a headhunter asking if I would like to interview with an up-and-coming semiconductor company in California. I told him I had no desire to live and work in California. He explained that the company was building a new plant in Chandler, Arizona and was looking for experienced personnel to help in startup. My interest piqued immediately. Sure, let's interview. When I explained to Margaret that I'd been called to interview for a new job, she just rolled her eyes. She knew of the changes going on in MOSTEK and how they had affected everyone. But she was not too keen on moving again after living in Carrollton for almost five years. I flew to San Jose, California for an interview with Intel Corporation. I'd heard of them, of course, but knew little about them.

It was during one interview that I learned why I'd been called. A former supervisor in MOSTEK's Boston branch had read my training materials and had seen pieces of the new hire orientation program. He figured I could be of value in hiring and training new operators. I had no idea my materials had been sent to Boston and I asked how he had gotten them. He wouldn't give me a direct answer, just that he'd had them. An entire day was spent in interviews with production management and engineers. After being grilled for a day I was tired but felt positive about my chances for a job offer. Candidates get a gut feeling when interviews go well and can sense a forthcoming offer.

49
Joining Intel Corporation

I was offered two jobs by Intel managers. One was looking for an experienced manufacturing supervisor and the other wanted a training supervisor. I opted for the training position. The salary offer was excellent. I was to train in California for six months and then move on to Chandler. I could bring my wife and kids with me to California and then move to Arizona. Something just told me that Margaret would not buy into two moves. When I talked to her about the new job and what it entailed she agreed that I should go on to CA without the family and then we'd hook up in Chandler. I explained that would mean I would be gone for up to six months. I think she actually looked forward to that.

I was beginning to be aware of a problem that Margaret was having. I observed that when I came home from work she always looked like she had just gotten out of bed. What I didn't know until much later was that she had acquired a drinking problem. After I left for work she would go to the store to buy beer or alcohol, proceed to drink herself into a state and then sleep it off before I arrived home. The kids knew about it but would not say a word. Catherine told me about it years later. Rather than help her by telling me what was going on, they remained silent. Why wasn't I aware of this? Weekends she would not drink a drop and this lulled me into thinking everything was OK. We had good friends, we went to church regularly, we ate out as a family often – I just did not see the magnitude of the problem in front of me.

I did learn of the seriousness of the problem after the move to Chandler and we sought help to take care of it. We spoke about what was happening to our marriage and I stated that I could not accept her drinking. She must get help. I think our relationship as husband and wife took a serious hit and it seemed to me that we had an uncoupling of our marriage at that time. It was never quite the same again. I welcomed her hospital rehabilitation and held no ill feelings. Margaret, however, never seemed to relate to me the same way after that. She insisted on smoking in our home and it bothered me very much. Not only was it harming her but I was getting the second hand effects from the smoke also. Thinking back I believe it was the effects of moving several times that had changed her. She just couldn't seem to get settled after our move from Austin. I assume fault in my changing jobs had caused it.

After receiving the job offer letter from Intel, I announced my resignation to Richard who was sorry to hear it but not surprised. Quite a few employees were leaving the company and moving on to other jobs. Several managers talked to me and said I was making a mistake going to Intel. I didn't agree. I liked what I saw and heard about the company and was happy to be joining them. It was the best decision I ever made regarding a job change.

On January 7, 1980 I flew to San Jose, CA to start my new job. I was to be met at the airport by a trainer in the new group. No one was there. It was Sunday evening and it was raining very hard. I had no idea where I was to go or how to get there. I did have a car, and loading the luggage I got soaked. The agent at the car rental counter directed me to a motel. She drew a map for me and I drove off, only to get thoroughly lost. I managed to get back to the airport and get onto the correct road to the motel. I spent a restless night wondering where I was to go on Monday. Then I remembered the manager's name. I called Intel and was able to hook up with the office where I was to go. Dan G, the manager, directed me to the office and I arrived late for work on my first day. When he heard that the trainer had not met me at the airport, he called Dawn M into his office and chewed her out. She had forgotten about meeting me at the airport. Nice start!

I learned that I was to go to an older Intel Fab in Santa Clara for training and was to report to a manufacturing supervisor and get my instructions from him. I found the man and received a less than welcome reception. "You are supposed to do what for me?" was his greeting. He hadn't the slightest idea of who I was or what I was to do. Calling Dan, I explained what was happening. "Come on back to the office and we'll go from there." What in hell was going on? I learned later that the forming of the new group for Chandler had not been disclosed to many people and few knew what we were doing in Santa Clara. I met Harry H, the new Fab 6 Manager, and liked what I saw. Outspoken, direct and very organized were my first impressions. One could not help but like him.

Other trainers included John C, Doug U, and Dawn M. All three had worked for Dan in Boston. We talked a lot about what we wanted to see in training operators, having a new hire orientation and eventually supervisory training. We had some new ideas and we wanted to implement them. Harry would get all of the new Fab 6 personnel together occasionally to pump us up and keep momentum going for the startup. Dan made phone calls trying to find training positions for all of us. He finally hit pay dirt talking to Intel Fabs in Aloha, Oregon. They would gladly take us to help them in training operators. All of us flew to Portland to see where we fit in. My first encounter with the training manager, Paul, was to be asked, "What do you hope to accomplish here?"

Intel Corporation had a different approach to work. Set high goals, work your butt off achieving them and get richly rewarded. It was a new learning process for me. The company recognized the need for professional training and paid well for it. I was amazed to learn that Intel had its own university within the corporation. There was a staff of nearly fifty employees located at several sites that taught university grade courses. Corporate Education and Development (CED) had a manager, administrative staff and program developers/facilitators located in Santa Clara. CED Site managers in Oregon and California reported to the Santa Clara manager. Each Intel site had its own staff that developed and facilitated university grade training courses. On a somewhat lower level each manufacturing facility had its own staff of trainers who worked with operators and supervisors. CED often contracted qualified professionals to deliver programs of value to managers and supervisors. These intensive, productive sessions often lasted 2 to 4 days at an off-site location.

50
Family and Work Issues

Living away from my family for an extended period of time left a mark on me. I missed them very much. I called Margaret every day to check in and see how she and the kids were doing. It was winter in Oregon and it rained almost every day. I became tired of the damp, dark weather especially on weekends away from the plant. Not having much else to do, I would drive to the sea coast to sightsee and try to relax. I loved the coast, walking along the beaches looking for souvenirs. It was dramatically beautiful scenery. Becoming a beach bum crossed my mind several times!

Just before spring school break Margaret mentioned that Dan was having problems with school as he was not applying himself to studying. We agreed to send him to Portland where I would pick him up, spend time with him, and do a little talking about school. I explained to Dan G that I would like to take a few days off work to show my son a little of Oregon. He agreed to a couple of days off but not a whole week. My son and I spent a lot of time on the road taking in the scenery including the beaches.

We stopped one day at the University of Oregon's School of Oceanography. During a student's lecture about ocean life, we walked to a small pool to see some sea creatures. A small octopus was placed in the pool and the student talked about its habits and life. I was not paying attention to where Dan was until I saw a hand opposite me reach over the edge of the pool to touch the octopus – it was Dan's! Nothing happened of course but it startled me. He was a very inquisitive boy. We had a great time visiting and travelling about the western part of the state. It was a sad day for me to put him on the plane to head back to Dallas.

Meanwhile, Margaret was trying to hold the family together in Carrollton. I could tell by talking to her each day that she had her hands full and I felt a lot of guilt because of it. Harry granted each Fab 6 person a short visit to their family once each month – I called it the "conjugal visit" event. I would fly to Dallas and spend 2 or 3 days, usually over a weekend. Each visit to my family I could see the wear and tear reflected on Margaret and it bothered me. Leaving each time only increased the feeling.

Talking with John C one day he let slip the fact that he had gotten a $2000 bonus for signing on with Intel. He knew as soon as he saw the look on my face that I had not been given the bonus. I marched into Dan G's office and confronted him. He stuttered and stammered about how some got a bonus and others didn't. I was furious, especially since I was the only one in the group of trainers who had had actual experience in developing and delivering training on a semiconductor manufacturing floor. Dan said he would check into it. He never said another word about it but two weeks later I received a $2000 bonus check. John told me later that he had been thoroughly chewed out by Dan for telling me about the $2000. There are times when you gotta speak up!

51
Intel's Fab 6 Group Forms

At least once a month Harry H would call a Fab 6 group meeting. This meant the three trainers in Oregon would fly to San Jose and spend two days in meetings, ending in a big dinner and party. It was fun and exciting. I was absolutely amazed at the money being spent not only in salaries but also in housing and per diem. Each of us had our own rental car and apartment and a $30 a day living allowance. I couldn't spend $30 a day for food! Consequently, I managed to save a good portion of that money and send it to Margaret each month.

Near the end of the training period in Oregon I was told to make arrangements with my wife to meet in Phoenix for a house hunting event. Margaret arranged for friends to look after Cathy and Dan and flew to Phoenix to meet me. We spent three intensive days looking at houses and finally agreed on a vacant house in Dobson Ranch in Mesa. We made an offer and it was sent to the owner, who had transferred to Colorado. His immediate response was a resounding NO! He had lost touch with the housing market in Arizona and wanted more money. We stuck with the offer and the real estate agent reasoned with the man until he finally agreed to the price. Intel was buying our house in Carrollton and we had no problems in closing the deal for our new home.

In June, 1980, the Fab 6 start-up group assembled in Chandler, AZ. Intel had leased a nearby building which would be our home until the manufacturing building was completed and turned over to Fab manager, Harry H. All fifty of us were crammed into what was called an office but was little more than a large garage. The day finally came when we were allowed to enter the new Fab office area. The manufacturing area was still closed to all but construction personnel. At least we could spread out and do some actual work in producing training programs. I was assigned the job of creating a new hire orientation program and started putting together classes similar to what I had done at MOSTEK with minor changes. John and Doug were given the task of organizing the group for on-floor training. Dawn was to assist in setting up record keeping and ordering office supplies. We were busy and liking it. Dan G pretty much left us alone and only asked for results each week in our group meeting. He was out of the office most of the time meeting with engineering and manufacturing personnel.

Intel's corporate policy was to have each employee define a job or project, set goals, develop schedules and then report results to your manager on a regular weekly basis. Miss your goal or schedule and you had better have a defense ready for the weekly meeting. Of course, there were understandable circumstances that could prevent meeting a goal on time but one had to work around them and get back on track. I missed one goal in my 15 years with Intel and I paid a huge price for it. But that story will come later.

The manufacturing area was eventually turned over to Intel personnel and we began the process of qualifying equipment. This entailed bringing each piece up to operating conditions and then running small quantities of wafers to verify engineering specifications. Training personnel worked with engineers and equipment technicians to qualify individual pieces of equipment. It was like old home week for me getting back into wafer processing. It was a very satisfying time.

John and Doug were interviewing operators for training positions. Dawn was setting up our allotted area in the office and we were nearing the point where we could begin operations. When I could, I would write programs for the new hire orientation. I had the plan well in mind on what to do since I had already done it at MOSTEK. Dan G seemed pleased with what we were doing and Harry was ecstatic. I don't know if he had never had a well organized training group while at Texas Instruments-Houston but he really liked what we were implementing. Intel was infusing a ton of money to get Fab 6 up and running. We were all on a tight schedule, but great progress was being made in becoming operational.

Operators had been hired and were being trained by our group, engineers and equipment techs. We were on a fast track to begin producing semiconductors. Test results were exceeding planned schedules and it looked like we were ready to go. The first group of production wafers were introduced into the line and we were off and running. Initially we began with just one shift but plans had been put into place to expand into a three shift operation. Additional operators were hired and new hire orientation began. I administered the program to about 20 operators a week and results proved to be acceptable. The level of competency of newly hired operators was much higher than what I had seen in Carrollton due to the fact that most operators had worked at other semiconductor companies in and around Phoenix and were eager to get in on the ground floor of Intel. All had heard about Intel and its reputation for excellence.

I had introduced a black UV light into the Clean Room Class to demonstrate how humans can contaminate wafer manufacturing. Turning out the lights in the room, I would switch on the UV lamp and show how organic particles fluoresce on the body and clothing. It was a dramatic and very convincing demonstration. That part of the program always impressed new employees. I was working at top speed to orient the new hires, complete paperwork and get them into manufacturing supervisor's hands. It was fast, furious and rewarding.

Dan G came to me one day and told me that I must develop a safety program for all Fab 6 personnel, including engineers, process technicians, equipment technicians and even safety personnel, anyone who had business in the manufacturing area. Harry had deemed it necessary after a minor chemical accident in the Fab. This meant a program for more than one hundred personnel.

With Dawn's help, I developed a one hour, lecture type program. Handouts showing all of the chemicals used in the Fab and their effects on humans were prepared for each participant. All Fab 6 personnel were to attend one of three classes. Harry pronounced the edict that all must attend and I heard a lot of moaning and groaning from people who felt too busy to go to a safety class. I was to have each sign in at a class to record the attendees. Harry wanted proof that everyone had gone through the class.

With the help of Intel qualified safety personnel, all three classes were held as scheduled. After the first class, Dan G asked for the attendance list and I gave it to him. At the end of the three classes, Harry wanted to see who had attended. When the first list could not be found, guess who Harry came down on – me! What Dan G had done with the list I don't know, but I'm the one who caught the flack. From that time on I became very wary of my manager.

A year into operation of the Fab, all employees were given a performance review. Supervisors were to write and administer a review for each of his/her employees. Since I was operating alone, I did not have to write a review. Dan G painted a glowing review for me and I was happy to find I was exceeding expectations. Talking with John later, I discovered that key employees had been awarded Intel stock options. He had shot off his mouth again and realized that I had not gotten any options while he had been given some. My first reaction was to go into Dan G's office and let him have it. Calming down, I decided that would only make conditions tough not only for me but also for other trainers who had not gotten awards. By now I was very carefully watching my backside for any kind of offense by my manager. He was a sly person and my respect for him was dwindling rapidly.

52
Intel Encounters a Big Problem

Fab 6 operation and yields were exceeding expectations. We were making big bucks for Intel and the future looked rosy. However, by mid-1985 semiconductor sales were skidding downward. Intel hit a critical point in its business cycle. All employees, including managers, were asked to give a 120% effort by working longer hours and taking a 10% cut in pay. IBM, finding that Intel was in financial trouble, awarded a contract for production of several different integrated circuits to be used in its large scale computers. The contract was a lifesaver! With it and cost savings realized by cutting employee salaries and reducing purchasing of supplies we were still in business. It was a rocky road for more than a year but it proved to be successful for the company. In 1986 Intel awarded a bonus for every employee, helping to make up the losses incurred with the cutback. Life was good again.

In 1986, Harry H was promoted to a higher position on the Vice President of Manufacturing's Staff. A new Fab manager was hired, again from Texas Instruments–Houston. Bob P was the opposite of Harry. He was stern, driven and not at all friendly. He was also a drinker. He brought in an entourage of buddies that quickly changed the way business had been conducted. He was establishing his mark on the Fab. But he got results.

212

Soon after the change, manufacturing management met with Dan G, complaining about line trainer's work and scheduling. They felt that John and Doug were doing an inadequate job supervising and scheduling trainers. Later, Dan called me into his office and told me (he didn't ask) I was going to take over the supervision of line trainers for all three shifts. I was taken aback but looked at it as a challenge. Developing training programs had grown to be weary work and I needed a change.

Manufacturing supervisors apparently approved of the change in supervision. I met with each supervisor and discussed their needs for training. Dan hired a second shift training supervisor and she and I laid plans for getting the job done. I discovered that she was a hand-picked star of our new Fab manager from TI–Houston. She was an attractive woman with a Bachelor of Arts degree. She was very bright but also very self centered. Her husband had been hired to a position somewhere in the bowels of Intel. What she and Bob P's relationship had been at TI could only be guessed. Meanwhile, John and Doug had become developers in the group.

Two other developers were hired and programs started coming out in high gear. One of the new developers quit within a year. John and Doug had made plans to take a one year leave of absence to go on a motorcycle trip around the USA. I told John he was making a mistake because the economy was not doing well and jobs were not easily available. He felt in a year things would ease up and he would come back to work at Intel.

After John and Doug left the company, Dan G transferred to another job as manager of the Equipment Training Group. Their function was to provide training for equipment maintenance techs. The Fab 6 manager then brought in a new training manager from Oregon. It was questionable what training background he had, but he immediately took each of us into a meeting to get acquainted and lay out his plan for us. All of us continued in our current jobs but change was a comin' – you could just sense it.

Randi A and I were now supervisors in Fab 6 training with a whole new group of production line trainers. Randi took over the development group and I held the line trainer supervisory role. She had zero experience in semiconductor manufacturing but was able to produce programs with the help of line trainers. Next thing we knew, our relatively new manager left the Fab 6 training group to join Dan G in equipment training. We never knew if there had been a conflict with Bob P or what the real reason was for his transfer.

Bob P called Randi and me into a meeting and told us he would choose one of us as the new training manager. Subsequent meetings with Bob did not go well with me. He and I got into a heated discussion in one meeting when he asked me a question about my presence in the Fab. I replied, "To tell the truth, I only get into the Fab about once a week." His face became crimson and he yelled that I had better always tell him the truth. I replied, "My answer was truthful and I would never lie to you or to any manager!" Then I said something that I probably should not have said. I told him that operators had commented in Fab meetings that neither he or his first shift manufacturing manager were ever seen much in the Fab.

I figured you hand it out, you should be able to take it as well. He exploded! I was definitely on his S--t list from that time on! I believe he had made his mind up long before our initial meeting. Soon the announcement came that Randi had been chosen to be the new manager of the Fab 6 training group. I discovered later that she had been seen many times with Bob at a local watering hole long before the announcement.

Randi drove me nuts in our group meetings. Her agendas were all over the place and had little continuity. Meetings limped along for what seemed like hours. After a month of this I told her that it would be best if I left the group and she immediately agreed. I began looking for another job in the Chandler operation but it was still tight with few openings available. Randi called me into her office one day and told me she had made arrangements to transfer me to a Chandler group associated with Corporate Education. I was taken aback and told her I appreciated her effort. A week later I was gone from Fab 6 training.

53
My Stint in Corporate Education

I began working for a lady, Peg S, whom I had met months before. She had been hired by Intel to work one summer as an intern while studying for her doctorate at Arizona State University. She liked Intel so much and impressed managers so greatly that she was asked to stay on as a permanent employee. I was immediately impressed with her. I could tell just by talking to her that she was forthright and honest – no BS. She had a project in mind for me and we laid plans to develop it. Mind you, the Corporate Education Group worked in the same building, same room, and in very close proximity to the equipment training group. I was only a few feet away from my old manager Dan G and his short-lived replacement Fab 6 training manager!

I began to enjoy my work again and I especially enjoyed working for Peg S. She stopped by each day for a few minutes to see how I was doing on my new project. At lunch one day she asked if I would like to take a walk outside around the facility. We talked about a lot of things including my work with Fab 6. We soon developed a relationship of taking a walk after lunch and discussing work, politics and life in general. There was never a hint of a personal, intimate relationship. Peg was married, as I was, and our talks and walks were about work and life, just that, nothing more. I developed a great respect for her and I think, she of me.

Upon completion of my first, and minor, project I was asked by the assistant manager, Myron W, if I would work with him to develop a paper he wanted to deliver at an Engineering Conference in Boston in December. It had to be completed in three months for delivery to the IEEE conference review board by the middle of November for approval. Of course, I jumped at the opportunity. I found later that I was second choice. Another developer had been asked but refused because he didn't like the subject matter. He missed a great opportunity!

Myron and I began work on the paper, he feeding me pieces for the article and expecting me to fit it together. He asked me if I could develop graphs given data for illustration purposes. Sure I could. I'd had a mechanical drawing class in high school and did well at it. He gave me data and I converted it to a graph. And he loved it! His paper dealt with Henry Ford, the building of the Model 'T' car and how Ford had developed economies of scale to mass produce the car for a reasonable price. I never knew that! Not only was I learning about real industrial engineering but I was helping to produce a paper for an important engineering conference. We completed the paper well before the deadline, produced a professionally printed copy and sent it off to the IEEE Board for review, and hopefully approval. Mid-November we received the approval!

Myron took me aside just a few days before leaving for Boston and told me that I may have to deliver the paper at the conference! He was ill and looked it, and felt so badly that he couldn't speak in front of a group of engineers. I was shocked! I had developed the paper but I didn't feel qualified to speak to engineers about the topic. We went ahead with plans to travel to Boston hoping that Myron would mend enough to speak.

On the day we left Phoenix he said he felt better but I still may have to speak to the group. Good grief! On our arrival in Boston it was a very cold, blustery December day. Myron felt good enough to have dinner so we went to Faneuil Hall for sea food. He was getting better, I kept telling myself. Early to bed and hopefully he would feel better for the conference starting the next day. Myron's paper was not to be given until the second day. Next day he was feeling much better and said he could handle the delivery of the paper. Hallelujah! What a relief.

The conference was very interesting and I sat in on several speakers' presentations. We spent a little time visiting Boston, Myron taking me to Harvard University, Faneuil Hall, and Marblehead. He had lived in Lynn, Massachusetts, and was familiar with cities nearby. We went to lunch in a little restaurant run by two sisters in Marblehead. I had the best clam chowder and fried Cod that I had ever eaten! We sat looking out over a small bay, watching seagulls flying about in a snowstorm. It highlighted a delightful, though short, tour of the Boston area.

Next day Myron delivered his paper to a group of about twenty-five engineers and it went off beautifully. I say that because there were several questions from attendees that led to good discussions. The paper was a success and Myron and I were happy and satisfied. He and I had developed a great friendship working on the paper. We had one more delicious meal in Boston in celebration and then we were off to Phoenix and back to work.

Peg took me aside after getting back to work and talked to me about an important project that she wanted produced. Specifically, it was Statistical Process Control, or SPC. Intel had hired a professor from the University of Utah who was renowned for his knowledge of statistics. The company wanted an SPC program to be developed and administered throughout the entire corporation. What I knew about statistics could be hand printed on one's fingernail. I knew it to be important but I was leery of getting in over my head. Peg assured me that I would work with an expert and I was to use my expertise in producing the training program. After discussing the project at length with her I agreed to help in any way I could. The SPC professor could have cared less who was to help develop the program. He had hired one of his assistants from University of Utah, Cynthia B, to lead and direct the program, with his input of course.

I first saw Cynthia when she walked into our building. She was drop dead beautiful, looking like a person out of Hollywood! Dressed completely in white clothing with a white hat, she was an imposing figure! Heads turned when she walked to her boss's office. I didn't formally meet Cynthia until several days later when her boss introduced her to me. We discussed the direction of the program and made plans to start the next day. As we talked I came to the conclusion she was, indeed, knockout beautiful, very well versed in statistics, but absolutely disorganized as hell! I realized this was going to be a tough project to co-develop.

We developed an outline. I should say Cynthia developed it after a great deal of talking and my recording it. She tended to talk in circles. I was on a huge learning curve. We met every day for several hours with her giving me written materials and much information about statistics. I furiously wrote pages of notes. As I began putting words on paper I would bring them to her for review. She would make changes and I would revise the copy. This went on for weeks and slowly the program began to take shape. Some of her data would be made into graphs and that seemed to please her.

Our first review of the course with her boss was about due when she called me saying she had injured her ankle in a fall.

We still had work to do to present a draft. Saying she was unable to come to her office she asked if I would come to her apartment to continue work. This didn't look good to me – I was very suspect. I had learned as a supervisor, or manager, never to put oneself in a possibly compromising situation. Peg told me it would be OK to meet at her apartment, but I was still doubtful. Arriving at her place I found her roommate also in attendance, providing some relief for me.

At the beginning of the project I believe she looked upon me as a grunt who would do computer input and produce copy work. As we progressed I felt her attitude change with a degree of respect for me. As I said, she was beautiful but very disorganized. I helped keep her on track and kept sequence in place. And I was learning about statistics to the point that I began to understand. Peg kept abreast of the project and communicated with the professor on a regular basis. She seemed pleased with progress being made. It took over four months of intensive work before the project was ready for review.

My first inkling of the importance of the SPC program came with a note written by Craig Barrett, Intel Vice President of Manufacturing, thanking me for the work I had accomplished. I'm sure he sent one to my colleague as well. Cynthia was to initiate teaching of statistics to manufacturing groups throughout the corporation. I was now without a project.

54
A Family Gathering

An unexpected phone call in Spring, 1982, informed me brothers Erve and Bill were coming to Arizona for a visit. Margaret and I quickly made arrangements to host them only to find out that Erve and his wife Edna would be staying with her brother in Chandler (we didn't even know she had a brother living only four miles from us!). I informed Bob that Erve and Bill were coming for a few days and we needed to get together at our house. It was wonderful having all four "Scheske boys" together in one place again. Brother George had died several years earlier. We spent a lot of time catching up on our lives and families, telling stories and jokes.

Bill and I walked one day along a canal bank in back of our home in Mesa. He remarked how bleak it was with few trees and shrubs and asked how I tolerated it. I replied, "This is out West – wide open spaces in the desert." He was not impressed with Arizona or the desert. We had two good visits as a family and then Erve, Edna and Bill left to return to Waukegan.

55
Family Matters

While living in Mesa, Cathy, having graduated from high school in Carrollton, was finishing her college work at Mesa Community College. In June, 1987, she was awarded her Associates degree in Social Science. Cathy was dating a boy, Bill, she had known for some time and he had asked her to marry him. Margaret and I were less than thrilled with him. He was a nice looking boy (man?) but appeared to have little ambition. Bill had only a high school degree with no special skills. He thought he was going to work for an uncle in Texas who had a small business. He and Cathy travelled to Texas after her graduation to check out his potential job. Apparently it didn't take long for him to determine the job was a loser position with little, if any, future.

After their return from Texas, both families got together for dinner and to talk about the forthcoming marriage. Bill's mother was a royal pain in the butt and the father wasn't far behind. Margaret and I later talked seriously with Cathy about the impending marriage and I believe she began to see the light. We did not want to hurt the boy but we just as surely did not want to see our daughter married to someone who we felt had a dismal future ahead. Several weeks later Cathy gave the engagement ring (which she had helped pay for) back to Bill. His parents were very angry and demanded to talk to us. The meeting was heated and not productive and Cathy's decision did not change. Sometime later I was awakened by the ringing of our door bell at 2 am. A Mesa policeman was supporting a very drunken "boy" who had been found loitering outside our house. He asked if I wanted to press charges and I said no, just send him on home. We never saw or heard from Bill again.

Dan had graduated from Dobson High School, the first class to graduate from the newly built school, and had enrolled at Northern Arizona University in Flagstaff to begin mechanical engineering studies. His cousins, Robert and Jeanne Scheske, were attending classes there and had influenced Dan to enroll. Margaret and I agreed to support Dan in college just as we had Cathy by paying tuition and books and an allowance for room and board. He would have to secure a part time job to fill in the rest, which he did by working at a nearby golf course as a groundskeeper.

In his sophomore year he called me one evening and told me he wanted to change his major from mechanical engineering to computer science engineering. I told him, "That would be an excellent choice, but I have one request." He said, "OK, what is it?" I told him I had worked with computer gurus for some time and most were nerds completely oblivious of fine arts. "Will you take at least one course in english, preferably a literature course?" "Dad," he replied, "I am taking an english course." Immediately the question came to mind to ask, "Well, what is the english course?" He replied, "Report writing!" I started laughing and let him know how I felt about fine art courses, how they round out your education in the hard science courses. Dan graduated with a Bachelors degree in Computer Science Engineering from NAU without having one fine arts course!

Cathy secured a job at Intel after her breakup and began working in the Assembly & Test area. Her job was to run integrated circuits through a programmed computer test to determine its pass or fail status. While there she met an engineer, Paul W, and they began dating. Long story short, they became engaged, planning to marry in a year. I worked near Paul's office at Intel and saw him often. He had worked hard to earn a degree in electrical engineering from DeVry Institute and proved his value at Intel working in the IC Test Area. I began to see a side of Paul that was of concern. He had a fiery temper and had been called for it several times in his department. Talking to him one day he read a memo sent to him by a female engineer in his group. He tore the memo into pieces and threw them into the engineer's cubicle. It took me by surprise to see such a childish act by a professional engineer.

Margaret and I met Paul's mother and grandmother at a family dinner one evening. Both were classic older California women: overdressed, loaded with jewelry and loud of mouth. His mother provided some eye rolling comments during the dinner. I learned later that Paul's father had committed suicide and Paul was the one who found him in the garage. From the image his mother projected I could see how it could happen.

Paul and Cathy's marriage took place in a Lutheran Church near our home. It was a lovely wedding. Margaret and I had made arrangements for the wedding dinner at a Holiday Inn Hotel in Mesa. They had an attractive room for the reception and prepared an excellent dinner for about 40 guests. We had offered to give the kids $1500 in lieu of providing alcoholic drinks for everyone and they happily agreed. Paul's mother made a snide remark in passing about our being too cheap to provide alcoholic drinks for the reception. I blew it off, considering the source. After their honeymoon, we helped Paul and Cathy move into and set up housekeeping in their new home in Chandler, Arizona.

56
Time For A Change?

After completing work on the SPC project, I'd gone into the break room for coffee one day and met an old friend whom I hadn't seen in years. He told me he had transferred to the New Mexico facility in Rio Rancho and loved working there. I learned that a new Fab was in the making and that managers were looking for qualified employees. That was most interesting! I looked up job openings for the Fab 9 start-up and noted there were openings in manufacturing training. Margaret was not thrilled when I approached her about living in New Mexico. She had had enough of moving about. I explained that I was temporarily at an end in Chandler but I would stay on if she did not want to move again. We talked at length about New Mexico and what it was like. I had been there once before for a training session and liked it. She finally agreed that I should look into openings in the new Fab.

I talked with Peg S about moving and she agreed that I could apply for a transfer and see what was available in jobs. I filled out an application and sent it to Human Resources. Within days I got a phone call from the new Fab 9 Training Manager, Peggy L. I'd met her years before on a trip to California. She had moved from a manufacturing management position into training some time back and was looking forward to starting a new training group. Peggy asked me to visit the new facility, which was still in a construction phase, but open to the point where one could see the inside of the building. Travel arrangements were made to fly to Albuquerque for an interview. The Intel facility in Rio Rancho is a good drive from ABQ airport, but an easy one. Fab 9 personnel were temporarily housed in a leased building north of the plant that looked out eastward over the valley toward the Sandia Mountain range. It afforded a spectacular view.

Visiting the still under construction Fab 9, I was stunned at the size of the building. It was large enough to hold three football fields, end-to-end! Interviews went well and I got a very positive feeling for the group. I left for Phoenix with a sense of an upcoming offer for a new training job. One week later I received a substantial offer for a supervisory position in manufacturing training program development under Peggy. I'd prepped Margaret that I felt positive about a job offer and here it was. She surprised me by agreeing to another move, saying that she had had enough of the hot summers in Arizona.

57
Buying Another House

Albuquerque was much smaller than the Phoenix metropolitan area and driving about was a snap. Real estate was in a slump and housing was readily available for reasonable prices. I had to leave quickly for the job and arrived in ABQ to seek temporary living quarters and found a nice apartment on the west side overlooking the city. Each evening I drove about with an agent looking for a home. We came upon a new home in Taylor Ranch on the west bank that fit the bill nicely. Albuquerque is bisected by the Rio Grande River. The place was a three bedroom, partial brick home with a brick fireplace and a two car garage on a large lot. The builder had put in landscaping in front trying to sell the home. It had been on the market for some time. He wanted $84,000, bottom price.

I called Margaret and gave her an idea what was in the place. She suggested and I agreed to offer $80,000, period. Take it or leave it. The agent swallowed hard and went into conference with the builder. The builder and his brother went outside to his truck and did some figuring. Fifteen minutes later they came back into the house and announced we had a deal. The agent couldn't believe it! I was happy and immediately called her with the good news. The area was new with only a fifteen minute drive to Intel's Fab 9 plant. Papers were signed and arrangements made to move Margaret, the dogs and our household to Albuquerque. I felt life was good again.

Intel took over the house in Dobson Ranch and moved our household to New Mexico. Margaret's first reaction to the new home and to Albuquerque (ABQ) was positive. After unpacking and settling in we drove about the city taking in the new sights and getting acclimated. ABQ is a little behind times in development but it is a very interesting city with strong Hispanic heritage. We loved the view of Sandia Mountain and the valley below. Living in the west elevation, we had three extinct volcanoes within two miles. Three blocks away from our home was an open area where one could view hundreds of petro glyphs, examples of Indian artwork on large dark rocks.

Several months after relocating to Rio Rancho Fab 9, Peg S called me and told me I was to come to Phoenix for an award dinner. I was to be honored, as was the SPC guru Cynthia, in receiving an award for our work in developing the Intel SPC Program. Peggy L quickly authorized my travel to Phoenix and I was on my way. Imagine my surprise upon entering the restaurant to see many faces I had never met before. Who were all of these people? Turns out they were in one way or another connected with SPC training at all of Intel's sites.

Having been given a copy of the newly printed Intel SPC Training Manual, I was stunned to see that my name was not listed as co-developer of the program. Somehow my colleague had assumed all credit for developing the book! When I inquired about it I was given some half-hearted reason why my name was not listed. But I had received a $200 award for my effort, hadn't I? Miss Beautiful would not even speak to me that evening. Less than a year later she left Intel, I was told, to join another company with her newly acquired fame as a published SPC expert.

I fell in love with the Albuquerque's southwest architecture. ABQ is a city with many wooden fences and gates of differing styles. Gates make an interesting format for photos and I soon became captivated with them, taking 35mm pictures of a great variety of gates (this was before the advent of digital cameras). On the west side of Sandia Mountain one can ride a tram from the base to the 10,500 foot crest and enjoy a magnificent view of Albuquerque and the valley. There is also a pleasant restaurant at the top of the mountain to enjoy a meal with the view. Potable water is hauled to the top each day in the base of each tram and piped to the restaurant for use.

New Mexico is called the "Enchanting State". It grew on me and I still have a great admiration for the state. Like Arizona, it has high country with tall pines, aspen, piñon, oak trees and of course, cold weather and snow in the winter. Lower elevations have desert fauna and high temperatures in the summer. ABQ is in between with moderate temperatures in the summer and winter. The majority of homes have air coolers, referred to as swamp coolers, as the source of cool air in the summer. We found it refreshing as it not only cools but also adds moisture to the very dry air.

Because of its high elevation (average of 5500 feet), Albuquerque does not get hot in the summer and cools off rapidly in the evening. I can only recall having to leave the air cooler on twice during the night in the five years we lived there. However, winters are a different issue. The coldest temperature we experienced was 8 degrees above zero and that lasted for one day. It snows infrequently and when it does it is usually gone in one day, melting very quickly. The wind is incessant in the early spring, blowing in from the west or northwest at speeds of 20 to 40 miles per hour. Tumbleweed can usually be seen blowing around all over the west side of town in the high winds.

In October of each year ABQ hosts the world's largest hot air balloon festival. Balloon owners and enthusiasts come from all over the world to participate in the festivities. It is impossible to secure a hotel room in the city and surrounding areas since most reservations are made a year or even two years in advance. As many as 1000 balloons of varying colors and designs can be seen vying for prizes for design and performance. One night during the week is devoted to glow up, when the balloons are tethered to the ground and the propane burners are ignited, illuminating the balloon in the darkness. It is a dazzling sight when viewed from the height of the west bank.

ABQ is a perfect site for the balloon events because of something called a box effect over the city. Rising above the launch site, balloons can travel in one direction flowing with the wind. Rising yet higher, the balloons catch a reverse flow of wind and travel in the opposite direction. It is an unforgettable sight to see upwards of 1000 colored craft in the sky over ABQ. Kodak made a fortune selling 35mm film for the festival (before digital cameras became a reality).

The training group began forming and assuming roles in the upcoming Fab 9 startup. I was assigned the program development role and given authorization to hire two developers. I was fortunate to hire a seasoned operator and a college degreed teacher with a distinguished background in computer operation. We clicked from the start. Annie H and Beth P worked tirelessly in developing and producing training programs. One of our first assignments was to produce a safety program (where had I heard this before?). We put our heads together and designed a booklet listing all of the chemicals used in a Fab, their properties and safety issues for each. It took weeks to develop and print the booklet. Next we scheduled meetings to deliver the session. The program was a success and the booklet was a smash hit with manufacturing. We had made a mark right at the start.

Peggy L was doing an excellent job promoting and establishing the training program in Fab 9. Being the oldest member in the training group, I believe I was looked upon with respect as a father figure. Peggy treated me exceptionally well, awarding me stock options and excellent raises over the years. A side note: Had she not granted me the stock option awards I would not have been able to live the retirement lifestyle I now enjoy. I shall always be grateful for her generosity. As the years went by training became the baseline for manufacturing excellence. Our Fab 9 group was rather large by Intel standards but we earned great respect and recognition.

A newly hired accredited teacher, Lynn W, came into training and was assigned to my group as a developer. Looking upon me as the old conservative guy, she met with Peggy and objected to working for me. Peggy told her that was her assignment and to give me a chance. Initially she was distant and had little to offer in our group. When I was asked to work with another part of training in setting up and administering a huge program for managers promoting teamwork, Lynn came with me. We worked side-by-side for several weeks planning with Eric, the manager of the program.

I began to notice a change in Lynn's attitude as we put the program in place. She came to me one day and asked how to gauge a yield for the participants. How were we going to rate the effectiveness of the three day training event? I explained how we would assess each team's effort in getting a prescribed job done. Dividing a team's output by the time spent and by the number of participants in the team would give us a good measurement of production effectiveness. She did not know how to set up a mathematical equation, or model, and work with it to arrive at an answer. I was surprised and showed her how to develop the equation using fake numbers and how to calculate an answer. From that day on she and I became a team. It became our responsibility to acquire the tools and materials the teams needed to do their work for the program and set up work stations. During the event we monitored the teams and kept track of their progress. It was demanding but in the end very rewarding. The team building program was a huge success and became another feather in Fab 9 Training's hat.

59
A Family Calamity

Margaret received a phone call from Cathy one day telling her that Paul had physically abused her, stolen her charge cards, emptied their checking and savings accounts and left her. It was another example of Paul's fiery temper. He exclaimed he was angry and upset that he had not been able to impregnate her and that he wanted children very badly. We felt it was a blessing that she had been unable to have children. I believe Paul's mother and grandmother had pressured him into wanting a family.

Paul had left Intel two years before to accept a job at Hewlett-Packard. They had found a home in Houston, TX and resumed their life there. Perhaps it was additional pressure from his new job or their marriage that had set him off.

Cathy was in a state of panic and Margaret was not far behind. We sent money and assurances to help her get back on her feet. We found that Paul had also charged several thousand dollars in purchases using Cathy's charge cards. We advised her to see a lawyer immediately and start divorce proceedings, feeling the lawyer would put a stop on any more charges made by Paul. It took six months for the lawyer to get an annulment of their marriage and straighten out the debts Paul had incurred.

Cathy moved from Houston to Dallas and found an apartment

not far from where we used to live in Carrollton. She was able
to find a job quickly and set about to renew old friendships
there.

60
Another Fab Retrenchment

After four years, Fab 9 had matured and the need for manufacturing training began to diminish. Yields were meeting targets and product was moving and selling at the expected rate. There comes a time in manufacturing when costs become a target so as to maximize profit. And, training is one of the first places to look for reductions in costs. We knew it and expected it. So, people started to look about for opportunities. Peggy had stated we were allowed to look for another job within the corporation.

Intel had set up a computer system that listed all jobs available throughout the entire company. I began searching for training positions and found several available. Only one was open in Arizona and it was with Corporate Education and Development in Chandler. My eyes nearly popped when I saw who the hiring supervisor was: Peg S! I quickly updated my resume and filled out the required application for transfer, getting Peggy to sign her OK. The transfer request was sent to Human Resources and the waiting began.

Knowing that I would probably have to fight for the position, I dressed up a safety training program I had written in Fab 9, and bound it with an attractive cover. I compiled a short note to Peg listing some of my training accomplishments and sent it with the bound program. What I wasn't aware of was that Intel would pay for moving employees to other sites when downsizing was being implemented at any factory. Peg S knew it and convinced her manager, Tracy in Santa Clara, I would fit in with the CED Group, citing my previous work with her. And the moving expense would be handled by the corporation. Peg called me about two weeks after I had applied for transfer and told me that I could have the job. When can I move to Chandler? Now the tricky part came into play – convincing Margaret that we should move back to Arizona.

Her first reaction to telling her that I had an offer to move back to Arizona was, and I quote: "I am not moving!" I explained that Fab 9 was going through a cutback and I had no place to go as a training supervisor. I had to find another job by going back into manufacturing or stand the possibility of a layoff. There were no training jobs available at the Rio Rancho site. Yes, I could go into manufacturing as a supervisor and would wind up on second, probably third shift. I did not want to do that. Margaret was less than convinced that was the case. Our discussions became more and more heated.

Talking to Peg, I explained that Margaret was refusing to move. She became upset and said either I am moving or I am not, because the job must be filled quickly. Then she suggested something that I had not thought of. Our health insurance plan allowed psychological treatment and she suggested Margaret and I get help from a counselor.

I suggested it to Margaret and was met with a cold shoulder. I went ahead and met with the counselor, explaining the situation and Margaret's reaction to a move. After two meetings he explained that resolution could not be achieved unless Margaret attended a meeting. As a couple we met twice with him and discussed the move in great detail. On the last meeting, he told Margaret nicely that she had not thought the situation clearly through and that I would be penalized if I did not accept the job in Chandler. Our continued life in ABQ would be difficult at best if I took just any job to avoid the transfer. After quietly thinking for a few minutes, Margaret agreed that our future would be better if we moved to Chandler. But I could see that she was very unhappy.

I called Peg the next day and told her that we would move and that I could be there within two weeks. At home, however, the situation was one of coldness and distance. Margaret was not going to move without my knowing that she had had enough. And I saw her point. I could literally see the fabric of our marriage unraveling. Our marriage was in serious trouble. I promised her I would call every day and find a house that she would love. I got little response in return.

I knew I had about five years of work remaining to get our financial house in order before retirement. We had been frugal throughout our marriage but had not been able to put aside a lot of money for the inevitable day of leaving the work force. That would be my primary goal while finishing my work career at Intel.

I would leave ABQ with a feeling of despair. I very much wanted to move to assume the new job but I felt a gulf developing between Margaret and me. I knew she was fed up with moving again and having to start life in another city. I also knew that I could not continue working at Intel's ABQ site. I tried to assume a positive attitude and hope that we could make a good life back in Arizona. It was not going to be easy.

61
A Fab 9 Real-Life Story

Having lived and worked in ABQ for nearly five years I had become aware of some people not being happy with their work or with Intel. I often saw a display of what I called the "manăna attitude". Hey, if we don't do it today, we'll do it tomorrow – or maybe the next day – or some other time – what's the rush? The weak work ethic bothered me.

In fact, one of my training colleagues did not seem to think that schedules were important and often blamed others for his missing deadlines. Peggy was about to fire him when I asked to have him work for me. In meetings Louis B would tell me his problems with his project and I kept advising him how to gather data from individuals to be able to finish on time. Near the end of time for his project completion he still was not nearly done. He began offering excuses again when I stopped him and laid it on the line. He was very close to being terminated for his inability to complete projects.

Louis became angry, began swearing and got up to leave the room. I stopped him with, "If you leave this room, you might just as well walk out of the plant because you are fired! Now, calm down and let's finish this meeting." He sat down. I explained that I had coached him for six weeks, offering advice on how to complete his project. "You did not complete it. Why?"

He explained that his wife had left him and he was going through tough times. "Why had you not told me this before?" I asked. He snapped, "I didn't feel it was any of your business!" "Louis, as your supervisor it was my business, especially when it affects your work like it obviously has."

We talked at length and I readjusted his completion date, scheduling daily meetings to review his work. With that, Louis successfully completed his project on time and moved on. Peggy was happy that Louis' problem had been solved.

The manǎna attitude was something I had not seen or experienced at other Intel sites. Excuses for not meeting goals were not tolerated. If anything, the Intel attitude was one of getting projects or jobs completed on time and done effectively. That was a quality that impressed me and inspired me in my work. It had been rewarding for me and I could not understand why some employees in Fab 9 were not following the norm.

62
It's Back to Arizona!

I moved in September, 1991 and found the quarters that Intel had arranged for in a Chandler apartment. I had one month to find a house and try to settle in before moving Margaret and our dogs. A real estate agent was recommended and I called to arrange a meeting to discuss our needs in a home. She seemed like a nice lady with years of experience in real estate. I laid out our preferences for a home in the east valley area and was told that she had some places already in mind. Our first trip out to view homes was a total zero. Whereas I had set a price limit of $100,000 for a home which I felt to be attainable, she immediately showed me several homes well above the limit. I reiterated our top price and she lined up several homes for showing two days later – another zero. I began to wonder if she had a hearing or comprehension problem.

While out on my own one day I found a very nice home in Mesa near where we had lived previously. She seemed peeved when I called her about the home but set up a visit the next day. Inspecting the home, however, left a negative feeling. It did not meet our needs. The lady showed me one more home on the far edge of Mesa in a neighborhood that was less than desirable. I'd had it with the agent and decided I could do better on my own.

Near the end of the month of my allotted stay in the apartment, I walked to a new home development just one block away. I spoke with the realtor/agent in charge of sales and explained I was in need of a home quickly. He gave me keys to a nearby house still under construction and told me to take a look. The house still needed kitchen completion, carpet, tile, etc. But it definitely met our needs. He made a phone call when I returned to the sales office and spoke with the person who had bought the house with a down payment. Unfortunately the person could not sell his current home and did not have the money to complete the sale of the house under construction. The buyer relinquished his right to the house with a promise of getting his down payment returned.

I quickly called Margaret and told her of my find in a house. She asked many questions and finally agreed to our buying it. The salesman was happy to have made the sale in a market that was very slow. Later I met with the interior decoration coordinator to order cabinets, carpet, etc., and selected all components while speaking long distance with Margaret on the phone. It was done!

When I called the realtor who had shown me several older homes in Mesa and told her I had bought a house under construction, she became very angry. She told me in no uncertain terms that she felt I had cheated her, she had spent many hours lining up homes for me to see and now she was not going to earn a commission. I let her go on her tirade for several minutes and then asked, "Why did you not show me a new home like I was able to find?" She hung up the phone.

63

Corporate Education and Development

My position in Corporate Education and Development was as Professional Development Training Specialist. Doesn't that sound grand? But it was much the same responsibilities as I had had before, just that the programs were designed for supervisory and management personnel. We were part of Intel University. Peg S assigned a project that was fairly easy to accomplish and I was off and running. Mix this in with making arrangements to move Margaret and furnishings to Chandler and I was very busy.

Time came when I had to travel to ABQ, watch the loading of household items, pack up a rented GMC van with family and drive back to Arizona. The trip was uneventful and we arrived in Chandler later that day. I noticed that Margaret became less and less talkative as we got closer. By the time we got to the new house, now finished and livable, she was not talking. Inside the house she walked about carefully inspecting every room. She came back into the kitchen, looked at me and angrily said: "This is nothing but a damn patio home!"

It was not. It was not connected to another house and had a large fenced back yard. I was speechless and decided not to begin an argument. She was absolutely furious! I had clearly explained the dimensions, square footage, number of rooms, etc., while talking to her on the phone. We did not speak to each other for several hours. I was definitely on her S--t list again. I reasoned that Margaret was letting go of her pent up emotions and I was the brunt of them. We continued limited talk for several days while unpacking, moving furniture around and putting kitchen items in place. It took weeks for Margaret to come to terms with the move and the new home. Slowly we resumed our positions as husband and wife.

64
Becoming Grandparents!

Our son, Dan, had graduated from Northern Arizona University with a Bachelor of Science degree in computer engineering and was now working for a small software firm in Scottsdale. He called one day and asked us to accompany him to look at two home sites he had narrowed to in search of a new house. We looked at some homes in northeast Phoenix and some in Scottsdale. Asking our opinion, we pointed out that the Scottsdale home won hands down. He later bought a three bedroom home in Greyhawk, a lovely subdivision in north Scottsdale. It was a wise decision and it proved to be a winner for homes in the city.

Meanwhile Catherine had married an old friend, Scott Dallal, from Dallas and they had purchased a home in Plano, Texas. Scott was employed by State Farm Insurance Company and was a member of the firm's Catastrophe Response Team. As a team member, Scott often traveled to cities that had experienced extensive fire, flood, storm or hurricane damage. Consequently, he was not home in Plano more than four months a year.

Soon Margaret and I became grandparents to two beautiful children, Fred and Deanna. Margaret had flown to Texas to help Cathy after the delivery of each baby. Things were looking up and life was moving on. Years later, with both kids in school, Cathy decided to return to college and earn her Bachelor's degree. After several years of study and hard work, Cathy was awarded a Bachelor of Social Science Degree from the University of Texas-Dallas. Dan continued his college work and later was awarded a Master's Degree in Business Administration from Arizona State University. Margaret and I were especially proud of both kids, each having attained a higher degree of education than either one of us had earned. She and I had often talked about and encouraged both children to complete college work.

65
Coping With A Job Transfer

Peg asked me to attend a meeting in which a contractor was espousing work he had done regarding the personal feelings managers experienced transferring from site-to-site. I was unaware of the emotional and psychological effects workers experienced when transferring from one work place to another. Dr. Bill D, a psychologist who studied how families were affected by corporate transfers to other sites, had developed a four day seminar to deal with such moves. Peg had gotten information about the seminar and had put two and two together on how it could apply to Intel managers.

Intel had to respond quickly to changes and demands in the semiconductor market and frequently moved key managers and supervisors to other sites to effectively meet those manufacturing challenges. Gordon Moore, one of Intel's three founding scientists, had predicted those vast changes in semiconductor design and manufacturing in what became known as "Moore's Law". The swiftly moving progress in design and manufacturing resulted in key employees relocating to meet the need for implementation. Peg recognized the need for education in coping with employee's needs for aid in making moves to other sites. I was amazed at what Dr. Bill revealed during the meeting. It made sense to me having made several moves in my career and having dealt with personal issues related to the moves.

Peg met with higher Intel managers and got the OK to contract with Dr. Bill and move ahead with the educational program. She asked me to work with him and absorb what he taught during the sessions, her reasoning being that we would eventually develop our own program. Obviously we had to pay an enormous fee to secure Dr. Bill's training. As the program's administrator, I had to make all internal arrangements for the four day seminar, including securing an off-site facility large enough to accommodate 20 to 30 management participants, lunches, handouts and reservations for the seminar.

During each seminar I listened carefully to what Dr. Bill was telling managers. He and I developed a close relationship after several seminars. He had given me a copy of his entire work and I read through all of it. In the end I felt I could revise his program by adding a few Intel twists.

Essentially what Dr. Bill had done was to modify the grieving process one goes through upon the death of a loved one after studying how people felt upon moving to another job. The negotiations, anger, frustration, despair, loneliness, coming to grips and finally acceptance of the move were the same emotions one feels after a loved one's death or after a divorce. I had experienced all of those feelings with each move. What I had overlooked were the emotions and feelings that Margaret had felt. Now I understood why her anger was so pronounced.

How does one cope with the emotions and feelings after a transfer? Dr. Bill pointed out that simply acknowledging what the individual was experiencing after the move was paramount. Coping methods (he called them tools) included periodically having a treat such as a movie or dinner out, talking at length about your feelings with someone (counseling), taking care of yourself with adequate sleep and rest and knowing that eventually there was light at the end of the tunnel. He spoke of the personal transaction lasting six months to a year. His diagram of the process displayed a loop where one descends to hit bottom and then moves upward again, hopefully to a normal, stable life.

About a year after Dr. Bill's seminars had begun, Peg asked me if I would develop a condensed version of the seminar lasting two days instead of four. Her thought was to shorten the program so that supervisors could attend. Most groups within the company did not look kindly upon training courses that took supervisors away from their work areas more than two days. She knew this. Dr. Bill stated he did not want to shorten his seminars, feeling that would take away the effectiveness. He did not understand time restraints corporations like Intel placed upon employees.

So I began the condensing work on the seminar and presented my plan and schedule to Peg for her review. She approved the plan and I was in business. Of necessity, I spoke with Dr. Bill telling him I was shortening his program and he was not at all happy with my plan. He realized that his gravy boat with Intel was coming to an end. After weeks of work, the program was shortened to two days, was reviewed and turned over to Intel University personnel for delivery. Peg was happy and I was happy.

One evening leaving work I passed by Peg's office and noticed she was still at her desk. We chatted for a few minutes and she remarked that her back was giving her great pain. I suggested she get home and apply heat while in bed. Next morning we all wondered why she had not come in to work. A call from her husband saying she had collapsed and was now in Intensive Care at Desert Samaritan Hospital in Mesa shocked everyone.

One of the developers left immediately to go to the hospital, but was refused entry to Peg's room.

We waited a day for news about her condition when her husband again called to say that she had suffered an aortic rupture and had died. We could not believe what we had just heard. Here was a vital, seemingly fit woman, a former Olympic swimmer, dead at the age of 48! Our CED Group was in mourning, as were many other people in the company.

A huge throng attended a memorial service for Peg, including VP's and high ranking Intel officials. In memoriam, an oak tree was planted in her name at the Intel headquarters in Santa Clara, California. It took weeks for us to really get back to productive work. She was not only a good wife and mother, but an excellent manager who could see potential in an employee and help shape them into happy, productive workers. Unquestionably, she was the best manager I had ever worked for.

Things changed rapidly after the funeral with the appointment of a new manager for our Chandler group. Sheila W met with our Chandler group and explained that she would reside in Santa Clara and would visit our group one day each week. I had met Sheila years before when she was training manager at the Livermore, California facility. It had not been a pleasant event. She was distant, abrupt and not helpful concerning our training for eventual placement in Chandler. Several weeks into her new job as manager of the CED developers, she asked me to assist her in supervising the group since she was only in Chandler one day a week. I was to sign necessary paperwork for her, interface with HR, facilities and other groups when needed and in general, help keep the group up and running. It took little time from my assigned work.

66
Scheske Family Events

September, 1991, I received a phone call stating my older brother Erve had died of lung and heart complications. I quickly arranged a flight to Chicago and got to Waukegan just in time for the funeral. I had not seen Erve in nine years and I was shocked to see how he had aged. I knew he had had a stroke and that his lungs were frail, but I did not anticipate his physical condition. He'd had wavy hair all his life and now it was cut very short. It was a jolt for me. I did get to meet Edna and their children and it was good to talk and reminisce with them. Erve was buried in North Shore Garden of Memories next to my parent's grave sites.

I spent a few days with brother Bill after Erve's funeral and we talked about family history and events. Bill still had his hackles up about my not attending brother George's funeral years before in northern Michigan. When I explained that I was in the midst of making a job change when George died and could not make the trip, he calmed down somewhat. Bill had a hot temper and it took time for him to cool off. I recall parking my Volkswagen Bug on his driveway one time while visiting my parents. When he came home and saw the foreign car in his drive he shouted, "Get that GD piece of crap off of my drive and never park it there again!" I parked it on the street in front of his house, telling him that was public property and I could park there any time I wanted to. He was steamed.

I returned to Phoenix. Two days after Christmas, 1991, I received another phone call telling me that brother Bill had died from a massive aortic rupture. I couldn't believe what was happening! Flying again to Chicago, this time in the midst of a winter snow storm, I arrived a day before the funeral. The rental car at O'Hare airport had been washed and the door locks were frozen shut. Just what I needed! Finally getting the car unlocked and warm, it was tense for me driving in a darkening evening snow storm.

At the funeral home I spoke with his kids and then willed myself to go to the casket. Bill and I resembled each other very much and when I saw his body in state I broke down. Two family funerals in three months were more than I could handle. He and I did not often agree on issues but we were still close. It was a very sad time for our family. His wife Norma had died several years earlier. I spent time with his two boys and reminisced some more. Bill was buried next to Norma alongside my parent's grave sites. Brother Bob and I were now the only Scheske family members left.

67
Nearing the End of My Career

My next, and last, assignment was to co-manage a project with a young lady on loan to our Santa Clara CED Group. Laura was a very pleasant lady, attractive and college educated. We were to work with Corporate HR groups, calling upon their expertise to assemble an "Employee Handbook" which would be used to guide employees on Intel procedures regarding work conditions, discipline, safety and legal issues with jobs. The plan was to assemble a printed book and also make it available online for easy access. We drew up a plan and time schedule and submitted them for approval.

Little did I know that this project had been attempted several times before and had never been completed. We got the go ahead and set off to meet with experts in given HR fields. Laura spoke with HR personnel in California and I met with Arizona and New Mexico personnel. Everyone voiced approval of the project, citing the need for it. Projected completion dates were agreed and we set off to pull it together. Less than two months after starting Laura informed me that she was being removed from the project by her boss, leaving me on my own. The significance of her leaving did not register with me until later. Her supervisor was a lady who had treated Arizona trainees, of which I was one, like dirt when we came to California to begin our work with Intel in 1980. She was uncooperative, sly and cunning while smiling to our face when dealing with us, and could not to be trusted. We learned quickly at the time not to voice our opinion on anything because it would come back to bite us. Apparently she saw something in the employee handbook project that did not please her and pulled her favorite, Laura, to protect her.

Several months into the project I had received copious amounts of material that were to be placed in the handbook. However, one California manager in particular was not responding to my phone calls for progress status on formulating legal procedures. I notified my manager that I was not getting responses to my calls and that I would have to go to Santa Clara to confront her. No suggestions from my manager, who worked in the same building as the Legal department, on how she could help me. I finally was able to arrange for a meeting with Patty, Manager of Intel's Legal Staff.

Her response to me in the meeting was that she could not begin work on the handbook project until at least six months out, which would totally blow my scheduled completion date. Laura had assured me that when she met with the legal manager that she was told Legal would hire extra help, if needed, to meet our completion date. I told Patty that I could not accept a date that late and I would be happy to come to her office and work with her employees to meet the scheduled completion date. Her response was that she would not do that, she had other work to complete first and repeated her suggested date for the handbook work. She got up and left the meeting. I told my manager that Legal was not going to meet their obligation and consequently the completion date would not be met. Sheila's response: "Keep working on it and try to finish on time!" Did she not comprehend what I had just told her?

Several days later I received an anonymous phone call from a California Intel employee telling me I had better watch my back, that I had been eviscerated in a meeting that discussed the employee handbook project. I had a pretty good idea what had happened. The CED manager, Tracy, had met with the HR Group in California and when the topic of the handbook came up, Legal tore me apart. I called my manager, Sheila, to try and find out what had happened but she was not in her office – nor did she return my phone call.

I wish I could change what I did following that incident. I spoke with the Chandler HR manager, Judy, explaining what was going on. She was very much involved in the project and was concerned. She did nothing to help me or the project as it turned out. What I should have done is meet with Intel's Human Resources Manager and explain what was happening. At the least I would have been protecting my backside. What happened next was unbelievable.

68
My Performance Review

At my annual review in mid-November, 1993 I was approaching age 65 and knew that I was near the end of my career at Intel. But, I had no idea what was lying ahead. Sheila called me into an office to administer my performance review. Reading through the review I could not believe what she had written. I was being placed on employee probation for being unable to complete a major project on time! The project completion date was not due for another six weeks! I had received two-thirds of the information from HR experts and it had been entered in a computer base. The major component still missing: Legal Issues! I became angry and I gave the review back saying I would not sign it. She replied this was very difficult for her. Difficult for her? What did she think it was for me? I got up and left the room. I don't know what she did after that but I was told she quickly left the Chandler facility.

After returning to my office, I sat for a few minutes trying to collect my thoughts. I had in the past delivered disciplinary measures to a subordinate. But I had never in all of my working days been on the recipient end. My mind was in a state of complete confusion. How had it come for me to be put on notice for failure to complete a project? I could not think straight! It took at least an hour for me slow down my thinking and realize I was in deep sauce. What to do?

I spoke to a confidant and briefly explained that I was on disciplinary notice for failing to complete a major project on time. And the expected finish date was still six weeks out! She had many questions and we talked for almost an hour. She advised me to write a letter immediately to Intel's Employee Ombudsman, Cheryl. I compiled a three page letter relating my experience with the employee handbook and the outrageous performance review I had been given (which I had not signed) and sent the letter to Cheryl. I never got acknowledgement of receipt of the letter nor did I get to speak with her. I was in a real funk. For the first time in my career I felt fear. I felt frozen in time, not being sure of what to do. The thought kept running through my head – over 30 years work in the semiconductor industry without incident and it had come down to the possibility of being fired at age 65!

I demanded a written formal charge of incompetence since I had not been given a verbal or written warning before receiving the performance review. That was a violation of the corporation's disciplinary process. I did receive an email notice that I was no longer to work on the handbook project. Another developer had been hired to complete work on the project. As I came to work each day wondering what I was supposed to be doing an Arizona HR manager called me in and talked to me about the situation. Somebody, I believe, realized that CED management had made a serious mistake in writing and administering my performance review, but no action was being taken to remedy it. Clearly, the review was not going to be rewritten or changed. I told HR that I was entitled to a corrective action plan to clear the charges. And, they agreed. My manager, Sheila, was not to be seen or heard from while this was going on.

While this was happening, I heard that Intel was again going through downsizing. I felt CED management decided that I, being the oldest member in the group at age 64, could be sent on my way out the door to help meet the group's cutback total. I also found out that Intel was about to offer employees an incentive to voluntarily leave the company and based on years of service, each employee would receive appropriate compensation. The policy would go into effect February 1, 1994. If I could successfully complete my corrective action project sometime after February first, I would be eligible for the program. There was no way in hell I was going to fail meeting the conditions of the project! Further, I was eligible for sabbatical leave, having completed 14 years of service. Intel's policy was to grant six weeks of sabbatical leave with full pay for every seven years of employment.

I don't think Margaret understood the gravity of the situation I was in. I found it very difficult to talk about the issue and she appeared to not want to hear about it. Had Tracy pushed the issue with Human Resources, I could easily have been terminated. That would have meant no benefits, including separation pay. While we were not hurting financially, we would have had to tighten the belt and retirement could have meant having to find a part time job to meet our obligations. I would probably have had to file suit against Intel and take my chances in court for an award. While I did not speak openly about filing a discrimination complaint with the EEOC, I think HR realized there was room for cause.

69
My Corrective Action Plan

I spoke with Tracy about the corrective action project (she was so nice over the phone!) and proposed that I submit a plan to her within the week. She agreed (where was my manager?). I subsequently surveyed all of the CED site facilitators and determined that the "The Role of a CED Facilitator" on how to facilitate a training program was badly in need of revision. I worked a plan and schedule for completion (mid February) and sent it to Tracy. I received a phone message from her saying she approved the plan and I was off and running. I traveled to California several times interviewing facilitators for input on changes. CED trainers in Arizona were also interviewed. All of the input data was assembled and the rewrite began. Mid-January, 1994, the revised version was sent to site facilitators for review. A few changes were suggested and were incorporated into the program. I attended the first session of the revised program in early February, facilitated in the Folsom, California plant. It was a one day event and the facilitator was happy with the rewrite. Tracy got the word that I had successfully met the conditions of the corrective action plan and my "satisfactory" status was reinstated mid-February.

Intel had indeed announced the voluntary termination package to its employees early in February. I informed HR that I was entitled to sabbatical leave, with full pay, and that I would retire upon returning from sabbatical. Tracy respectfully informed me that I was not retiring, but that I was being terminated. I didn't care what she called it. I was leaving with six weeks of full pay while on sabbatical and then would return to turn in my badge and leave – retire – entitled to six months of compensation based on my fourteen-plus years of service. It was not a golden parachute package, but was certainly adequate.

I enjoyed my sabbatical, but the performance review incident was always on my mind. Margaret and I travelled about Arizona and relished our first taste of retirement. The day of reckoning came in May, 1994, to clean out my desk, turn in my badge, say my goodbyes and leave the Chandler facility. Even then my final paperwork had not been completed and sent to HR in Chandler. I had to call Tracy and remind her that HR was waiting for the final forms to release me to the world. She said she had sent it, but I didn't believe her. She again reminded me I was being terminated, that I was not retiring from Intel. Her secretary faxed the forms to HR and after a short exit interview, I left the plant. Walking to my car, I realized that I could no longer enter any Intel facility unless I had an escort. My retirement had begun! In the words of a famous philosopher: "Goodbye Tension, Hello Pension!"

70
Ah, Retirement!

The entire incident surrounding the employee handbook project kept popping up in my mind long after I left Intel. I asked myself: Was I without fault in this matter? Of course not! I knew I was in trouble after several meetings with the Legal Manager had produced no results. Instead of trying to negotiate a way to still meet my deadline and receive the materials I needed from the legal department, I should have gone to the CED Manager and discussed the problem. As it was, Tracy obviously listened to only one side of the story and formed her decision from the meeting when the Legal Manager tore me apart. As a good manager she should have called me in and laid it on the line.

To make decisions based on only one input is indicative of poor management skills. Was her action a way to protect herself and form an alliance with an up-and-coming Vice President of HR, the then current Legal Manager? Well, it was over and done with. Thirty-three years in the semiconductor industry had come to a very distasteful end. The incident left a bitter taste in my mouth for months afterward, however. It was especially hard to forget the matter and it remained stuck in the back of my mind for a long time. Finally, I realized it was not doing me any good to relive the events and that I must forgive and forget. It took a while but I did just that.

About three weeks after retiring I received a phone call from an Intel colleague asking me to have dinner with some of my former co-workers. I did not anticipate a roast in which I would be the brunt of bald face lies and funny stories. There were fourteen of my former colleagues at the dinner and each of them took a whack at me. I have never laughed so hard or so long in my life! A large notebook of photos and stories was presented after the roasting that was a compilation of my career at Intel. The tribute was touching and heartwarming. I had to try very hard to keep from crying several times. What a wonderful group of people! I miss them to this day.

I learned during the dinner that the replacement hired to complete work on the employee handbook had quit and left the company. My former manager, Sheila, also had left Intel (quit, fired or retired?) to set up a training consultant business. The Legal Manager had indeed been promoted to Intel Vice President of Human Resources. To my knowledge the employee handbook was never completed.

I missed reporting for work. My father had instilled a good work ethic in all five of the boys. Work was a form of enjoyment for me, and in fact there were jobs that I loved. That's not to say my life was all work and no play. I prized the time spent with Margaret and our children. But think about this: I was a liberal arts major who had worked more than forty years with chemists, chemical, electrical, mechanical and industrial engineers and other scientists. Work was not only challenging, it was fulfilling and educational. Work colleagues were interesting and inspirational. I had not only accomplished work, I had received an education along the way! Giving that up at retirement was not easy and I knew that I had to find stimulating projects or hobbies to remain physically and mentally active.

I had formed many friendships while at Intel but none quite

as fulfilling as the ones with former colleagues Marc Burhans and Dan Jaggers. Over the years we worked together at various times in training groups at Chandler and Rio Rancho. We now meet for lunch every two or three months to maintain our friendship, to recall events at work and keep up to date with Intel's business. Also to tell a few jokes and laugh at old work stories. Dan still works at Intel while Marc has also assumed the retiree role.

Things I Learned During My Work Career:

To succeed, give an employer more than is expected on the job: time, effort and loyalty

Exercise discipline in everything you do

Ask yourself periodically: Is this the best I can do for my career?

Persevere – don't ever, ever give up trying to better yourself!

Think positively – negative thoughts will drown a person and a career

When you sense problems in your job, meet with your manager or supervisor and resolve the issue(s)

71
Reflections

Abbott Laboratories is a very conservative corporation. Having to meet and stay within Food and Drug Administration (FDA) rules and regulations makes it so. A job at Abbotts was a lifetime job, assuming you met job expectations. There were no layoffs. Excellent management provided the job security employees looked for in work. My nearly twelve year career with Abbotts was challenging and fulfilling.

Motorola Semiconductor on the other hand, flew by the seat of its pants. The original Chicago TV and Radio organization was better organized but as the corporation expanded operations and moved into the semiconductor and government product fields, management philosophy changed. Phoenix operations fostered a political structure that hampered employee satisfaction, I believe. You could expect workforce cutbacks on a regular basis. Whenever market or economic downturns occurred, layoffs were a certainty. I lived through several of them in my nearly fifteen years with Moto and, in fact, experienced a two month layoff.

MOSTEK seemed to always be in a growth mode during the five years I spent with the company and never saw a layoff. Good management encouraged a small company atmosphere, loyalty and job satisfaction. My management role in Training was stimulating and very rewarding.

Intel was a gung-ho company from the time I started with them in 1980. The company had a very aggressive business plan in place to become number one in manufacturing integrated circuits. Innovation and execution were foremost in their plan. Management worked tirelessly to avoid work force reduction. At one point in 1985, everyone in the company, including executives, took a ten percent cut in pay and agreed to work longer hours to get through a very tough period for the semiconductor industry. We did this with the company's assurance that compensation would be given to all employees when the economy came back up. We were rewarded handsomely less than a year later. Intel is a company that takes employee welfare seriously. I never experienced a layoff in the fourteen plus years I worked for the corporation. My growth and development as an individual and team member reached a peak with Intel. I am proud of my achievements and contributions made to a company I consider to be one of the finest in the business world.

72
On the Home Front

Margaret had decided not to attend my retirement dinner. She had excluded herself from Intel events years back. I'm not sure why she did that other than to remind me that she had had enough of my work adventures. We were getting along but that was it. There was not a lot of loving taking place. Talking with other retirees, I was told that is not unusual for people in their 60s and 70s, but I'm not sure I agree with that bit of wisdom. When golf, tennis, athletic events, drinking, dining, gambling or card playing becomes the driving force in any marriage there is a significant problem within, I believe. I noticed that Margaret was aging rapidly and that her memory was definitely going downhill. Her short term memory was very bad, yet she could easily recall events from childhood and our early marriage. Our family doctor felt she was in the early stages of Alzheimer's disease and prescribed the drug *Aricept*. It did little to help improve or retain her short term memory.

I set up an office in our home complete with a used office desk, file cabinet, a new computer and printer. I realized that some form of work was needed to keep my brain actively functioning. What I found interesting was Margaret's refusal to work on the computer. She had been an executive secretary while working at Abbotts and was an excellent typist. She decided she wanted nothing to do with a computer, however.

The first project I set out to work on was research and write about my family's ancestry. Brother Bill had talked to me about family history the last time I saw him before his death. We knew our father had changed his name from Olshefski to Scheske sometime after a row with his father, but we didn't know exactly when. We also knew he had come into the United States from Germany as a young boy via New York, moving on to Milwaukee, Wisconsin with his family. After a family quarrel he travelled to North and South Dakota, working for farm groups reaping grain. Later he returned to Milwaukee and began working for Johns-Manville in their paper mill.

My mother was born in Milwaukee shortly after arrival there, her family also emigrating from Germany. After school, she went to work for Gimbel's Department Store in downtown Milwaukee. That is where my father and mother met. So I had some information to work with when I got to the genealogy library of the Latter Day Saints (Mormon Church) in Mesa, Arizona. A kindly gentleman explained how to find the information regarding any family name. The church has a large library full of historical microfiche documents. He explained if I could not find the information I wanted he would show me how to get it from the Mormon Temple in Salt Lake City, Utah. It took several trips to the library to gather all of the information I could find.

The links of information went back as far as my father's last known place of residence in Posen, Germany. I could find no more data preceding that city. His family had arrived in the USA in 1892. I didn't get much more information regarding my mother's family either. They had emigrated from Hamburg, Germany in 1892. Reviewing Census data for 1910 and 1920 I found information about both families. The Census Bureau will only release data every eighty years, the expected life cycle for citizens, to protect their privacy. I gathered enough data to write about my parent's wedding in 1912 in Milwaukee, their move to Waukegan in 1920 and the birth dates of my three older brothers. Altogether, the material I wrote produced a fifteen page document. Six months had elapsed since I began the work. Upon completion I printed copies for everyone in the Scheske family still living and sent them off. The response I got was underwhelming. Cathy and Dan did thank me for the effort. Nephews and nieces did not respond at all. So much for that project!

Margaret and I had to make some big adjustments with my being around the house all day. She loved to read and spent time with books and her bible. We had joined Epiphany Lutheran Church in Chandler and had made a number of friends among members. Pastor Larry Stoterau was an inspiring preacher who made sermons come alive. We attended social functions in the church and fit in nicely. Rev. Stoterau left after serving the church for about ten years for a LCMS synodical position in California. A young, vital pastor took over and things began to change. He and his wife were very much youth oriented and they organized groups of teenagers within the church. One group became a rock type band that played at the late service each Sunday. It was an immediate success in bringing more teens into the church. Old time Lutherans began to grumble about kids taking over the church, even when two traditional Lutheran services were offered each Sunday. Lutherans do not accept change easily. I thought the pastor was doing a great service to the church and to teenagers.

Talking one day, Margaret and I decided we had better get our affairs in order and set up a living will. We'd heard about a lawyer in Phoenix who would create a living trust for a very reasonable fee. Arranging a meeting with the lawyer, he asked many questions and told us he'd have a trust ready for each of us in two weeks. We were impressed when we saw the trust document that he had prepared for each of us. It was one item out of the way. Next we met with the funeral director at

Green Acres in Scottsdale and finalized arrangements there. The second item was taken care of. We felt we had covered the bases, easing decisions for Cathy and Dan upon our demise.

I had set up a program on the computer, courtesy of <u>money.com</u>, to regularly track our investments. I had acquired a lot of Intel stock through an employee stock purchasing plan and through stock option awards. I watched in dismay as the value of the Intel stock climbed in value almost daily. I had set a financial goal, investing in mutual funds, stock and bank CDs for our retirement. Less than a year after retirement in 1994 the total value of our investments had nearly doubled in value! It would nearly quadruple in six years! I was absolutely stunned. I had no idea that we could amass such a fortune in our lifetime. I showed the astounding figure to Margaret one day and she thought I was kidding. Nope, that was a real figure!

Retirement became routine for us, taking things easy, enjoying our good fortune. Margaret's health continued to decline, however. Her back was causing much discomfort. She insisted on driving her car to shop and do errands. Margaret told me one Saturday morning that she was running an errand and would be home for lunch. She had not come home at lunch time and I began to be concerned. Around 1:00 p.m. I received a call from the Chandler Police saying Margaret had been in an accident and was taken to Scottsdale Health Care Center. I drove immediately to the hospital and entered the Emergency Room. I was directed to an area where she was lying on a gurney in a hallway. ER was jammed and all rooms were full. I spoke with her and asked how she felt. She had no recollection of being in an accident. She was still in a state of shock. A doctor came up and told me that she had a broken right leg and was due to go into surgery within the next hour. They were also concerned about her chest, feeling there had been injury there as well, and were scheduling her for an x-ray. I called our children and related what had happened and both quickly drove to the hospital. We talked and realized there was not much we could do at that time. Margaret was taken away to surgery and we left the hospital.

73
The Beginning of a Long Hospital Stay

Chandler Police had little to offer about the accident, saying it was still under investigation. They did say that Margaret apparently had made a left turn in front of an oncoming truck, probably causing the accident. Her car had been transported to a lot in Mesa. I did see Margaret Saturday evening after her leg had been surgically repaired. An Orthopedist proudly informed me that he had installed a steel rod in her leg to repair the damage – apparently the lower leg bone had been shattered. From surgery she had been moved to Intensive Care and was in an induced coma. I saw her but could not speak to her before I left to return home. I had dogs that must be fed and watered.

I visited her each day, but as she was in a coma we could not talk. Monday I drove to the lot where her car was being held. First sight, I could not believe what was before me. The car, a little Dodge, was now in a slight V shape, the right front bent to the right. Obviously it could never be repaired or driven again. I removed any personal items from the car. Speaking with the lot attendant, a real gentleman he was, I was informed that I could not remove the car unless I paid any and all charges. And charges were adding up by $30 a day. Towing the car was included in the daily charges.

I remembered that Father Joe Ministries had TV commercials asking for donated cars, trucks and motorcycles. They would tow the car at no cost and one could take a tax write-off for the vehicle. I called and they agreed to get the car the next day. I met the tow car driver at the lot and showed him the car. It would not be easy to load her car due to the way it had been parked in the lot. I went in to the office to pay the charges only to be told they would not accept a VISA charge card or a check. The bill must be paid with cash. It was nearly four o'clock in the afternoon and I could not get to a bank in time to get cash and return before the lot closed. The driver was very understanding, saying he could come back the next day. We agreed on a time and I went home to gather cash for the payoff. The removal of the car next day went smoothly. The wrecked Dodge was now part of the past.

Trying to get information on Margaret's condition was very difficult. Finding a doctor to give me her status was next to impossible. Nurses were reluctant to tell me how she was doing, saying only that she was making progress. Of course, I could not speak with her because she was still in an induced coma. I left the hospital each day concerned and downhearted. After nearly two weeks in Intensive Care, Margaret was released to a monitoring unit for care. She remembered absolutely nothing about the accident; in fact, she kept telling me she thought she had hit a curb. I knew that she had collided with a red pickup truck and I asked her if she remembered the truck, but she had no recall.

After several days in the monitoring unit, a CIGNA insurance representative took me aside one morning and said Margaret must be moved from the hospital before evening. I thanked her for giving me so much time to find a care facility. In response she gave me a list of facilities to look into in the next six hours. All were in the Scottsdale area and I drove quickly from one to another scoping them out. I found one that appeared to be nice but they had no room for any more patients. I settled on a facility directly across the street from the hospital and made arrangements to have her admitted late in the afternoon. The facility's manager showed me her room and I left to return to the hospital.

Margaret was transported by ambulance (less than a half block from the hospital) to the facility. I proceeded to her assigned room expecting to see a nurse or at least an attendant, but could find no one. I waited for the ambulance attendants who arrived about thirty minutes later. One went off to find a nurse to make the transfer. He spent nearly fifteen minutes before he found her administering drugs to patients. The transfer was completed and Margaret and I waited for an attendant to let us know what was going to be done. She needed attention and I went off looking for the nurse again. When I found her I asked what was being done to help my wife. This nurse was either on drugs or medication because she was spacey and had little to tell me. She called a Nurse's Aide who took me to her room and kindly explained the routine of the place. Their doctor would examine Margaret the next day and prescribe medication for her. Meantime she would continue to receive food via a tube into her stomach. I left a very unhappy Margaret after visiting an hour, saying I would be back the next morning.

Sometime during the night, Margaret had removed the feeding tube and liquid food had spilled onto the bed and floor. The nurse was not happy. A physical therapist had explained to me, and I assume to the nurse, that she was not to be given solid food to eat because her throat would not be able to handle it, being that she had had a feeding tube installed weeks before. I was outside when the facility's doctor came into the room the next morning. He was an older, imperious gentleman, dressed like a fashion plate and very talkative.

I was told the attendant explained that Margaret had pulled

her feeding tube out during the night. The doctor told her that was OK and put her on a light food diet. The therapist's cautionary note was thrown to the wind. And what do you think happened? They gave her a light lunch when I was not there which she attempted to eat. When I came into the room, Margaret began having trouble breathing. The nurse was called and, checking her heart rate and pulse, immediately left the room and called 9-1-1.

She was rushed to Scottsdale Health Care and placed in Intensive Care again. Some of the food which she had attempted to eat had bypassed the throat and had gotten into her lungs. Later, I spoke with the care facility's administrator and related what had happened from the time Margaret entered the place until she was rushed back to the hospital. She was shocked (feigned?) and apologized profusely. I told her that their doctor needed to get his act together and not ignore a therapist's instructions. I left amid her continued apologies, to return to the hospital. While in Intensive Care she had a tracheotomy performed to ease her breathing. Every day as I left the hospital I prayed for her, asking God to ease her pain and, if it was His will, to grant her recovery.

Two days later, I received a phone call near midnight, asking me to come to the hospital immediately. A change in Margaret's condition required immediate surgery. A doctor explained to me that they had found "free air" in her abdomen and they had to operate to find the problem. Nearly three hours later the surgeon found me in the waiting room and explained they had inserted a tube into her colon. He had also removed her appendix (just a little something "extra" for a late night operation). By this time I was so wound up that I had to get out of the place before I began screaming. I believe that it was during this operation an event occurred that had a serious, debilitating effect on her. Now, as I left the hospital, I told God that what Margaret was going through was unfair. She was a good Christian and I felt she should not be subjected to such treatment.

About a week later I was told that they could do no more for Margaret and that if I agreed she could be sent to Mesa Lutheran Hospital that had a unit to treat difficult pulmonary problems. I was not aware that she had a serious pulmonary problem nor had I been told that she required special treatment. Of course, I agreed to the transfer to Mesa Lutheran. A wing of that hospital had been turned over to a private treatment group. I was impressed immediately with the administrator and nurses. We were greeted and informed exactly what they were going to do to help Margaret. Very professional medical people! I could see that Margaret was regressing physically and mentally, but had not given up hope that she could be made whole again.

Next day a pulmonologist took me aside and told me what his examination had revealed. Somewhere in her episodes with surgery she had been deprived of sufficient amounts of oxygen and her brain had been seriously affected. He could not pinpoint the time but said it had probably occurred during her previous hospital stay. I was shocked! His diagnosis: she would never be the same person again!

Physical therapists went to work immediately to help restore her mobility. Progress was very, very slow. It now had been eight weeks since the accident and Margaret was in very bad shape. I spoke with her each day and I could see she was making no progress. She was given a swallow test using barium liquid before an x-ray to see if she could indeed swallow without anything getting into her lungs. She failed the test. The administrator took me into her office and said they had exhausted all forms of treatment and that Margaret had not responded to any. She recommended that Margaret be taken to another facility for rehabilitation. I didn't catch the meaning of rehab until I saw the facility she was transferred to. It housed the long term care and hospice unit for Mesa Desert Samaritan Hospital.

During her first night at the new facility, Margaret pulled the traech tube from her throat. Nurses had tried to reinsert it but failed. The third day another CIGNA hospital representative took me aside and said they had tried every antibiotic known to clear the raging infection in her lungs and that nothing had worked. She recommended taking her off medication and transfer to the hospice unit within the facility. My mind went numb! I was being asked to give permission to stop administering medication and food, allowing her to die! I needed time to get a grip on this and told her I would decide the next day. I stopped to see Margaret before I left. I held her hand and she saw me crying. She tossed my hand away, from anger or what? I literally staggered out of the building.

I called Cathy and Dan and told them I needed to talk with them that evening. We agreed after long discussion that we had to let her go. After ten weeks of treatment she had suffered enough and prognosis was that she could not defeat the lung infection and inevitable death. Sleep was very limited that night.

Monday morning I gave permission to transfer Margaret to a unit of Hospice of the Valley within the building. She was given excellent palliative care by nurses in hospice and she died from pneumonia on Wednesday afternoon, May 24, 2000. Dan was at her side when she died. I had gone home to feed the dogs and was on my way back to hospice when she took her last breath. As soon as I walked into the room I knew that it was over. As I left the hospice unit I felt relief that her ordeal had ended. I was not prepared for the coming events, however.

74
Funeral and Aftermath

Funeral arrangements had to be made very quickly. The Memorial Day weekend was coming up and Green Acres Mortuary in Scottsdale was fully booked for funerals that week. We were able to arrange an early Saturday afternoon funeral in the chapel at Green Acres. Our Assistant Pastor agreed to officiate and conduct the service. I was pretty much out of it, just going through the motions at the time. The kids and I each said our last goodbyes to Margaret before the service. We had been married forty-eight years and it was hard to realize that our life together was over. It struck me then how much I loved this woman. Our earthly marriage had ended.

Pastor conducted a wonderful service memorializing Margaret and then it was finished. We did not have a graveside service. I simply could not have held it together for one. Cathy had a "wake" at her home in Chandler and we all celebrated Margaret's life.

I went home to an empty house and talked to our dogs. I was in the depths of despair. It is while in this darkest part of life that one has to trust in God for strength to get through the ordeal. I had no idea how I was going to cope with life without her at my side but I knew that my faith would help me deal with it. It was then that I acknowledged how emotionally and physically exhausted the last ten weeks had left me.

Wrapping up affairs with Social Security, banks and insurance companies took up most of my time for the next several weeks. Everyone wanted a death certificate proving her demise. I had not ordered enough from Maricopa County and I had to take care of that little item. It struck me that Intel could have provided a much needed service for retirees about settling estates. I had no idea what had to be done to change or close bank accounts, deal with Social Security, deal with her trust, or handle insurance issues among other items. Needless time was wasted running from one place to another filling out forms and talking to agents and clerks. All of this while trying to get a grasp on life after a death.

Questions arose: What do I do with all of her clothing? What do I do with her jewelry? And what about all of her memorabilia about the house? What do I do with it? What do I save, and what do I donate? When do I remove the wedding band from my left hand? Or do I?

Little by little I began donating her clothing and personal items to charities. I'd asked Cathy and Dan to take whatever they needed or wanted. It took weeks to empty her closet and dresser drawers. The house seemed very, very empty.

75
Hospice of the Valley

I received a phone call one day from a lady who said she was a grief counselor with Hospice of the Valley. We spoke for several minutes and I told her that I could handle Margaret's death by myself (typical German male response!). I thought I knew what to do to get through the grieving process. After all, I had helped teach the process to Intel managers, hadn't I? Thank God, two weeks later Sally M called me again to see how I was doing. I was not doing well, I admitted. She asked to meet with me in my home and talk about how to deal with my grief. We met the next week and I liked her immediately. She was gracious, soft spoken and obviously well trained as a counselor.

We met once each week for about three months before cutting back to once every other week. She had induced me to come to weekly grief support group meetings to talk with others about feelings and emotions. The first two meetings I could not speak for fear of crying but eventually started revealing how I felt about Margaret's death. Each time it became easier to let it all hang out, as they say. Listening to others voice their feelings revealed each had similar emotional reactions to death of a loved one.

I knew that losing one's parents or a sibling is emotionally tough. I'm told that losing a child is extremely hard. But, I believe losing one's spouse is infinitely more difficult, forging a void in life that cannot be filled. Margaret's death left a hole in my heart. The sudden adjustment one has to make living life alone is seemingly overwhelming. I learned that the best way to cope with grief is to talk about feelings and emotions with others who have suffered the same experience. I also learned to cry. In the privacy of a shower I discovered how to scream to vent pent-up emotions. It also helped to cope.

When I felt capable of talking about her death, I met with our pastor, Rev. Stoterau. One always asks after the death of a loved one: What happens after death? Is the person in heaven? Does one's soul continue on after the body dies? We talked for nearly a half hour, but I did not get the assurances I had sought. I finally got up to leave and went out into the hallway. I realized I was extremely angry and that pastor had done little to answer my questions or to comfort me. I very nearly put my fist into the wall! My thoughts and feelings about God and religion took a serious hit that day.

It was only much later that I realized that Rev. Stoterau had had no training or experience with people dealing with grief. He did not know what to do to console me. It is well known that men do not talk about feelings or emotions. They talk about cars, jobs, fishing, sports, etc., but never about their feelings. Women, on the other hand, always talk about their emotions. Feelings and emotions are precisely what men need to talk about when grieving. Group therapy is the ideal venue for men to do that. Individual counseling and group therapy were of tremendous help in my period of grief.

76

The Feds, Taxes and Lawyers

I had met with a Phoenix law firm recommended by my financial advisor to finalize Margaret's living trust and to get her trust's financial affairs taken care of. The house was to be transferred to my trust. Assets were divided and placed within our individual trusts, hers to be administered by our children. Federal and State taxes had to be paid. I called the lawyer repeatedly to learn the status of the transfer. Always the answer: it takes time to finalize estates. I learned later that the law firm was a high powered unit that dealt with very wealthy clients. I was just small fry to them. Many months later when it was finally done I was presented with a bill for $18,000! I almost gagged. The lawyers had really stuck it to me. And I still had to pay federal and state taxes on the estate! A different estate lawyer told me that the entire procedure should have cost no more than $2000, excluding taxes!

And, while all of that was going on, the stock market took a gigantic dive (2001). I had not paid close attention to investments and had not communicated much with my investment broker during Margaret's 10-week hospitalization and the funeral. But then, he had not communicated with me either. When the stock market had finally hit bottom, I had lost nearly half of our retirement estate! I was in a fog. What else could go wrong? I awoke to the fact that I had better get a handle on my financial affairs and quickly. Calling my financial advisor one day I was told he had left the firm to join the FBI. Great! His manager informed me that he was personally taking over my account, noting that he was aware of the losses I had sustained and would watch over my holdings.

I soon recognized that much of the money my stock holdings represented had vanished into thin air. Well, that is not entirely true. I later learned that stock market money just doesn't disappear – someone, some people, some group had gained handsomely from my loss (and other people's loss). It left me very wary of the stock market. Hadn't I learned the hard way in the Army not to gamble if you don't understand the risk of the game? It was a hard lesson in life again.

77
Grief Counseling and Therapy

Sometimes after a group therapy meeting we would go to a restaurant for coffee or dessert. At one of the coffee sessions, I was asked to go with several others to a dance the following Sunday evening. My reaction was, "Are you nuts?" No, they were not nuts! It was a form of therapy and it will be helpful, they said. I finally agreed to meet them and go to a dance held in Sun Lakes Retirement Village in Chandler. We had a good time dancing, talking and listening to the 40's and 50's music. The band, all retired musicians, was excellent. I found over the next several months that talking about our experiences with death at these social events was more intimate and revealing than the weekly group sessions with a counselor. I was taken aback, however, when a woman in the group revealed to us that her husband had died nearly five years ago and she missed having sex. I was in no position to help her with that problem.

Sally M offered many suggestions for dealing with grief. She urged me to write a letter to Margaret and tell her how I felt about her absence in my life. I asked, "Are you kidding?" She replied, "No, I am not!" I thought it was a goofy idea. How could I mail a letter to Margaret? She was adamant about the letter and kept encouraging me to do it. So, one lonely Saturday evening I sat at the table and wrote a letter to Margaret, letting her know in no uncertain terms how I felt about trying to cope with life without her and leaving me with five dogs. It was cathartic. I wrote five legal sized pages "letting it all hang out". The mere process of writing about feelings and emotions is very healing. I have since encouraged others who have lost loved ones to try writing a similar type letter.

I had found some of Margaret's poems while cleaning out drawers. One in particular struck me profoundly. She spoke about being tiny in God's eyes but was looking forward to meeting Him. I designed a framed memento with her photo, her poem and a small wooden cross that she had received from her mother at her first communion. I hung it on the wall of honor in our living room.

78
That First Christmas

The kids and I agreed that we needed to get out of town for Christmas. Someone suggested we go to Lake Tahoe to enjoy the holidays, ski and maybe check out the casinos. Cathy made travel arrangements and I arranged rental of a condo in Incline Village for a week. Husband Scott, Cathy, Freddie, Deanna (their children), Dan and I flew to Reno, Nevada and rented a big van for the drive to Tahoe. Our condo was ready for us, minus only a stash of wood for the fireplace. We had no holiday decorations for the condo but we enjoyed the festive decorations in the village. Sightseeing the entire Lake Tahoe area proved interesting.

Each night one of us would make dinner. My turn brought forth spaghetti with meat sauce, right out of the container. Thank goodness for the Safeway store nearby for having all of the food supplies we needed. There were two casinos a short drive away and one offered a great prime rib dinner for $9.99 and we ate there one night. We did not gamble much. There was too much to do and see. Everyone wanted to ski so I drove them to the ski area and left them to shop around in Tahoe.

Trips into Virginia City and Carson City proved to be entertaining for all of us. We decided to eat out on Christmas day. There was a beautiful restaurant situated right on the shore of Lake Tahoe that offered dinner that day. We made reservations for noon only to find out that dinner would not be served until 5:30 pm. So, we ate delicious sandwiches for our Christmas feast! It was delightful dining, looking out over the beautiful lake. We gave gifts to Fred and Deanna and had a good family fete Christmas evening.

Since we were only a two hour drive from San Francisco, we went in to the City by the Bay day after Christmas. We took the ferry from Sausalito to the City and shopped in China Town. It was charming visiting the many shops, talking with many people. Time to leave, we caught the last ferry back to Sausalito. We were tired but happy when we got back to our condo. It was a great day! Like all good things, however, the Tahoe trip had to come to an end. Flying back to Phoenix I knew I had the same empty house to deal with.

Picking up the dogs at the Vet's, I had one who was very sick. Hercie (short for Herculena) had gotten so upset in a strange kennel that her heart was about to give out. She had never been a healthy Chihuahua, but I had to do something to help her. I agreed with the Vet to euthanize her. Six weeks later her brother, Herbie (he looked like Herbie the Volkswagon as a pup), had to be put to sleep. I was now down to three dogs. Under my breath I uttered a solemn word for Margaret. I still harbored some anger at her for taking in so many dogs, leaving me to fend with them.

79
A Trip to Ireland

The kids and I talked about a trip to Ireland. Cathy, a former travel agent, arranged all flight, hotel and tour accommodations. In May, 2001, Cathy, Dan and I travelled to Dublin, Ireland for a 10 day trip touring the Emerald Isle. We toured the "Ring of Fire" in southern Ireland by bus complete with a lovely Irish Lass as tour guide. Not only did we see places of interest, we heard stories about each city and points of interest along the way. Dan was the official photographer for the trip and he took many interesting photos.

Our vacation included several extra days looking about Dublin. One of our first visits was Guinness Brewery in Dublin where, after the plant tour, we received a glass of its famous frothy dark beer. We visited Trinity College and looked upon the Book of Kells housed in a specially lighted room (to avoid bleaching the book's print and paper). Cathy and I attended a moving Catholic worship service in St. Anne's Church, a small picturesque building on a very narrow side street off of Grafton Street.

Our bus tour included a stop at the world famous Waterford Crystal factory and we stood not ten feet away watching glass blowers and glass engravers doing their work. The factory was clean as a whistle and bright with light. We stopped in Cobh to visit the Heritage Center where millions of Irish immigrated to the New World in ships. Cobh was the last port of call for the Titanic before its fateful voyage to America. Of course, we visited Blarney Castle, famous for its "Blarney Stone". One had to lie on their back to kiss the stone, which I attempted to do. A quick look at the stone showed me it was greasy black, and I faked the kiss. Getting up I conked my head on the stone wall, knocking me half goofy. It took several minutes for me to regain my composure. Looking out upon the countryside from the top of the castle, I could envision warriors running toward the castle with their swords and spears and shouting, ready for battle and looting. The knock on the head had nothing to do with my imagination.

My favorite city was Killarney, a beautiful town with lots of interesting shops and restaurants. I told the kids I could live in that charming city. We had a rest stop on a view point overlooking the Bay of Dingle. I couldn't stop chuckling over the name. Dan took a picture of Cathy and me with Dingle Bay in the background and it was framed as a memento of our trip. Our 7-day bus tour ended in Limerick. We spent an extra day sightseeing and shopping. We also visited a local watering hole located in the basement of a building that resonated with music and laughter. We spent a wonderful evening there. I got feeling pretty good drinking iced Bailey's Irish Cream, a lovely Irish liqueur!

We left the charming and scenic Emerald Isle on a morning flight out of Shannon Airport, arriving in Phoenix early evening. We all were totally refreshed from our vacation. My only regret: I hadn't taken Margaret there while she was still able to travel to see the village near Dublin where her father was born. After returning from the trip, another dog, Lady, was found ill having advanced cancer and had to be euthanized. My grief recovery process was taking some serious hits.

80
Life's Decisions

After a year the personal counseling ended, but group meetings continued. I was still having problems with the empty house syndrome, however. The two dogs, Sugar and Sparkle, were very good listeners but not very good conversing. I had asked Sally M before our last counseling session when a person knows they are ready to begin dating again. Her reply: "You will just know." Well, I'd had enough of going to dinner or to a movie alone. Have you noticed when dining out that most are couples or groups? Or going to a movie? A single person stands out.

I had progressed through the grieving process with the help of a counselor and fellow grieving friends. It was a daunting trip but I had made it. There was indeed light at the end of the tunnel as Sally had promised.

I met a lady at one of our group dinner meetings who also had toured Ireland. We talked at length about the Irish and how much each of us had enjoyed vacationing there. Later, I asked her out and we had a nice evening with a movie and ice cream after. We dated several times after that and one evening at dinner she told me that she did not want our relationship to continue. I did not seem to fit her idea of a suitable suitor. Timing of her pronouncement surprised me but I didn't get upset. So much for that encounter I thought.

I did something after that I never, ever thought I would do at age 72. In September, 2001, I cranked up the computer and joined <u>match.com</u> with a six month subscription. I carefully worded a personal resume and included a recent photo, placing all of it online. Within a day I had many hits, as they are called, from women in the southwest. Over time I realized there are many unusual (perhaps wacky?) folks reading and responding to one's data placed on the web site. I responded to several hits and began emailing several women. One turned out to be a real kook living in New Mexico and fortunately that ended quickly. A woman in California, Patty, and I became quite friendly in our emails and eventually we began talking over the phone. Her site photo showed her to be very attractive and quite petite. Our online and telephone relationship reached a point where we agreed to meet in Las Vegas for an introduction.

I must admit I had some misgivings about meeting a stranger in Vegas. Was I really ready for the meeting? And what if it turned out to be an unpleasant encounter? I was concerned that in our frequent telephone talks Patty had coughed many times. She said she did not smoke but I was not certain of that. I wanted no part of the smoking scenario again. However, curiosity got the better of me and I planned to make the trip.

81
My Last Brother Dies

Just four days before our scheduled meeting in Vegas, I received a phone call from the Chandler Police telling me my brother, Bob, had been found dead in his apartment. The same day I received a letter from Patty with an enclosed photo holding her grandson. Petite? The woman had to weigh at least 200 pounds! The photo she had posted on match.com must have been taken when she was in high school. Her obvious deceit angered me! How could she mislead me with an undeniably very old picture on her resume? I sent an email calling off our meeting, explaining that my brother had died and that I was in no condition to travel to Las Vegas. Patty went on the defensive in an email, cursing the photo she had sent me. That ended the brief, misleading meeting with a match.com patron. I had learned a valuable lesson. Ask personal questions and always ask if the photo with the resume was current. The encounter did not help with my grieving process.

I had taken Bob shopping to the grocery store two days before the call from the police. He appeared to be OK and we spent some time talking after returning from the store. I was again in a state of shock. Dealing with Bob's unexpected death only exacerbated my state of mind. I made arrangements for his funeral in Chandler. Bob was a US Air Force retiree, having served 21 years. He and I were fairly close as brothers, closer than each was with our three older brothers. I went about the next few days in a fog, not thinking clearly. Was this death thing ever going to leave me?

Bob had not been on the best of terms for years with his former wife and four children, but they all attended the service. A nephew Ken, whom I had lost track of, attended as well. I had arranged for a retired Lutheran pastor to conduct the funeral service. Following, we drove to the United States Veterans National Cemetery in north Phoenix for a graveside service. Arrangements had been made for an Air Force Honor Guard's military salute during the service. I broke down after Taps had been played and the 21-gun salute. Taps is an integral part of military life. Each evening it is played at U.S. military installations around the world, signifying the end of the day and retirement of our flag. At military funerals it salutes the end of life for a fallen comrade.

Enough already with this death business! It was later that the thought struck: I was now alone, the only living member of the original Scheske family!

82
One Last Try On match.com

I decided to try one more time before my six month subscription with <u>match.com</u> came to an end. I discovered a lovely woman's resume and photo on site and sent an email. Two weeks elapsed and I had not heard from her. Well, nothing lost I figured. I had tried. Incidentally, she was the first and only female I had inquired about during the six months. In that time frame I had gotten over 1500 hits.

A day later I received an email reply from her. She lived in Las Vegas and asked if I knew anything about new retirement homes being built in Sun City Grand. No, I did not know anything about them but I would be happy to drive out there to take a look, I replied in an email. Sun City Grand (SCG) was located in the boondocks, at least thirty miles northwest of Phoenix. I lived in Chandler, about 50 miles from Surprise where the retirement community was located. A long drive one Sunday afternoon took me to SCG and I inspected all eight of the new models. The community had everything: four 18-hole golf courses, a softball stadium, three pools, a spa, two fitness centers, a library, twelve lighted tennis courts, lawn bowling, Bocce courts and even two restaurants. My email to her the next day explained what I had seen and liked.

From that point we began communicating regularly. We

exchanged names. She told me hers, Michelle Madoff, and I told her mine. Soon we reached the point where emails were not sufficient and we spoke over the phone. We spoke at times for more than an hour, talking in general terms about likes and dislikes. Michelle was very interested in the arts, live theater, opera, symphony, movies and museums. I admitted that I, too, liked them but had not patronized them for some time. Truth be told, I had not been to live theater in years, months to see a movie and many years since I had last been in a museum. But, I had learned a long time ago when it is best to shut up and listen, right?

When she learned that I had two dogs, she was thrilled, for she had a miniature Poodle. Many long phone conversations followed and it became apparent that we had many common interests. She was a former Councilwoman from Pittsburgh, PA, serving for 16 years. I had worked for several prominent corporations for over 40 years. Soon we were talking about meeting in Las Vegas (yikes!) where she lived. Michelle told me one day that she was Jewish. I replied I was German. There was a pause before we continued talking. We agreed on a date to meet in Vegas.

I placed my two dogs, Sugar and Sparkle, in a kennel for a few days and drove to Las Vegas. The five hour drive went smoothly and I managed to find the Hampton Inn where Michelle had reserved a room for me. I called as soon as I unloaded the suitcase and Michelle told me she would pick me up in about 15 minutes. I waited anxiously outside the hotel until I saw her pull up in a Lexus. Wow! She was as beautiful as her photo had shown. We shook hands when I got into her car and talked about my trip to Vegas. She put me at ease immediately.

She owned a lovely home in Summerlin, a Del Webb retirement community in Las Vegas. We talked and talked and I began to like what I saw and heard. At dinner time, Michelle insisted on making the meal rather than going out to eat. I will never forget the meal she prepared: tossed salad with strawberries and pecans, Veal Marsala and steamed vegetables. I thought to myself, man, this woman can cook! Mind you, I had dined on frozen dinners for over a year and this was a royal treat. After cleaning up, we sat about and continued talking. It was refreshing for me to listen and talk about issues with government, the economy and retirement rather than emotions and feelings.

Michelle showed me around Las Vegas, parts that I had not seen. I had been to Vegas once many years before with friends and I felt it to be a make believe town. It was brilliant lights, gaudy signs, and phony people. But on our tours I saw lovely homes, wonderful restaurants and terrific shopping. We ate out several times, enjoying food and each other's company. My last evening with Michelle was quite romantic. After dinner we talked and ended with Michelle reading to me. I had never had that kind of experience. We kissed as I said goodbye and I agreed to return soon. Leaving Vegas the next morning, I stopped on the way and called her. We had a short, endearing conversation and she invited me to stay at her house and to bring my dogs on the next visit. Yesssss….. man, I was pumped!

We spoke on the phone at least once each day and made plans for my return to Vegas for a stay. A month after my first visit, I locked the house and with the dogs drove on to Vegas. My stay with Michelle developed into a relationship that promised to be long term. We discussed many important subjects: living together, finances, medical care, a home, investments, dogs, and what we wanted to do the rest of our lives. Sugar and Sparkle quickly made friends with Michelle's miniature Poodle, Sammy Davis Jr.

Our <u>match.com</u> relationship was turning into a lifetime undertaking.

We discussed our life's work. Michelle had been an environmental activist in Pittsburgh.

After her marriage to Dr. Henry Madoff in Boston, they moved to Pittsburgh where he entered practice as a Cardio/Pulmonary Surgeon. Several years later they divorced when Michelle discovered her husband's infidelity.

Soon after arriving in Pittsburgh, Michelle developed a serious asthma condition. The source of her health problem was air pollution and she began action to force the steel mills to clean up their smoke problem. The mills were the major source of pollution. A meeting in her home with the city's most influential citizens formed the action group, GASP (Group Against Smog and Pollution). While she was in her kitchen preparing drinks, members elected Michelle as their leader (lesson: never leave a meeting when important issues are up for a vote!). I was impressed and admired her accomplishments in cleaning up smog and pollution in Pittsburgh, widely known as "Steel City".

We talked at length about a retirement community in Surprise and about Anthem in Henderson, NV. Several visits to Anthem to seriously consider living there proved to us that it was not our place of choice. Sales personnel were not amenable to making changes in house plans. Their motto was: this is what we offer in a house, take it or leave it. They would however, finally acquiesce to consider several minimal changes for an added fee of $10,000! We walked out of the sales office.

Michelle called a contractor/friend who drew up expansion plans for her current home in Summerlin. The changes would add another 400 sq. ft., bringing the total to just over 1800 sq. ft. The contractor's work would cost a mere $35,000, an $87.50

sq/foot charge! There was a major problem, however, in that the city of Las Vegas could not provide sufficient water pressure to the house. All nine of the houses on her street suffered from inadequate water pressure due to the size of the water main serving the street. She was told the city was unable to increase the size of the supply pipe. Our conclusion was to look into the retirement community in Surprise, Arizona.

Reservations were made to visit the community, staying at one of their vacation homes. We met with a personable sales lady who was eager to accommodate our ideas in a house, a completely different attitude from agents in Anthem. We soon settled on a house plan after spending time viewing all of the models. We chose the Ashbury, a 2100 sq. ft. house and made several changes which included adding a second closet in the second bedroom and expanding the kitchen. After several long discussions about minor changes and additions, we signed a contract. A down payment was made and the house was put on the construction schedule for a start in May, 2002.

We asked about someone who could look after the building while we were back in Las Vegas. An unlicensed contractor was recommended and we spoke with him. He agreed to watch over construction while we were gone for $500. We verbally agreed to have him do the inspection work for us. It had to be the easiest $500 he ever earned because, as we found out later, he did little to nothing to earn the fee. He sent us two Polaroid photos of the foundation. Every other day I would send him an email and I would get maybe one each week from him telling us he was actively watching the construction.

The same contractor later fleeced us for construction of a built-in barbeque on our patio. He hired an illegal immigrant to do the work and while it looked decent it was really an unprofessional job. Installation of a gas line to the BBQ was found to be in violation of Surprise City code, in that he used the wrong gas pipe. In order to meet code, we had to hire a licensed plumber to reinstall approved pipe at a cost of $500. We had to threaten the contractor with a law suit before he finally reimbursed us the cost of the approved pipe. Not a nice guy!

Back to Las Vegas, we put Michelle's house on the market with a real estate agent. He talked a good game convincing us he would work hard to sell the house. Her backyard was beautifully landscaped with shade trees, a little grassy area, a brick paved patio, a fountain and a shaded bench to meditate and take in the beauty. We waited for buyers to view the house. An open house brought zero results. No one came to see her place. Several weeks went by and nothing happened with no potential buyers and certainly no offers. It was now October, 2002 and construction of our retirement home was moving toward completion.

While shopping, Michelle met another real estate agent, a lady who had a different approach to selling homes. We talked about putting an advertisement in a Los Angeles newspaper, which she did. One day after the ad and picture appeared in the paper, we had a couple from California inquire about the house. Several days later they inspected her home and made an offer! The housing market was slow in Vegas and the offer was less than Michelle had hoped for, but it was reasonable. A little bargaining and she settled on a price. We quickly lined up a moving van and began packing up some of her valuables for the move. We left the furniture and large items for the packers and movers.

Just before moving, we attended an auction house that Michelle had frequented many times. I was looking for some baseball sport cards for my grandson, Fred. We found much more than that. Before we left we had purchased a framed, ¾ life-size oil painting of Troy Aikman and much memorabilia of his college and professional football career with the Dallas Cowboys at an unbelievably low cost. Michelle fell in love with the oil because it had a lot of blue in it which matched her kitchen set! I saw it as a valuable painting which could be sold for a nice profit later.

We had also attended a furniture auction in another business and bought a 19th century walnut Hunter Cabinet with hand carved figures. It was a magnificent piece that would serve us well in the dining room. An outstanding find, it has awarded us many compliments. Michelle loved to attend auctions and I soon found it to be interesting and challenging when bidding on prized pieces.

Before leaving we began looking for flooring for our new house. We soon found ceramic tile at Home Depot made in Italy that looked like wood. We were referred to a flooring dealer who stocked a wide array of the tile. The dealer showed us a variety of the tile and we selected a dark version. He had contact with a flooring contractor in Kingman, Arizona and recommended we talk to him for installing the tile. On a trip to Surprise we stopped in Kingman to see the contractor and discussed the installation. He assured us he not only could do it, but he would complete it as if it were his own mother's house. Sounded great! We signed a contract and left a deposit for the installation.

I had turned my house in Chandler over to a realtor to affect a sale. He quickly found a buyer. We negotiated a selling price and while I made a reasonable profit, I felt I had been pushed into a corner by the buyer. I was told they were going to put the house up for rent. That was something I did not want out of consideration for my neighbors. Then I got hassled to empty the house quickly. Fortunately Cathy and Dan were of tremendous help in cleaning out the house.

83
Our Surprise Home

The final walk-through in November, 2002 with the construction supervisor showed the house was ready for tile to be installed. We specifically instructed the supervisor to merely lay the carpet on the floors (he cited an FHA regulation that the house must have carpet on the floor), but not attach it because tile would be installed the following week. We had arranged to give the carpet as a donation to a needy family.

When the tiling contractor arrived he found the carpet securely attached to the floor. It would take more than a day to remove the carpet and tools to remove the spiked attachment strips secured to the concrete floor. The first word we got that there was a problem came after we had returned to Vegas. Further, we found the contractor we had signed to do the work had given the job to a Kingman subcontractor who in turn had given it to a Phoenix subcontractor. We had no idea who was doing the tile installation! We were given a cell phone number to call the subcontractor and we spoke at least once a day with him. The move to Surprise was coming up fast and the tile installation was no way near being completed.

The subcontractor completed his tile work one day before we were to move into the house! When I opened the door on December 7, 2002 with the moving truck in front of the house, I was appalled! The entire tiled flooring was filthy, having been wiped only with a dirty wet mop. We called the construction supervisor who came immediately to the house and contacted a man who could come quickly to hand mop the floors. Meanwhile the movers were impatiently waiting to unload the truck.

I went to the garage and was shocked a second time. The person we had made arrangements with to give the carpet to a needy family had left the entire pile in the center of the garage! He told us in a quick phone call that he didn't know anything about it. His buddy apparently had forgotten to move it and he wanted nothing to do with it. We gave new carpet to any contract worker who would take it away.

It was the start of a long, ongoing battle with contractors. When we threatened to withhold some of the final payment to the tile contractor, he drove to Phoenix, ready to do battle. A discussion with him got very heated and he made several threats to go to court. We finally settled on a price, paid him with a check and he left with an utterance of never doing business in Phoenix again. Hooray!

Our dealings with contractors became more and more frequent and vociferous. It seemed that every week another problem surfaced. Most problems were fixed after days of waiting, but the dealings became more and more heated. The major difficulty centered on our heating/air conditioning system. The first indication of a screwed-up installation came when an AC consultant found we had the wrong thermostats in the house. The thermostats did not match the variable blower speed unit we'd had installed. We wouldn't be able to get sufficient heat in the winter or cooling in the summer. The AC unit would often shut down on 110° days, usually on weekends when maintenance or repair was hard to obtain. It eventually came down to a defective heating/cooling system, and after

20 months of complaints with little resolution, the heating/AC manufacturer finally agreed to replace it with another unit of our choice.

We chose a Trane unit and its installation revealed the major problem with the previous system. A ¾ inch copper pipe had been crimped during its installation, restricting the flow of cooled refrigerant from the compressor to the blower unit. It was no wonder the unit could not perform as expected! It was a defect that was difficult to find or see since it was behind a wall. We have never had a problem since installation of the Trane unit!

The building contractor agreed we had been through many trials with our new house and stated they wanted to do something to "make it right". We requested granite countertops be installed in our kitchen and they agreed. Our kitchen was torn up for a short time but the black granite with white cupboards proved to make the room spectacular. It did make things right with us.

84
Back to the Past

An article in the local newspaper piqued Michelle's interest. While living in Pittsburgh, Pennsylvania, she had been the driving force in founding a group (GASP) to eliminate smoke and pollution in the city. The Phoenix newspaper article pointed out that sand and gravel operations in the Agua Fria River bed near our home in SCG were producing unsatisfactory levels of dust in the air. She went immediately to the site and began talking to nearby residents and even truck drivers for the mining concern.

A reporter for the *Arizona Republic* accompanied Michelle to the site on a second visit and took photographs of her talking to a truck driver. A subsequent newspaper article spoke about her actions and displayed the photo. The article and photo was seen by a former environmental advocate in Pittsburgh who was living in Surprise. Bill Wilson could not believe his eyes when he read the paper! He and Michelle had gone head-to-head many times while he was working for Jones and Laughlin Steel Company in Pittsburgh. A phone call re-established their relationship and friendship. Bill's wife, Diann, is an old friend of Michelle's. It really is a small world!

Michelle and I lived as an engaged couple for five years. Can you believe it? It was something I never, ever thought I would do! I felt marriage was the only way two consenting adults should live together. And here I was living with a woman, engaged but not married! We had talked about marrying many times but never got around to making arrangements to legalize our union. I'm sure there were comments made about our relationship. When I spoke to a pastor of a Lutheran church nearby our home in Sun City Grand about joining the church, I told him about living with Michelle and not being married. He replied that he had seen this type of relationship many times with older, retired couples. He indicated it would not be a deterrent to membership in the church.

Michelle and I talked about marriage one day with Diann Wilson and she said she would arrange it for us. In less than three hours she had made hotel reservations in Las Vegas, arranged for a pastor to marry us in a wedding chapel and set up a wedding celebration dinner! Michelle and I were bewildered how quickly Diann had made the arrangements – and perhaps with the realization that she and I were to be finally married! In June, 2007, we traveled to Las Vegas and began the process of obtaining a wedding license. It took all of about one hour to secure the license and we were ready to get hitched!

The next day, June 20, 2007, we drove to "Little Chapel of the Flowers" and met with the pastor, Rev. Bradley Gilbert. He immediately put us at ease and even joked about weddings. Now picture this: Here was Michelle, a Jewess, and Fred, a German Lutheran, being married by a Black Baptist pastor! Talk about ultimate integration, that was it!

Diann Wilson served as Maid of Honor and Bill Wilson served as Best Man. Two former Las Vegas neighbors of Michelle, Richard and Mimi Blaine, attended the wedding as witnesses.

The wedding ceremony went off beautifully with Pastor Gilbert making memorable remarks during the service. We were impressed! Immediately following the wedding, photographs were taken. Then it was off to a wonderful wedding dinner at The Space Needle (a slowly rotating restaurant 30 stories above the street!). Michelle has a fear of heights and could not look down at the Las Vegas Strip during dinner for fear of becoming ill. The dinner and conversation with wonderful friends made it a memorable day for Michelle and me.

85
Second Marriage

With our marriage, I inherited another daughter, Karenlin Madoff. Karen had also returned to college and at age 40 earned her degree in law from Pepperdine University in Los Angeles. Karen practices estate law in Los Angeles. And, Michelle inherited two children as well, Catherine and Daniel. Incidentally, Michelle is not related to Bernie Madoff, the infamous ponzi scheme financial broker.

Our marriage has been remarkable. Michelle is still involved in air quality environmental issues, but has met resistance from Maricopa County and Arizona State officials. It seems no one wants to force polluting businesses to clean up their places of work. Dust and pollution continue to plague the Phoenix metropolitan area. There is a lot of talk but very little action. Even with EPA citations, the air in Phoenix, and in the Valley, is dirty. The issue is not paramount with people because you can't smell or taste the pollution. If it were smoke with its attributes of smell and taste, perhaps people would get up in arms. And politicians simply will not push for cleanup of sand, gravel, concrete and asphalt business operations.

Michelle has been of great inspiration to me. She spoke about joining a group of retired engineers in the west valley, encouraging me to join also. I resisted but she joined. Hearing her many positive comments about the club, I attended a luncheon meeting and later joined the West Valley Engineers Club. As an active participant, I offered to write articles for their monthly publication. The club's newsletter editor asked me to interview club members and to write a short article about each. I submitted several articles for the letter and they have met with great interest.

Later I was asked to be on the slate for the Vice President's position. This post required the acquisition of a noted speaker for each of the nine monthly luncheon meetings for the year 2008. I agreed to the nomination and was elected to the post. I found the position to be very challenging and difficult to find qualified speakers but managed to fill the monthly programs for the year. The position to follow, of course, was the President's post. I was reluctant to run for the position but finally concurred. It turned out to be much less demanding than the VP's position and I was able to successfully fill the post of President for the year 2009. I must admit that I often questioned my election to head up the group. I was not a graduate engineer. However, having worked with and for engineers for more than thirty years, I had come to think and work as they had. Both club positions were marvelous opportunities and I grew as a result. Had it not been for Michelle's insistence that I join the club I would have missed all of that experience.

Michelle also reintroduced me to live theater and we regularly attend shows that have been rewarding as well as fun. She is also what I call a movie nut, loving to see interesting and fulfilling movies. I trust her to pick good shows since she reads reviews regularly. She loves to dine out and we eat at good restaurants at least once, sometimes twice a week. Our retirement in Surprise has been pleasant, but not completely rewarding. Most retirees here play golf, some playing every day. My knees do not allow me to play, which provides a viable excuse. The game is expensive and does not interest me. To hit a little white ball with a club and then go traipsing after it is boring, I think. Other retirees play a variety of card games: Bridge, Poker, Mah Jhong, and Cribbage to name a few. Those games hold little interest for Michelle or me.

So, what do I like to do as a retiree? I enjoy reading, and working on a computer. At least twice, usually three times each week, I work out at a fitness center to help keep the old joints working. It helps. I walk our dogs each day to keep them in shape. At times I take them to the dog park and let them run about. Recently I spoke with a gentleman from Cicero (Morton High School) at the dog park who had graduated from Northwestern University in Evanston, IL. He spoke of two football players on the NU team from Waukegan: Jim Blumberg and Chuck Petter. I knew both as they were in the WTHS graduating class of 1946. Small world!

I still have a desire to teach and facilitate learning programs. For example, after Margaret died I spoke to my pastor and asked if I could conduct a program for people grieving the loss of a loved one. I did facilitate several eight week programs at the Lutheran church in Chandler with the blessing of the pastor. And I found facilitating the sessions to be rewarding and fulfilling.

Soon after we moved into our new home, Michelle formed a group called Fun Diners. The intent was to meet and become friends with residents while dining at a nice restaurant. We'd hoped to form a group of 20 to 30 people who enjoyed good food, conversation and companionship. Our initial notice in the retirement community's magazine met with great success. Initially ten couples signed up to meet for dinner at a local restaurant once each month. Michelle was not one to settle for just any restaurant and she was able to find and check out very good establishments. Within two years the group had expanded to 140 members. Of course, not all attended every dinner, but we had at least 20 to 30 at each monthly gathering.

Michelle was always able to negotiate a reasonable cost for each meal and the restaurateurs would often add coffee or some delight with a meal at no extra cost. It was a very successful venture but after three years the wear and tear began to show on each of us. The effort of finding a restaurant, checking it out, negotiating a price and date, maintaining a membership list, notifying all members, taking reservations, and greeting each as they arrived for dinner became physically and emotionally draining. We gladly turned the group over to Phyllis Schwab to carry on the good work for several more years.

The second marriage for Michelle and me has been gratifying for each. We've had our moments of course, as all couples have, but we are adult enough to know that marriage is a give and take venture. She has enriched my life and has brought out my better qualities. Conversely, I believe I have enhanced her life. We rely heavily on each other for support and gladly give strength and encouragement when needed. And the love we have for each other is readily apparent. We have no compunction to kiss in public or to hold hands. For Octogenarians, we are not afraid to display our feelings for each other and to tell each other, "I love you." And that is what helps make life fulfilling and wonderful!

own at the completion through the G.I. Bill of the schooling while in the service. Those were college time; persisted, my early schooling gave me the base that I built upon... later I discovered the fruits of the... the kindled in me a desire of the accomplishment; persisted... reflected in the... screen of my life.

86
Personal Reflections

If there was one thing I would change in my life, it would be to have stayed in closer contact with my family after moving to Arizona. Money was tight but a phone call once a month could have been afforded. I did speak to brother Bill occasionally but I always seemed to be on the defensive when we talked. It was a feeling that being junior man in the family I was always to heed the directions of my older brothers. Frankly, that was one of the factors considered in making a decision to move from Waukegan. The move to Arizona liberated my thinking and I felt free to live without their input.

Margaret and I made decisions jointly during our marriage. We moved several times but always with her consent. Granted, it was grudgingly given at times. Each move was to better my ability to provide for my wife and children. I did not force my thoughts upon her. She was free to act and decide for herself. We reasoned our resolutions and we worked together in making decisions. However, I am keenly aware of the physical and emotional effects moving several times had on her. And it still troubles me.

I always had a much different philosophy of life than my brothers. They saw education as twelve years of schooling to be endured. I saw it as a way to a better life, even though I did not do as well scholastically as I should have. The opportunity provided by the WWII GI Bill was a gift I could not refuse. All four of my brothers simply ignored the GI Bill to seek work in a factory. Three years of college study provided many work opportunities for me in spite of the fact I did not earn a bachelor's degree. Yes, I regret not having completed college work. But I must state that my college experiences opened my mind and changed the direction of my life.

While I, too, worked in factories, all of them were of the ultra clean type. Abbott Laboratories, Motorola Semiconductor, MOSTEK Semiconductor and Intel Corporation were all super clean facilities, definitely high tech, requiring employees having great skills and knowledge. To say I was fortunate to be able to work and learn in each of these companies is an understatement. I look upon it as a blessing.

The faith that was kindled in Luther's Catechism class taught by Reverend Heise while in high school has only increased throughout my life. A strong belief in the Lutheran tenets of the Triune God has enriched my life. In fact, I marvel at the path my life has taken. It wasn't random thinking and good luck that got me to where I am today. I am absolutely convinced that God had a plan for me and I simply followed the path laid out before me. Of course, I wandered at times but He would always get me back on track.

Having been born and raised in Waukegan, the mid-western philosophy of life was deeply instilled in me. Respect for parents, family and professionals were part of life. Be a Christian, go to church, be kind and helpful to those in need. Vote in elections, participate in civic events – all of these are tenets of life. One doesn't lose qualities like that by moving to another part of the country. I am proud to be an American and, while I may not always agree with its leadership, I love and fully support the United States of America.

Now, at age 81, the question: what lies ahead? I know that I cannot do the things I used to do. Maintaining a car, doing yard work, painting a house or a room, or making house renovations are in the past. Our bodies let us know we aren't young anymore. I recently had a full knee replacement and it took months to get rehabilitated. But with good doctors and medical care we can make our golden years productive and rewarding. I wrote this book as a sign of that.

I can't predict the future, but I am convinced that life will be good. How can it be anything less? I want to travel more. We have not seen the Black Hills of South Dakota or Mount Rushmore. Yellowstone Park still beckons. Seeing the magnificent fall colors in the Northeast is on the list. And yes, another trip to Waukegan is definite. I feel there is still much left to see and do. But foremost, I know that God is in command and will continue directing my life. He is like that, you know.

Shall not He who led me safely
Through my footsteps of this day
Lead with equal understanding
All along my future way? – Adams

87
When Visiting Waukegan

Waukegan has many beautiful and noted landmarks. Anyone visiting the city must see Bowen Park on the northeast side. It is located on Sheridan Road just north of Greenwood Avenue. The Waukegan Historical Society operates the Waukegan History Museum and the John L. Raymond Research Library amidst the gentle rolling landscape. Whether you wish to view the Victorian décor of the buildings, enjoy an exhibit of Waukegan history or research history of a house or family, you will find that the Society offers something for everyone.

Another great city landmark is the Genesee Theater located in the heart of downtown Waukegan. This beautiful theater was designed by the famous architect Edward P. Steinberg. The original building housed the theater including a huge, magnificent pipe organ, eleven retail spaces and forty-four apartments. *"Man About Town"* debuted there on June 25, 1939. Jack Benny, a native Waukeganite, and Dorothy Lamour starred in the play. Restoration work on the vaudevillian theater began in 2001 and it was reopened to the public December 3, 2004 with the curtain raiser host, Bill Cosby. Star studded performances are scheduled each year.

The Waukegan Marina is located on Harbor Place on the shores of Lake Michigan. It is the mooring for hundreds of boats and water craft. A beautiful park, promenade and family picnic area are part of the marina.

A short drive to nearby North Chicago will find the Great Lakes Naval Museum located in the Great Lakes Naval Training Center. The Center is one of the largest training facilities for naval personnel in the United States.

West of Waukegan on Grand Avenue is Six Flags Great America recreation facility. It provides rides and fun attractions for all ages.

Fred Scheske and wife Michelle reside in the retirement
community of Sun City Grand in Surprise, Arizona.